Acknowledgments

No book is the work of one person, and *Flash! Creative Web Animation* is no exception. For the third time, I would like to recognize my wife, Barbara Moshofsky, for her unfailing support in the duration. My thanks also go to editor Karen Whitehouse for her steadiness and courage; designer Michael Nolan for amazing speed; Karen Tucker and Jane DeKoven at Macromedia for patience. Recognition should be made of the folks at Studio B and Peachpit Press as well. And last but not least, Peter Sylwester, fellow Flash fanatic.

Contents

Introduction _____ **vii**

Chapter 1 Flash Tour _____ **1**

What is Flash? 2

How Flash Works 3

The Guided Tour 7

Menus 7

Movie Window 13

Flash Windows 19

Chapter 2 Importing from and Exporting to Studios _____ **31**

Importing Vectors into Flash 32

Exporting Vectors from Flash 36

Importing Bitmaps into Flash 40

Exporting Bitmaps from Flash 42

Importing Sound into Flash 46

Exporting Video 47

Chapter 3 Drawing _____ **51**

Drawing in Flash 52

Changing Colors 72

Selecting and Reshaping Lines and Fills 78

Altering Shapes and Lines 87

Chapter 4 Overlays & Symbols _____ **95**

The Overlay Level 96

Text Objects 97

Bitmap Objects 103

Working on the Overlay Level 112

Symbols and the Library 116

Chapter 5 Animation _____ **121**

Frames 122

Frame-By-Frame Animation 126

Tweened Animation 131

Advanced Animation 138

Chapter 6 Layers _____ **145**

Working with Layers 146

Working with Artwork and Layers 150

Animating with Layers 155

Chapter 7 Scenes & Actions _____ **159**

How Scenes Work 160

Frame Actions 162

Buttons 165

Chapter 8 Actions _____ **175**

    Flash and the Web   176

    Button Effects   194

    Complex Actions   200

Chapter 9 Sound _____ **207**

    A Bit About Sound   208

    The Sound and the Flash   210

Chapter 10 Delivering Movies _____ **219**

    Exporting Movies   220

    Playing Movies   220

    Compression   228

    Size Reports   232

Chapter 11 Flash Sites _____ **245**

    How Much Flash Should You Use?   246

    Setting Up the Server   249

    Uploading Files to the Server   249

    The Payoff   250

Chapter 12 Flash Examples _____ **251**

    Macromedia, Inc.   252

    The Microsoft Network   253

    WebTV Networks, Inc.   254

    Becker Surf   255

    Hunterkillerdog   256

    Art Gallery of Ontario Edvard Munch Web Project   257

    Spumco's "The Goddamn George Liquor Program"   258

    Hide Needs Sake   259

    Aegagropila World   260

**Appendix A Configuring a Web Server to
Serve Shockwave Flash Movies** _____ **261**

Appendix B Transmission Speed _____ **265**

Appendix C <OBJECT>/<EMBED> Tag References _____ **267**

Appendix D Browser Scripting & Shockwave Flash Movies ___ **275**

Appendix E Hiding Broken Plug-in Icons _____ **283**

Appendix F Keyboard Shortcuts _____ **289**

Index _____ **297**

Introduction

One of the most satisfying

things you can do with a computer is make something that interacts with a viewer. A fundamental principle of art is to have an effect on others, and the ability to create computer-generated interactive artwork would seem to open a whole new world to the artist. With the advent of the World Wide Web, the potential audience is global.

Macromedia Flash is a tool designed for artists who want to use a computer to fulfill their visions for interactive art and show their works to the world. It incorporates many innovations from the way you draw artwork to how you make interactive buttons. It's easy to use, as well as extremely capable.

This book shows you step-by-step how to create artwork with Flash, how to animate that artwork, how to make interactive movies, and how to realize your dreams.

In this book you'll learn…

The Flash interface

Importing from and exporting to Macromedia Studios

Drawing in Flash

Flash animation

Symbols and overlays

Layers

Scenes and actions

Using sound with Flash

Delivering movies

Integrating Flash into your web site

The Dark Side of Multimedia

Creative artists have wrestled with the problems of designing interactive multimedia (kiosks, diskettes, CD-ROMs, etc.) for over a decade now. With the development of the Web and other forms of networked multimedia, online multimedia promised to be a boon for designers who wanted to push the creative envelope. Most of those promises fell short, though. The reality of file download times, the limitations of HTML layout capabilities, and designers' limited programming abilities have hindered that creativity.

For many people, design on the World Wide Web came to mean big downloads, the World Wide Wait—all of those logos, text blocks, and other graphics converted to bitmap GIFs and JPEGs to display! Most designers were forced to tone down their designs and trim down their files to work within the limitations of the medium.

There had to be a better way. There had to be a way that designers could get control over their layouts while retaining the fidelity of their original design concepts. Something that could solve the problem of big image files downloading over the world's networks. Programs like Macromedia Director and Macromedia Authorware exist as powerful, capable tools to create online and offline multimedia; but often they could be a little too powerful or a little too expensive for the average designer who simply wanted to tell a story, catch someone's attention, or just do something cool without dragging in the programmers. There had to be something.

Macromedia Flash: The Solution

Macromedia Flash combines simple methods for creating animation and interactivity with all the advantages of small file size that vector-based artwork allows. Its innovative drawing interface frees artists from the mechanics of other vector-based drawing programs without hampering their creativity.

Since its release, Flash has gained immense popularity because you can quickly put together a movie that looks like it took the hours or even the days it would take to create in other multimedia authoring programs. Because Flash has built-in drawing tools, there's no need to work in more than one program. Flash also recognizes and exports a variety of illustration and graphic formats.

You can play interactive Flash movies with a standalone Player or from HTML pages that use a Player controlled by a plug-in (Netscape Navigator or Communicator) or an ActiveX control (Microsoft Internet Explorer). You can export non-interactive animations created in Flash as QuickTime digital video, animated GIF files, or as a series of GIF, JPEG, EPS, or Adobe Illustrator-compatible files.

Flash is a tool designed for artists and designers to give them the power to create truly interactive multimedia. Flash movies incorporate graphics, animation, sound, and web connectivity with a fidelity to the design aesthetic that's unmatched by other multimedia programs.

Because of its small file size, resizable movies, and the accuracy with which the designer can predict what the movie will look like on a variety of screens. Flash's unique vector-based approach to multimedia makes it ideal for networked environments.

The interactive component of Flash movies is complex enough to handle most types of interaction without using programming techniques. Moreover, using browser scripting languages with Flash movies enables programmers to control Shockwave Flash movies with more precision.

Flash! The Book, the CD-ROM, and the Web Site

This book takes you through every step of creating Flash movies: from drawing to putting a finished movie into an HTML page. First you practice with the drawing tools and techniques to create images. In later exercises, you animate and turn it into interactive movies. Last, you'll incorporate your movies into HTML documents and framesets. All the projects in this book are designed to show you exactly how to accomplish the task at hand.

Also included is a brief tour of some of the most innovative web sites using Flash. The tour discusses the technology used, as well as what to look for when you're cruising the Web.

The CD-ROM accompanying this book contains the files for the exercises as well as samples of some of the other programs mentioned in these pages including Director, FreeHand, xRes, and SoundEdit 16.

You'll find this book contains a wealth of information notes, tips, and shortcuts. Even so, we couldn't show you everything about Flash that we would like to have shown you; it just wouldn't fit. So we've created a web site for the things that we wanted to show you but didn't have room for (plus the things we didn't know about when the book went to press). More exercises, examples, and up-to-date Flash information can be found there, at **http://www.macromedia.com/support/flash/**.

Moving On...

While Flash is a new player as a development program, it already has raised the bar for what people can expect from graphically oriented multimedia artists. It's truly an amazing tool. And a lot of fun.

The first chapter presents a tour of the Flash program, interface, and terminology to prepare you for a big trip into a new program. Prepare to be Flashed!

CHAPTER 1

Flash Tour

This chapter explores some

of the concepts behind the vector technology that makes Flash different from other forms of web animation. It also defines some of the terms used in this book as well as the scope of what Flash can do.

This tour introduces the elements of the Flash interface: the menus, palettes, and windows that you use to draw and animate movies. It's a quick course in the concepts and terms you'll encounter while learning to create Flash animation and interactive multimedia.

What you'll learn…

What Flash is

How Flash works

Flash Terminology

Macromedia Flash is like three applications in one: an authoring environment, an animation sequencer, and a vector-based drawing program.

Flash is an *authoring* program. You can use it to create *interactive multimedia* files, which are called *movies* in Flash. Interactive multimedia files usually incorporate graphics and sound (*multimedia*), and to some degree let the user determine the course of action (*interactivity*). Interactivity can be as simple as clicking a button to display a new screen or as complex as a cartoon animation.

Flash is an *animation sequencer.* You can use it to create or simulate motion or movement on screen. Flash uses a series of *frames* and a sequence of *scenes* to make its movies. Each frame of the movie can have one or more elements that can change position, size, color, etc. from the previous frame to create an animated effect. Using scenes, you organize sequences of frames within your movie. Digitized sounds may be imported into Flash and synchronized to specific events, or played as background music in your movie.

Flash is a *vector-based drawing program,* which means the program draws pictures on screen using points with specific coordinate values (*vectors*) to define curves. Vectors that connect together in a sequence describe a *path.* Flash uses all the vector information that describes a closed shape to create outlines and fills.

Graphics created as collections of vector information are mathematical equations. This gives vector graphics an advantage over bitmaps. The file size of an uncompressed bitmap image links directly to the size that it appears on screen. In a bitmap image you see the dots that make up the image so bitmaps appear pixellated—or jagged—when simply blown up to a larger size. In a vector graphic, the pixels are calculated every time the image is rendered to the screen.

Flash creates interactive movie files that play back through an application called the Flash Player. Movies also can be played back in web browsers, or as part of HTML (HyperText Markup Language) pages.

Individual frames of a movie can be exported as bitmap images (GIF, JPEG, and BMP), EPS (Encapsulated PostScript) graphics, as a FreeHand Xtra, a PICT (both vector and bitmap on Macintosh), or as illustration files (AI, DXF, WMF, and EMF) that you can use in other drawing programs like Macromedia FreeHand. Entire movies can be exported as QuickTime digital video files, animated GIF (Graphics Interchange Format) files, or as a series of individual bitmap, EPS, or illustration files.

Each movie scene is made up of *layers* that control how close the layer's images appear to the viewer. Layers are arranged from front to back; items on the front-most layers appear closest to the viewer.

Each layer has two *levels*: the *canvas* level and the *overlay* level. The canvas level contains lines and shapes. The overlay level contains text, bitmaps, and grouped items, as well as a special object type—the *symbol*. Objects on the overlay level have a *stacking order* that controls which object appears closest to the viewer.

Action!

Action commands give Flash interactivity. You assign actions to specific frames or symbols. When attached to a frame, Flash executes the action when it reaches that movie frame during playback. When attached to a graphic, Flash executes the action when the user clicks the graphic. Flash includes actions that can start or stop a movie, play a new scene or a different movie frame, or stop all sounds; and, when used in conjunction with a web browser, Flash can load new pages or movies into the browser window.

How Flash Works

Most multimedia animation programs depend on bitmap images for every element of an animation; so, if an image changes in size, shape, or rotation, it needs to be *pre-rendered* before the animation displays. A graphic that rotates 360° in 12 steps would require 12 separate bitmap images, each rotated 30° from the previous image.

Flash renders its images *on-the-fly*, as it needs them. When a movie plays, Flash uses the vectors of the objects in a frame to draw the picture right then and there. Flash then transforms the vector data into a bitmap image for onscreen display only when needed.

Vectors to the rescue

A picture displayed on a computer screen is made up of a series of dots arranged in a grid. The color of each dot, or *pixel*, is stored in memory as one or more numbers, which identify a particular color from a pre-defined list (or *index*) or by amounts of red, green, and blue light. A bitmap image is stored on disk the same way (see Figure 1.1). The size of a bitmap image in memory or on disk is directly related to its size on the screen, because each pixel requires a set amount of memory.

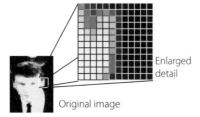

Enlarged detail

Original image

Figure 1.1
A bitmap image is stored in a computer's memory as a series of numbers with one or more numerical values representing a single pixel on screen.

Images created with vectors typically require much less storage space than bitmap images. Vectors are mathematical equations that define many of the same types of pictures created with bitmaps (see Figure 1.2).

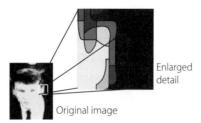

Enlarged detail

Original image

Figure 1.2
Vector programs use mathematical equations derived from a series of points to describe shapes and lines.

Vector-based images are not only smaller than bitmap images in most cases, but they can also be resized without any loss of resolution. The edges of an image drawn with vectors are just as sharp when enlarged as they are when when displayed at 100 percent of the original size. Bitmap images become jagged, or *pixellated*, when they're enlarged.

In Figure 1.3, the image on the left is a bitmap, the image on the right is made up of vectors. At 162 pixels across by 122 pixels tall, the bitmap image stores information for 19,764 pixels. Each pixel's color data is stored as a single byte, or about 20K (20,000 bytes) of memory for the bitmap. GIF data is compressed when the file is saved; this one is about 30 percent of original size, roughly 6K. The vector version, saved as a Shockwave Flash file is about 3K.

Figure 1.3
A bitmap (left) and a Flash movie (right) in which the Flash version of the image is half the size of the bitmap.

As a Flash movie plays, the vectors for the shapes for each frame draw outline by outline whenever they're needed. The same vectors can be used multiple times, enlarged, rotated, and moved, all without any loss of clarity.

Anti-aliasing

Because pixels are laid out on a grid, computers can display horizontal and vertical lines quite well. However, they don't always do a good job with curves or slanted lines. The human eye can see jagged edges in an image where one color meets another, a condition known as *aliasing*. Aliasing also can cause thin lines in artwork that displays at a small size to disappear entirely. *Anti-aliasing* is a process that visually smooths the edges between differently colored pixels by averaging the small colored areas to create the illusion of smooth-edged shapes. In Figure 1.4, the image on the left is aliased (no smoothing of the jagged edges occurs). The same image on the right is anti-aliased, which prevents some of the lines from disappearing entirely and smooths the boundaries between white and black by substituting intermediate gray pixels.

Figure 1.4
A detail from screen shots of the image in Figure 1.4 shows the effects of anti-aliasing at 100% of screen size (at bottom), and enlarged to 400% (above).

Most vector-based drawing programs focus on drawing a shape's outlines, using precise movements of a pen-like tool to lay down one control point after another to create the outline (see Figure 1.5). Flash takes an innovative approach to creating vector-based artwork by enabling the user to concentrate on drawing a line or shape with painting tools like a brush and paint bucket—the necessary control points are calculated automatically. Flash includes new techniques for reshaping lines and curves, simplifying complex shapes, selecting shapes, and combining shapes.

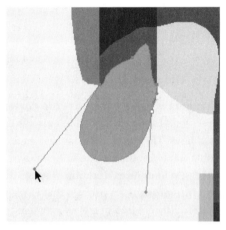

Figure 1.5
Drawing a shape in Macromedia FreeHand.

When vector drawings are not available, you can use bitmap images as pictures or as fills for other shapes; you also can trace bitmap images by using Flash's powerful automatic tracing utility that converts bitmaps to vector-based artwork.

Flashimation

Where Flash makes a radical departure from being just a very cool new drawing program is incorporating animation. Flash animation includes a *timeline* that you can use to create a sequence of events. A timeline is a series of *frames*, like a film strip, with a picture in each frame.

Creating animation in Flash includes creating *key frames*—points where change occurs (e.g., a shape's onscreen position, its color, or a sound plays)—and *tweening* (determining a shape's position, color, etc. between key frames). Tweening means that the animator doesn't have to make a picture for every frame. The animator sets a start position and time and an end position and time, and the program figures out the intermediate positions.

Flash on the Web

Flash incorporates *streaming*, which enables movies to play and display on screen before the file downloads completely from a web site. Even though vectors are usually very small, sound—or just a large number of graphics in a long movie—can mean that it may take a minute or two to download completely. With streaming, the movie starts to draw shapes as soon as the portion of the movie needed to draw the shape downloads.

Flash has made its biggest mark on the World Wide Web, inside HTML pages. To play a Flash movie inside a browser, the browser uses a special player plug-in called Shockwave. A Flash Edition of the Java Player makes Flash movies available on browsers that don't have the Shockwave Flash plug-in.

The Guided Tour

Flash is an easy-to-use program with a lot of capabilities. Because Flash movies incorporate so many tasks (drawing, animation, etc.), there are a lot of commands, windows, and terms related to creating movies with the program. This tour is intended to familiarize you with the basic elements of the program and make it easier to understand the exercises that follow.

Menus

This is a brief introduction to the functions available in the Flash menus. Flash duplicates some menu functions in tool modifiers, and on the toolbar in the Windows version.

File menu

The File menu contains commands used to create, open, and save Flash movies, illustrations, sounds, and bitmap files (see Figure 1.6). The commands on this menu deal with external files on the hard disk

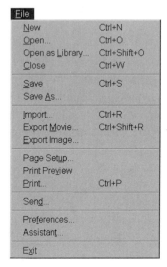

Figure 1.6
The File menu deals with file creation and external files.

Edit menu

The Edit menu contains commands that alter portions of shapes, objects, or scenes in a movie (see Figure 1.7).

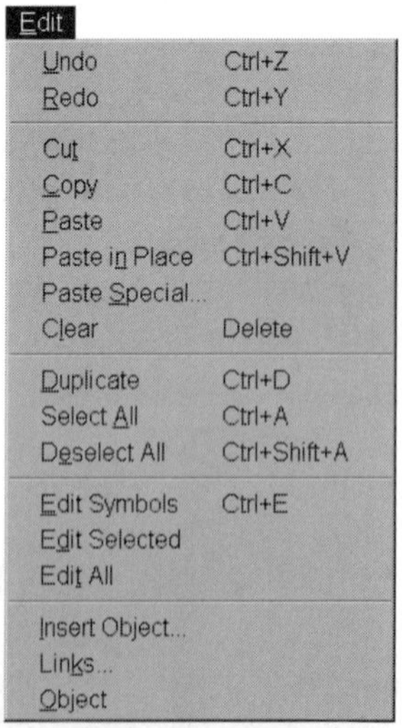

Figure 1.7
The Edit menu contains modification commands.

View menu

The View menu controls which scenes display, how they display, and what parts of the editing environment display (see Figure 1.8). The Goto submenu determines specifically which scene displays for editing (see Figure 1.9).

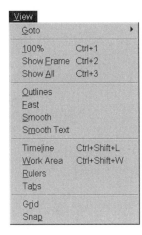

Figure 1.8
The View menu controls display.

Figure 1.9
The Goto submenu controls which scene displays.

Insert menu

The Insert menu commands add items to the Library, layers to the current scene, frames to layers, and scenes to movies (see Figure 1.10). Some items on the Insert menu are also available in the Modify Layers and Modify Frames pop-up menus in the timeline.

Figure 1.10
The Insert menu commands add or remove movie elements.

The Modify menu contains commands that alter whole objects, scenes, and movies (see Figure 1.11). It has four submenus: Kerning, which affects the space between type characters (see Figure 1.12); Transform, which affects the position, rotation, and scaling of objects and shapes (see Figure 1.13); Arrange, which modifies the stacking order of groups of symbols in a layer (see Figure 1.14); and Curves, which alters the selected shape's outlines (see Figure 1.15).

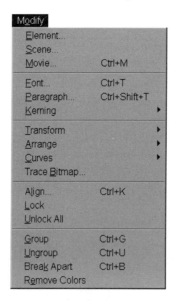

Figure 1.11
The Modify menu commands alter the appearance of objects.

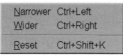

Figure 1.12
The Kerning submenu of the Modify menu controls spacing between characters.

Figure 1.13
The Transform submenu of the Modify menu affects objects and shapes.

Figure 1.14
The Arrange submenu of the Modify menu determines stacking order.

Figure 1.15
The Curves submenu of the Modify menu alters a shape's outline.

Control menu

The Control menu commands determine how the movie plays and responds to user interaction (see Figure 1.16).

Figure 1.16
The Control menu determines a movie's interaction and playback.

Xtras menu

The items on the Xtras menu depends on which files were installed in the Flash program's Xtras folder. Figure 1.17 shows the default Xtras for a full install of Flash:

Figure 1.17
The Xtras menu contains items from Flash's Xtras folder in its submenus.

Window menu commands arrange the various movie windows (see Figure 1.18).

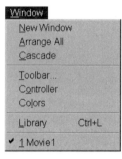

Figure 1.18
The Window menu determines the onscreen placement of windows and palettes.

Help menu commands access the online help files (see Figure 1.19).

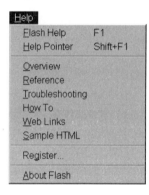

Figure 1.19
The Help menu gets answers.

Movie Window

Each movie window has two main areas. The lower half of the window is the *editor*, where the graphics in the current movie frame displays—along with its surrounding area, if you have selected Work Area in the View menu. The upper half of the window is the *timeline*, which controls how the movie operates and what displays in the editor (see Figure 1.20).

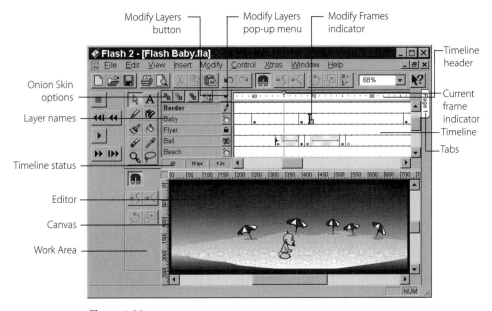

Figure 1.20
The movie window displays the editing window and timeline and other features of Flash.

Tabs also may appear on the right side of the screen. Use them to switch between scenes in movie editing mode and between symbols in editing mode. You can rearrange a movie's scenes by reordering its tabs.

The editor displays objects that appear in the current frame of the movie. There are two parts to the Editor: the Canvas and the Work Area (see Figure 1.20, above).

Canvas

The frame appears in the editor as a colored rectangle selected for the movie's background in the Modify > Movie menu. You can see only those objects that appear within the frame in the exported movie.

Work Area

If the Work Area appears at all (View > Work Area), it appears as a gray area surrounding the frame. Objects in the Work Area do not appear when the movie is exported; however, an animation can start or stop in the Work Area to give the appearance of moving outside the frame.

Timeline

The timeline displays information about the movie over a range of frames. It also shows the organization of the movie's layers (see Figure 1.20, above).

Onion Skin

Toggles the display of the onion-skinning feature. Onion skinning displays the graphics contained in a range of frames. Objects in previous frames are displayed in ghosted colors to register graphics in one frame to those in other frames, or to adjust the graphics relative to one another (see Figure 1.21). Items that appear in the frames—but do not move during the range of onion-skinned frames—display normally.

Figure 1.21
A range of frames displayed in onion skin.

Onion Skin Outlines

 Toggle the display of the onion-skinning feature. Same as Onion Skin, except graphics are displayed as outlines (see Figure 1.22).

Figure 1.22
A range of frames displayed in onion skin outlines.

Edit Multiple Frames

 If either Onion Skin or Onion Skin Outline is selected, this menu item enables editing the graphics in all frames of the onion-skin range.

Modify Onion Markers

Onion-skin markers set the range of frames whose graphics are displayed when onion skinning is on; you can modify the marker positions with the five options in this pop-up menu (see Figure 1.23).

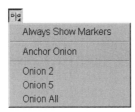

Figure 1.23
The Modify Onion Markers pop-up menu displays its options.

Modify Frame View

Controls spacing between frames in the timeline display (see Figure 1.24).

Figure 1.24
The Modify Frame View pop-up menu controls appearance of the timeline frames.

Timeline header

Extends over the timeline to indicate which frames are visible. The header contains the current frame indicator and the onion skin markers.

Layer Name

Identifies which layer is on a row of the timeline. Clicking and dragging the Layer Name vertically changes its stacking order with respect to other layers; layers at the top of the list appear in front of other layers (closer to the viewer). Double-clicking on the Layer Name makes it the active layer.

Modify Layers

Opens a pop-up menu that contains commands to alter layers. Each layer has its own Modify Layers button. Any command you choose from the Modify Layers pop-up menu affects only that layer whose Modify Layers button you click. The icon on each layer's Modify Layer button indicates that layer's state (see Figure 1.25).

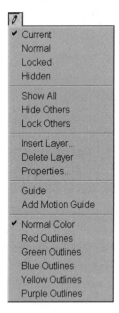

Figure 1.25
The Modify Layers pop-up menu determines where a button appears.

Frames

Indicates when objects appear in a layer and their status. Each layer has at least one frame: a key frame. A solid line indicates the layer's last frame. The default display mode for the frames is red or blue dots, but frames also can display thumbnails of the layer's objects (see Figure 1.26).

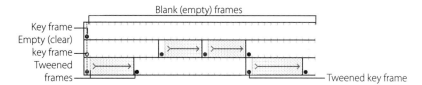

Figure 1.26
The Flash frame types displayed in the timeline.

Empty Frame

Indicates that there is no change from the previous frame on this layer.

Tweened Frame

Indicates an intermediate frame derived from two key frames through tweening. Tweened frames contain a red arrow.

Empty Key Frame

Indicates there are no visual elements in the frame on this layer. Empty key frames have an empty blue circle at the lower left.

Key Frame

Indicates that there are changes to visual elements in the frame on this layer. Key frames have a solid blue dot at the lower left.

Tweened Key Frame

Indicates that the key frame is derived from a tweened frame. Tweened key frames have a solid red dot at the lower left.

Action Frame

Indicates that the frame has an action associated with it. Action frames have a lowercase "a" in the upper left corner.

Sounds

Sounds in a layer are indicated by a thumbnail view of the sound wave, showing the length of the sound in relation to the timeline.

Modify Frames

Clicking a frame in the timeline displays an insertion point and a small gray box. Clicking the small gray box opens the Modify Frames pop-up menu to enable you to modifiy the selected frame. Select multiple frames and layers by clicking and dragging across frames and layers. The Modify Frames pop-up menu contains commands that alter the frames in the timeline (see Figure 1.27).

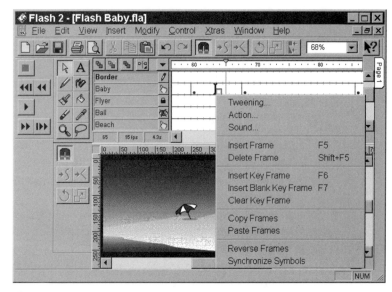

Figure 1.27
The Modify Frames pop-up menu items modify frames in the timeline.

Timeline Status

Contains numeric data about the movie (see Figure 1.28).

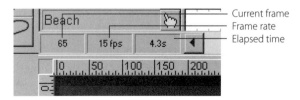

Figure 1.28
The timeline status bar provides information about the movie's playback.

Current Frame

Shows the frame number for the current frame.

Frame Rate

Shows the movie's desired playback speed (double-clicking on this value opens the Movie Properties dialog box, from which you can control the frame rate).

Elapsed Time

Shows how many seconds have elapsed when the movie reaches the current frame, at full speed (Elapsed Time = Current Frame / Frame Rate). This number does not vary, even if the movie cannot play at full speed on the current computer.

Flash Windows

The Flash program uses a number of floating windows that provide quick access to commonly used functions. Floating windows always appear in front of the movie and timeline window. In the Windows version of the program, they can be "docked" to the edges of the main Flash program window.

VCR Controller

Use the VCR Controller to play the movie and to move through the movie frames (see Figure 1.29).

Figure 1.29
The VCR Controller controls movie play.

Stop
Halts playback of the movie if it is running.

Rewind
Makes the first frame of the current scene the current frame.

Step Back
Makes the frame previous to the current frame the current frame.

Play
Begins movie playback from the current frame.

Step Forward
Makes the frame after the current frame the current frame.

Go to End
Moves the current frame indicator to the last frame of the current scene.

Color window

Use the Solid and Gradient tabs in the Color window to modify and add solid colors and gradient blends to the color palette for this movie.

Solid

Use this Color-window mode to modify and create solid colors to use with lines or fills. The default colors in the Solid colors list are the 216 standard, "web-safe" colors. These colors appear without dithering in most browsers (see Figure 1.30).

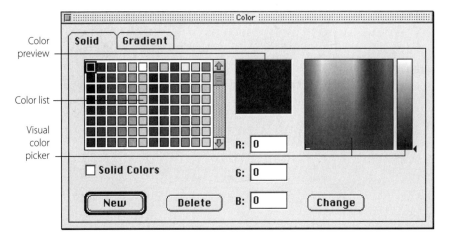

Figure 1.30
The Color window in Solid mode contains the default "web-safe" colors.

Color List
Displays current colors available and selected color.

Color Preview
Shows a large patch of the selected color.

Visual Color Picker
Click in the square to select a hue and saturation; click in the vertical bar to select lightness.

Solid Colors
When checked, enforces 216-color web palette on any chosen color by selecting the nearest match to the chosen color.

Numeric Color Picker
Select a color by typing in number for Red, Green, and Blue values. Values range from 0 to 255.

New
Creates a new position on the color list and selects that position.

Delete
Deletes the selected position on the color list.

Change
Verifies a change in color and applies it to the selection in the color list.

Gradient

Use this mode of the Color window to modify *gradients* (or blends) for use as fills (see Figure 1.31).

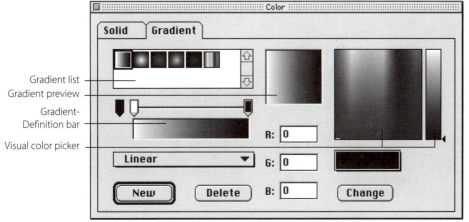

Gradient list
Gradient preview
Gradient-
Definition bar
Visual color picker

Figure 1.31
The Color window in Gradient mode used to modify fills.

Gradient List
Displays the current gradients and the selected gradient.
Gradient Preview
Displays a patch with the applied gradient.
Visual Color Picker
Select a color from the square (hue and saturation) and the vertical bar (lightness).
Gradient-Definition Bar
Sets the colors and positions along the gradient where the specified color appears. You can place up to eight color pointers along the line above the builder (there are always at least two pointers). You also can assign each pointer a different color from the Visual or Numeric color pickers or from the Color List. The Gradient Builder automatically blends the portion of the gradient between two pointers.
Gradient Type
This pop-up menu enables you to choose between Linear (straight) and Radial (circular) gradients.

Numeric Color Picker

Choose a color by typing in number for Red, Green, and Blue values. Values range from 0 to 255.

Color List

Enables you to select a color from the Solid Color List.

New

Creates a new selection on the gradient list.

Delete

Deletes the selection on the gradient list.

Change

Verifies a change in a gradient and applies it to the selection in the gradient list.

Library window

The Library window is a repository for a movie's symbols, bitmaps, and sounds (see Figure 1.32).

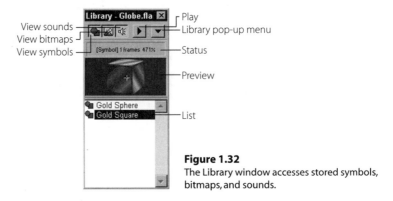

Figure 1.32
The Library window accesses stored symbols, bitmaps, and sounds.

View Symbols

Toggles viewing of symbols and buttons in the Library list.

View Bitmaps

Toggles viewing of bitmaps in the Library list.

View Sounds

Toggles viewing of sounds in the Library list.

Play

> When you select a symbol or button in the Library list, this button displays each of its frames in the Preview area. When you select a sound in the Library list, the sound plays.

Library pop-up menu

> Contains commands specific to the Library (see Figure 1.33).

Create Symbol...
Edit
Delete
Duplicate...
Properties...
Update...
Play
Smooth

Figure 1.33
The Library pop-up menu enables you
to create and modify symbols.

Status

> Displays information about the selected Library item. Indicates the item type (symbol, bitmap, sound). Symbols display the number of frames used for the symbol and how large the preview image is relative to the actual symbol. Sounds show length (in seconds) and the size of the uncompressed sound (in kilobytes).

Preview

> Displays the selected Library items in miniature. When you select a symbol and click the Play button, all frames in the symbol's timeline play in the preview window.

List

> Displays all Library items. You can limit this list by using the View Symbols, View Bitmaps, and View Sounds buttons.

Toolbar

The toolbar is a dockable or floating window under Windows, and remains a floating window on Macintosh. It contains all of the drawing and selection tools. Modifiers for the selected tool appear below the tool buttons on the toolbar (see Figure 1.34). More information about these tools can be found in Chapter 3, "Drawing."

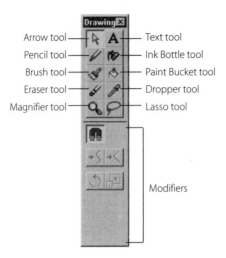

Arrow tool — Text tool
Pencil tool — Ink Bottle tool
Brush tool — Paint Bucket tool
Eraser tool — Dropper tool
Magnifier tool — Lasso tool

Modifiers

Figure 1.34
The toolbar with the arrow tool selected.

On Macintosh, the Zoom Control appears between the tool buttons and the modifiers. The Zoom Control appears on the standard toolbar on Windows machines. You can enlarge or reduce the apparent size of the frame by selecting a zoom level from the Zoom Control's pop-up menu, or by typing a value in the Zoom Control indicator.

Arrow tool

Use the arrow tool to select items by clicking, double-clicking, or click-dragging. You also can use the arrow to move and transform items by dragging on their handles. Arrow modifiers include the following:

Magnet
Toggles the automatic snap feature (same function as the View > Snap menu item).

Smooth
Simplifies selected lines and shapes (same function as the Modify > Curves > Smooth menu item).

Straighten
Simplifies selected lines and shapes (same function as the Modify > Curves > Straighten menu item).

Rotate

Displays handles for rotation of a selection (same function as the Modify > Transform > Rotate menu item).

Scale

Displays handles for scaling of a selection (same function as the Modify > Transform > Scale menu item).

Text tool

A Use the text tool to create and modify text objects on the overlay layer. Clicking in an empty area in the frame creates a new text object on the current layer; clicking an existing text object opens it for editing. The text tool has the following modifiers:

Font

Sets the default font and changes any selected text to that font.

Font Size

Sets the default font size and changes any selected text to that size.

Font Color

Sets the default font color and changes any selected text to that color.

Bold

Sets the default font style to the bold version of the selected font and changes any selected text to bold.

Italic

Sets the default font style to the italic version of the selected font and changes any selected text to italic.

Alignment

Sets the default alignment of text objects and changes any selected text to that alignment.

Paragraph

Sets the default paragraph properties for text objects and changes any selected text to share those properties.

Use the pencil tool to draw lines and the shape outlines on the canvas level. It uses the following modifiers:

Pencil Mode

The pencil has several different modes, depending on what type of line or shape you want. They include **Straighten**, **Smooth**, **Ink**, **Oval**, **Rectangle**, and **Line**.

Line Color

Selects the color with which the pencil draws.

Line Width

Selects the width of the line the pencil draws.

Line Style

Selects the type of line (solid, dashed, dotted, etc.) the pencil draws.

 Use the ink bottle to add a line to a shape or to modify an existing line by clicking on the shape or line. It uses the following modifiers:

Line Color

Selects the color the ink bottle applies.

Line Width

Selects the width of the line the ink bottle applies.

Line Style

Selects the type of line (solid, dashed, dotted, etc.) the ink bottle applies.

 Use the brush tool to paint filled shapes on the canvas level. It uses the following modifiers:

Brush Mode

Controls how the paint interacts with other painted shapes already on the canvas. Possible settings are **Paint Normal**, **Paint Fills**, **Paint Behind**, **Paint Selection**, and **Paint Inside**.

Pressure

Toggles pressure sensitivity on and off for the brush tool. When on, the size of the brush stroke increases with the amount of pressure on a pen. This modifier appears only if the computer has a pressure-sensitive pen tablet attached.

Brush Color

Selects the color with which the brush paints.

Brush Size

Selects the size of the brush stroke.

Brush Shape

Changes the shape of the brush stroke.

Lock Fill

Affects how Flash handles new areas painted with gradient shapes. If on, all shapes painted with the same gradient appear to be part of a single filled shape.

Paint bucket tool

 The paint bucket fills unfilled outlines and changes the color of existing shapes. It uses the following modifiers:

Fill Color

Selects the color that fills the paint bucket.

Gap Size

Controls how large you can make gaps in unfilled outlines before the paint bucket no longer recognizes them as closed shapes. Settings are **Don't Close Gaps**, **Close Small Gaps**, **Close Medium Gaps**, and **Close Large Gaps**.

Lock Fill

Affects how Flash handles new areas filled with gradient shapes. If on, all shapes filled with the same gradient appear to be part of a single filled shape.

Transform Fill

Displays handles on gradients and bitmaps used as fills so you can rotate, skew, or scale them.

Eraser tool

 Use the eraser tool to selectively delete portions of lines and shapes on the canvas level. It uses the following modifiers:

Eraser Mode

Controls and restricts what portions of lines or shapes are erased. Possible settings are **Normal**, **Erase Fills**, **Erase Lines**, **Erase Selected Fills**, and **Erase Inside**.

Faucet

Erases entire lines or fills. If you select a line or fill with the faucet tool, Flash erases the entire selection.

Eraser Shape

Modifies the shape of the eraser tool.

Dropper tool

Picks up a fill or line style from a shape or line. After clicking on the shape or line, the dropper tool automatically converts to the paint bucket tool (if a fill is selected) or the ink bottle tool (if a line is selected). The dropper tool has no modifiers.

Magnifier tool

The magnifier enlarges or reduces the view of the movie. Clicking in the frame with the magnifier tool makes the image on screen bigger or smaller, depending on the chosen modifier. Clicking and dragging a rectangle enlarges the enclosed area to fit the working area of the screen. Holding down the Alt key (Windows) or the Option key (Macintosh), shifts modes for the magnifier. It has two modifiers:

Enlarge

Sets the magnifier default to make the image larger.

Reduce

Sets the magnifier default to make the image smaller.

Lasso tool

The lasso tool selects irregular areas of the current frame by click-dragging an outline of the area you want to select. You can use it to split shapes, or to select only a portion of a line. It has two modifiers:

Magic Wand

With this modifier selected, you can use the lasso tool to select a portion of a bitmap image to use as a fill.

Magic Wand Properties

This modifier controls the magic wand's modifier tolerances.

Moving On...

This chapter introduced the menus and the tools used in Flash. By now you are more familiar and comfortable with the terms in this book and Flash's capabilities. The following chapters demonstrate how to use the tools and what they can do.

The next chapter introduces the various methods of importing and exporting graphics. Flash is a very flexible program, capable of incorporating a wide variety of file formats into its drawings. And while it's best known as a tool for making interactive animations for the Web, you can use it to create everything from graphics for print work to digital video.

CHAPTER 2

Importing from and Exporting to Studios

What you'll learn...

How Flash works with the Macromedia Studios

How to import artwork into movies

How to export frames and movies to other programs

Flash is an artistic creation

and design tool in its own right—

but it operates in a world alongside artwork that generally is created with other programs. It is easy to incorporate art and images created for print, video, and other media in your interactive Flash movies. Flash imports a wide range of file formats and can use artwork created in the era B.F. (Before Flash).

Flash is a useful tool for creating animations and drawing artwork because it exports to a variety of formats. Using Flash, you can export individual movie frames as vector artwork and bitmap files. You can export an entire movie as a sequence of files (vectors or bitmaps—it's your choice), as an animated GIF, or as a digital video file.

This chapter explores how Flash incorporates other programs in the Macromedia Studios by importing from and exporting to FreeHand, Fontographer, Director, Authorware, Extreme 3D, xRes, and SoundEdit 16.

Importing Vectors into Flash

Creating vector graphics in Flash is easy (see Chapter 3, "Drawing"). And, once you've mastered the Flash drawing interface, you may find yourself using it more and more—even for projects that aren't intended as Flash movies. If you're like most artists, though, Flash isn't your only drawing program. You probably have plenty of images that you would like to use in your Flash movies without redrawing them. In Flash you don't have to redraw your artwork because it can import artwork from many vector drawing programs.

TIP *Flash can create certain types of vector shapes more easily and quickly than most other illustration programs. Maps, for instance, require many adjoining shapes that share edges. However, taking a series of outlines (borders) and creating shapes for each of the countries (or other shapes) that are between the borders can be a daunting task—but not with Flash. In Flash you can import the outlines, use the paint bucket tool to fill the space between the borders, and Flash creates the shapes automatically.*

Flash also can use most vector-based clip art libraries. You simply import the clip art files into the program, where you animate and modify the files. Flash also can import vector artwork created by a variety of programs. The import process for each is slightly different, however, as described below.

Macromedia FreeHand

There are three methods for converting artwork from the FreeHand format to Flash: copying, importing, and using the Flash Export Xtra.

To copy artwork from one program to the another:

1. Open your artwork file with FreeHand.

2. Select the lines and shapes you want to copy.

3. Choose the **Copy** command from the Edit menu in Freehand.

4. Use Flash to open the movie in which you want to use the artwork.

5. Choose **Paste** from the Edit menu in Flash.

This sequence places the copied artwork on a single layer in the Flash movie. Flash imports each shape as an overlay object, which prevents you from modifying shapes accidentally.

Complex illustrations created in FreeHand can benefit from importing rather than simply copying the artwork. Importing preserves any layers that you may have created in FreeHand, with each layer in the original illustration duplicated in the Flash movie. In Flash, you can animate and modify objects on different layers independently.

To import a FreeHand document:

1. Open your artwork file with FreeHand.

2. Choose **Export** from the File menu.

3. Choose the **Adobe Illustrator 5.5** format from the Format pop-up menu and click **Export**.

4. Open a new movie in Flash.

5. Choose **Import** from the File menu to open the Import dialog box. Limit your choice of files to vector artwork files by choosing **Adobe Illustrator** from the **List Files of Type** pop-up menu (see Figure 2.1). Choose a file to import and click **Open**.

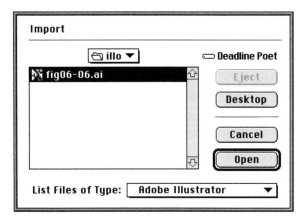

Figure 2.1
Using the Adobe Illustrator option displays only Adobe Illustrator files in the Import dialog box.

NOTE *When Flash imports the selected artwork file into the movie, all layers and layer items maintain their relative positions.*

SHORTCUT Invoke the Import command by pressing the Ctrl-R (Windows) or Command-R (Macintosh) keys.

You also can import two or more illustrations (and their layers) into the same Flash movie. Each successive layer of the illustration appears behind the existing layers.

TIP *If you choose an artwork file that is part of a sequence of numbered files (file001, file002, file003, etc.), Flash prompts you to import the entire sequence. Each file of an imported sequence occupies a single frame in one layer of the Flash movie—no layers import from the artwork file, and each layer of the imported file becomes an overlay object.*

Artwork imported into the movie starts in the first frame of the scene, and the last frame of each of the imported layers is the final frame of the scene.

NOTE *Bitmap images and gradient fills pose problems for imported artwork. To copy a bitmap image from a FreeHand document to Flash, select only the bitmap image (in FreeHand), copy and paste it into Flash. Copying a bitmap as part of a larger selection in FreeHand will not work, nor will attempting to import the image from a saved FreeHand file. Gradient (blended) fills created in other programs are copied and imported into Flash with each step of the blend drawn as an individual shape. Instead of applying gradient fills to shapes in FreeHand, fill shapes with solid colors and apply gradients after you have imported them into Flash. The resulting files are much smaller and easier to work with.*

The third method for importing FreeHand artwork into Flash is an Xtra included in FreeHand versions 7.0.2 and later. The Xtra saves a FreeHand file as a Shockwave Flash movie that you can use immediately with the Shockwave Flash Player or import into Flash.

To export FreeHand artwork with the Xtra:

1. Open an artwork file with FreeHand 7.0.2 or later.

2. Choose **Xtras > Create > Flash Image**. The Export File dialog box appears.

3. Click the **Options** button in the dialog box and choose the appropriate **Image Compression** and **Pages** options. Image Compression controls the quality of any embedded bitmap images; Pages specifies which pages of the FreeHand file export.

4. In the Save File dialog box, enter a name for the exported Shockwave Flash movie, and click the **Save** button.

5. Create a new movie with Flash.

6. Choose **File > Import**. Use the Import File dialog box to select the exported Shockwave Flash movie. Import the shapes created in FreeHand into the new Flash movie. Flash imports each FreeHand shape as a separate grouped object.

While this process converts shapes from FreeHand files, it does not preserve FreeHand layer information.

Macromedia Extreme 3D

Extreme 3D can create views of 3-dimensional shapes. You can use it to create vector files in the Drawing Exchange Format (DXF) as well as bitmap images (see "Importing Bitmaps into Flash," below).

DXF files imported into Flash provide a set of outlines that you can use as artwork or templates for new artwork created in Flash.

To import 3D shapes into Flash from Extreme 3D:

1. Open the 3D model in Extreme 3D.

2. Choose **File > Export > DXF** to display the Export File dialog box.

3. In the Export File dialog box, enter in the new file name for the DXF file and export the file.

4. In Flash, open a new movie.

5. Choose **File > Import**. Select the DXF file you exported from Extreme 3D.

Flash imports the DXF file into the Flash movie as a single group on one layer.

The Flash drawing tools were specifically designed so users could use tools similar to their "real-world" tools: brushes, erasers, and pencils (with unlimited resolution). This makes Flash easy to use for the person who isn't accustomed to computer-graphic tools. At the same time, Flash is powerful enough for the FreeHand expert to do sophisticated editing, such as trimming an illustration.

Macromedia Extreme 3D

You can import artwork created in Flash into Extreme 3D, where you can use the outlines as shapes to extrude, or otherwise manipulate in three dimensions.

To export shapes to Extreme 3D from Flash:

1. Open a movie with Flash.

2. Choose **File > Export Image** to display the Export File dialog box.

3. In the Export File dialog box, select **Autocad DXF** from the Save File as Type pop-up menu, and enter a name for the DXF file.

4. In Extreme 3D, open a new file.

5. Choose **File > Import > DXF**, and select the DXF file exported from Flash.

Flash imports the DXF file created in Flash into the Extreme 3D file as outlines that you can group and modify, or simply use as reference images for 3D modelmaking.

Macromedia FreeHand

If you need to provide artwork to someone who doesn't have Flash, or use a plug-in effect not available for Flash, you can export your Flash animations into an illustration program.

You have three options for exporting Flash artwork to FreeHand: copy individual frames to FreeHand; export frames as artwork files; or export entire movies to create artwork files with one file for each frame.

To copy artwork from one frame of a Flash movie to a FreeHand file:

1. Open the Flash movie, and select the scene and frame you want to copy.

2. Select the graphics you want to copy.

3. Choose **Copy** from the Edit menu.

4. Open the FreeHand file that is the artwork's destination.

5. Choose **Paste** from the Edit menu in FreeHand.

Copying artwork from Flash to FreeHand does not preserve the layers in the movie.

TIP *This is the only method for exporting files from Flash to FreeHand that handles both vector artwork and bitmap images.*

By exporting individual frames of a Flash movie as vector artwork files, you can preserve the layers of the Flash movie in the artwork file, which can help you organize the individual artwork elements.

To export a frame of a Flash movie:

1. Open the Flash movie, select the scene and frame to export.

2. Choose the **Export Image** command from the File menu.

3. Select **Adobe Illustrator** from the Save File As Type pop-up menu (see Figure 2.2), type in a name for the file, and click **Save**.

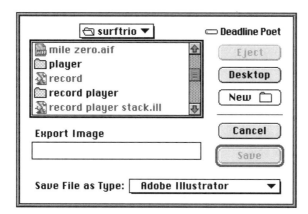

Figure 2.2
The Flash Export Image dialog box ready to export a Flash frame as an Adobe Illustrator-format file.

4. To preserve your layers from the Flash movie, select Adobe Illustrator version 5 or later in the Export Adobe Illustrator dialog box (see Figure 2.3). Click **OK**.

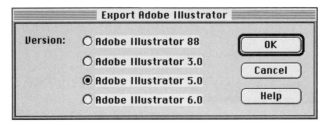

Figure 2.3
The Export Adobe Illustrator dialog box.

5. In FreeHand, open the file. The artwork (except for bitmap images) and layers in the Flash file are preserved.

You can export entire movies from Flash as well. Flash saves each frame of the movie as an individual file, gives it a name you choose, and numbers it to indicate its sequence in the movie.

To export an entire movie as a sequence of artwork files:

1. Open the Flash movie.

2. Choose the **Export Movie** command from the File menu.

3. Choose **Adobe Illustrator Sequence** from the Save File As Type pop-up menu (see Figure 2.4); type in a base name for the sequence of files, and click **Save**.

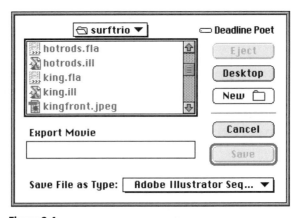

Figure 2.4
The Export Movie dialog box accessed via the File menu.

4. To preserve your Flash movie's layers, select Adobe Illustrator 5.0 or later in the Export Adobe Illustrator dialog box. Click **OK**.

5. With FreeHand, you can open each of the files separately. Artwork (except for bitmap images) and layers in the Flash file are preserved in each file.

Macromedia Fontographer

A somewhat overlooked use for Flash is as an accessory to Macromedia's typeface design tool, Fontographer. In many ways, Flash is an ideal tool for digital type design because it automatically joins shapes, unlike most other vector drawing tools.

You can use Flash to draw free-form or pictograph typefaces, or to join pieces of fonts together. If you build a library of parts, stems, bowls, serifs, etc., you can drag the necessary pieces together and let the program join them.

If you build each character of the typeface in its own frame, you can export the entire character set as individual files, and then import them into Fontographer as needed. Of course, you can export individual characters too.

When drawing characters to use in Fontographer, you should use black-filled shapes filled with no lines, outlines, overlay objects, or symbols.

To export a movie that contains characters for use in Fontographer:

1. Open the Flash movie that contains your typeface characters.

2. Export all of the characters as individual files by choosing **File > Export Movie**.

3. Choose **Adobe Illustrator Sequence** from the Save File As Type pop-up menu; type in a base name for the files, and click **Save**.

4. In the Export Adobe Illustrator dialog box, choose Adobe Illustrator 5.0 or later. Click **OK**.

5. In Fontographer, open the font for which you are exporting the characters, or create a new font file.

6. Select the character for which you are importing the outline file, and then choose **Open Outline Window** from the Windows menu.

7. Choose **File > Import > EPS**, and then choose the outline file for the selected character. The contents of a single Flash frame become the outline for the character.

TIP *If you've used the Flash drawing tools to create your characters, it may be necessary to use Fontographer's Clean Up Paths command from the Elements menu to simplify the paths. You can use the Flash Smooth and Optimize commands as well, but Fontographer's Clean Up Paths modifies the outlines by a lesser amount.*

Importing Bitmaps into Flash

Flash can use bitmap images as movie elements, as fills, or as templates for vector artwork. (For more specific information on using and manipulating bitmaps, see Chapter 4, "Overlays & Symbols.")

Flash imports GIF and JPEG bitmap images from both Windows and Macintosh platforms. The Windows version of Flash imports BMP files. The Macintosh version imports PICT (both bitmap and vector-based) files.

NOTE *While Flash can export animated GIF files, it can only import the first image from an animated GIF.*

Macromedia xRes

You can import a bitmap file created with Macromedia xRes into Flash, if you save it in one of the standard formats that Flash imports. Images with large areas of similar colors are best saved as indexed-color images in GIF, BMP, or PICT formats to conserve size. Photographic-style images with continuous color tones are usually smaller when saved as JPEG images.

NOTE *Don't compress a JPEG image before importing it into Flash. When Flash exports the bitmap image, it performs its own JPEG compression.*

To save an image from xRes for use in a Flash movie:

1. Open the bitmap image in xRes.

2. Choose **Resize > Document** from the Modify menu.

3. Enter values for the Width, Height, and Resolution. In most cases, you should use a Resolution of **72 pixels/inch**. Click **OK**.

TIP *The quality of some images may be adequate at lower resolution settings. Try saving the image at 50 pixels/inch to see if the quality meets your standards.*

4. Choose an export format from the **File > Export** submenu, and select any pertinent options in the dialog box specific to the file type. Enter a file name in the **Save Image** dialog box, and click **Save**.

5. Import the bitmap image into a new or existing Flash movie with the **File > Import** command.

NOTE *You can use bitmap images created with FreeHand in Flash; in general, however, it is best to import artwork created in FreeHand as vector images.*

Macromedia Extreme 3D

You can use Macromedia Extreme 3D on both Windows and Macintosh platforms to create a single, bitmapped three-dimensional scene, or a series of bitmaps depicting a 3D animation—either of which you can import into Flash. Because the file size of bitmap images is much larger than that of vector artwork (in most cases), importing long animation sequences into Flash is not recommended; but you easily can use individual 3D images or short (and small) 3D animations in the final movie, or as templates for artwork drawn in Flash.

To export bitmap images from Extreme 3D to Flash:

1. Open the scene or animation in Extreme 3D.

2. Choose **Render to Disk** from the Render menu.

3. If you only need one frame, choose **Single Frame** from the Render to Disk dialog box and enter the number of the desired frame. If you need an animation, choose **Multiple Frames**, and choose **All** or **From**.

4. Choose the **Final** option and a **Final Render Size**, and then choose **BMP**, **GIF**, **JPEG**, or **PICT** from the File Format menu. Click **Render** to begin rendering. Close the Render to Disk window.

5. Enter a file name and location in the Save File dialog box for the file or files. If you are saving a range of frames, each individual file is numbered in sequence, enabling Flash to import them in order. Click **Save**.

6. Depending on the format for the bitmap files, you may need to set options for your particular file type in a specialized dialog box.

7. Open a new or existing movie in Flash. Choose **Import** from the File menu, and select one or more bitmap files to import (see Figure 2.5).

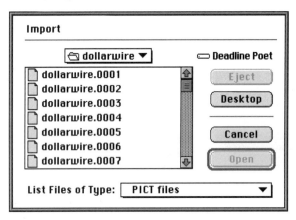

Figure 2.5
The Import dialog box displays a series of bitmap PICT images.

Exporting Bitmaps from Flash

With Flash you can create graphics that you can use with bitmap-oriented programs. Flash can help automate creating smooth, cartoon-style animations that you can use in multimedia authoring programs like Director and Authorware, as well as artwork you can import into xRes or Extreme 3D. Even FreeHand can benefit from this capability.

Flash exports bitmaps in the same formats it imports (GIF, JPEG, BMP, and PICT), as well as the Animated GIF format. You can export each movie frame—or an entire movie—as a bitmap. Flash converts the vector artwork to anti-aliased bitmaps. When you export an entire movie as bitmaps, you have the option to export as a sequence of individual files, or to export a single Animated GIF file that contains all of the frames in the movie.

To export a single frame of a Flash movie to a bitmap format:

1. Open the Flash movie, select the scene and frame you want to export.

2. From the File menu, choose the **Export Image** command to open the Export Image dialog box.

3. Choose **PICT file**, **Bitmap**, **JPEG Image**, or **GIF Image** from the Save As type pop-up menu, type in a file name, and click **Save**.

4. In the Export Image dialog box, choose **Dimensions**, **Resolution**, and any format-specific options. Click **OK** to complete the export of the bitmap image.

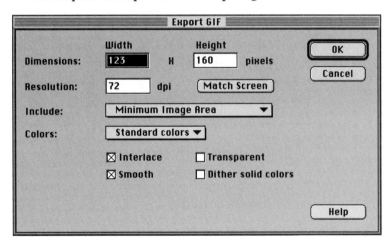

Figure 2.6
The Export Image dialog box displays the options for a single-frame GIF image.

To export an entire movie as a sequence of bitmap files or a single Animated GIF file:

1. Open the Flash movie.

2. From the File menu, choose the **Export Movie** command.

3. Choose **Animated GIF**, **PICT Sequence**, **BMP Sequence**, **JPEG Sequence**, or **GIF Sequence** from the Save As type pop-up menu, type in a base name for the files, and click **Save**.

4. From the Export dialog box, choose **Dimensions**, **Resolution**, and any format-specific options. Click **OK** to complete the export of the bitmap images or the single Animated GIF file.

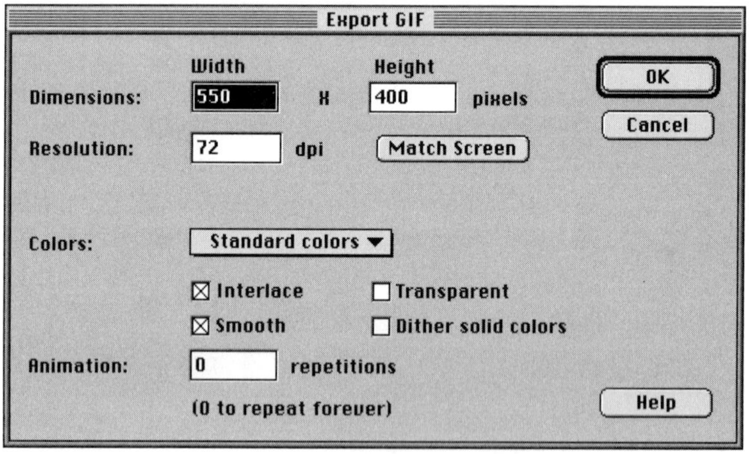

Figure 2.7
The Export Movie dialog box displays the options for an animated GIF image.

After Flash exports the sequence, you can import it into any of the programs in the Studios.

Macromedia xRes

You can combine Flash frames exported as bitmaps with other bitmap images in xRes. Simply open the files with xRes, which supports the opening of all bitmap file formats, except Animated GIF.

Macromedia Extreme 3D

You can use Extreme 3D to import bitmap images as backgrounds or texture maps.

To import a bitmap image created with Flash into Extreme 3D as a background image:

1. Open the 3D file with Extreme 3D.

2. Choose **Set Background** from the Render menu.

3. Click the **Load** button and use the File selection dialog box to choose the bitmap image.

To use a bitmap image as a Material element in Extreme 3D:

1. Open the **Materials** palette from the Windows menu.

2. Select the material **Default-Mondo Map** from the Materials in Catalog list on the right side of the window. Click the << button to load the material into the Materials in Scene list.

3. Select the material in the Materials in Scene list, and click **Edit** located below the list.

4. Modify the material by choosing an attribute tab and clicking the Map preview to open the Edit Texture dialog box. Clicking the **Load** button in the Edit Texture dialog box enables you to import GIF, JPEG, PICT, and BMP files as textures for Color, Specular, Roughness, Transparency, Luminosity, Bump, or Environment maps.

Macromedia Director

Director can import bitmaps created with Flash for use as backgrounds, graphics, and animated elements. Choose **File > Import** in Director to display the Import dialog box and select bitmap files to add to a Director movie's cast.

Macromedia Authorware

Authorware can import bitmaps created with Flash for use as backgrounds or graphics elements. Choose **File > Import** in Authorware to display the Import dialog box and select bitmap files to add. These will appear on the Authorware flowline as new Display icons.

FreeHand can import bitmaps for use with other illustration elements. Bitmaps are placed into FreeHand files with the **Import** command from the File menu. After selecting a file in the Import Document dialog box, click on the document to place the imported bitmap at the selected location.

Importing Sound into Flash

Sound is an overlooked element in many interactive presentations, but there's no reason to omit it from a Flash movie. One common tool on the Macintosh for manipulating sound for multimedia is Macromedia SoundEdit 16.

Sound in Flash movies exports only when you save the movie as a Shockwave Flash movie or as a digital video. Flash compresses the sound as it saves the file.

Bitmap and vector images do not contain sound.

Macromedia SoundEdit 16

When using sound files with Flash, high quality is desirable. If the sounds are short, it's best to work with audio CD-quality originals (44kHz sampling rates, 16-bit samples, stereo channels) until the time you export the movie (see Chapter 9, "Sound").

If you use audio CD-quality sound for longer sounds or if you import many sounds into the movie, Flash files can become quite large. In that case, finding a happy medium is the best policy. SoundEdit 16 is useful for creating sound files that optimize both quality and file size.

To save a sound for Flash from SoundEdit 16:

1. Open the sound file with SoundEdit 16.

2. Choose **Sound Format** from the Modify menu, and choose a Sample Rate, Sample Size, and Compression value from each menu. For Compression, the **None** setting is recommended because Flash performs its own sound compression when it exports a movie. Click **OK**.

3. Choose **Save As** from the File menu and select either **AIFF**
   or **WAVE** from the List Files of Type pop-up menu (see Figure
   2.8). Enter a name for the audio file and click **Save**.

Figure 2.8
The Import dialog box displays the AIFF sound files.

4. Import the sound into a Flash movie by opening Flash,
   choosing **Import** from the File menu, and then selecting
   the sound file.

Exporting Video

Flash can export digital video files (AVI and QuickTime) as well as
bitmaps, and you can use those files as part of Director or Authorware
presentations.

To export a digital video from Flash:

1. Open the Flash movie.

2. Choose **Export Movie** from the File menu, and then
   choose either **Windows AVI** or **QuickTime** from the
   Save As Type menu. Enter a file name for the digital video
   file, and click **Save**.

3. Select **Dimensions**, **Format**, and **Sound Format** settings
   and click **OK** (see Figure 2.9). Flash saves the entire movie as
   a digital video, frame by frame.

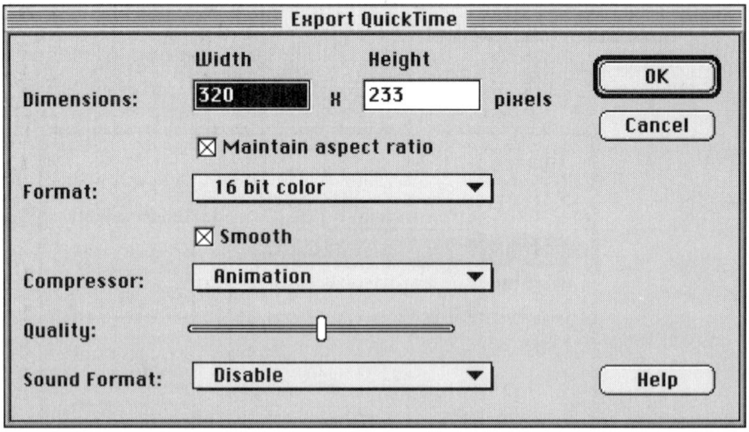

Figure 2.9
The Export QuickTime dialog box displays options for the export of QuickTime digital video.

Macromedia Director

Digital video files are often used in Director for animations that require tightly synchronized animation and sound. Flash saves sound and graphics in a digital video file frame by frame to prevent them from getting out of step with each other as the movie plays.

To import a digital video into a Director movie's cast, choose **Import** from the File menu, and select the digital video file in the Import File dialog box. Then click the **Import** button.

In addition, Director 6 supports the use of the Macromedia Flash ActiveX control in Windows 95 and Windows NT 4.0. This allows you to display Flash animations inside a Director movie. For more information on using ActiveX controls with Director, see the online help documentation included with Director 6 for Windows.

Macromedia Authorware

Authorware uses the same digital video formats as Director when working with animations that require tightly synchronized animation and sound. To import a digital video into an Authorware piece, choose **Import** from the File menu, and select the digital video file in the Import File dialog box. Then click the **Import** button to add the digital video file to the Authorware flowline as a new Movie icon.

In addition, Authorware 4 now supports the Macromedia Flash ActiveX control within Windows 95 and Windows NT 4.0. The Flash ActiveX control allows you to display Flash animations inside an Authorware piece. For more information on using ActiveX controls with Authorware, see the online help documentation included with Authorware 4 for Windows

Moving On...

This chapter covered how with Flash you can import from and export to other applications in the Macromedia Studios. You now should have some idea how versatile Flash is, as well as some insight into how seamlessly it integrates into the multimedia world.

The next chapter delves into the world of creating artwork with Flash using its innovative approach to vector-based drawing.

CHAPTER 3

Drawing

The Flash drawing environment is unique among vector-based

drawing programs. The overall "look-and-feel" of the Flash drawing tools is more like that of a paint program—you can use tools like a brush, a paint bucket, or an eraser in addition to a pencil.

With Flash, you can create original drawings for your interactive animation sequences, or modify and manipulate images imported from other programs.

This chapter shows you how to use the Flash drawing tools to get the effects you want.

What you'll learn…

How to create graphics with the Flash drawing tools

How to color graphics in Flash

How to modify graphics with the Flash drawing tools

There are three important aspects about drawing in Flash that you should remember:

■ Drawing happens behind all text, groups, and symbols (see Chapter 4, "Overlays & Symbols"). Drawing does not affect any text, groups, or symbols unless you convert them to editable shapes by breaking them apart.

■ All drawing on a layer happens on the canvas level (see Chapter 4, "Overlays & Symbols"); when you move a selection on top of another shape, the selection modifies the shape underneath, adding to it if it is the same color or subtracting from it if it is a different color.

■ Drawing one line on top of another line in the same layer causes the lines to join together as part of a single shape, if they are the same line style and color. A line that crosses over itself creates a closed shape.

Now it's time to start drawing in Flash.

Drawing lines with the pencil

To create a line or outline of a shape in Flash, use the pencil (see Figure 3.1). You can draw straight lines, curves, irregular lines, regular shapes, irregular shapes, or pretty much whatever you want with the pencil.

Figure 3.1
Use the pencil tool to create lines and outlines for shapes.

To define a straight line:

1. Choose the pencil tool from the toolbar.

2. Choose **Line** from the Pencil Mode modifier pop-up menu (see Figure 3.2).

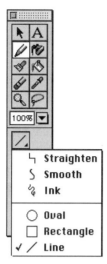

Figure 3.2
The toolbar and Pencil Mode modifier pop-up menu with Line mode selected.

3. From the Line Color modifier pop-up menu, select a color (see Figure 3.3).

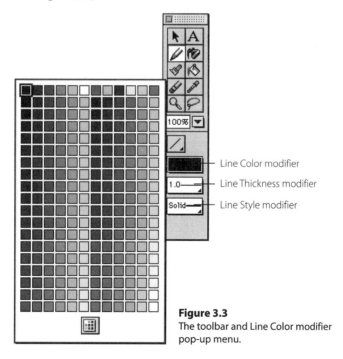

Line Color modifier

Line Thickness modifier

Line Style modifier

Figure 3.3
The toolbar and Line Color modifier pop-up menu.

4. Choose a thickness from the Line Thickness modifier pop-up menu (see Figure 3.4).

Figure 3.4
The Line Thickness modifier pop-up menu accessed via the toolbar.

NOTE *The line thickness setting H (or Hairline) always draws at a width of 1 pixel.*

5. Choose a style from the Line Style modifier pop-up menu (see Figure 3.5).

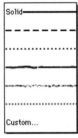

Figure 3.5
The Line Style modifier pop-up menu accessed via the toolbar.

TIP *In Flash you can define your own custom line styles by choosing options from the Line Style modifier pop-up menu. If you use custom line styles for more than one line, you can apply them easily to other lines by using the dropper tool in combinaton with the ink bottle tool. A solid line style results in a smaller file size than other line styles.*

To draw the straight line you've defined:

1. Move your cursor to where you want your line to start, click on the canvas and drag the crosshair cursor (see Figure 3.6).

Figure 3.6
Drawing a straight line with the pencil tool by clicking and dragging.

2. Move the cursor to where you want your line to end and release the mouse button. Flash draws your line with the thickness, color, and style you've selected.

TIP *Flash does not use the Shift key to constrain movement of the cursor as many other programs do. If you need to draw a perfectly vertical or horizontal line, turn on the Snap option in the View menu.*

You also can use the pencil tool to draw lines that aren't straight.

To define a curved line:

1. Choose the pencil tool from the toolbar.

2. Choose **Smooth** from the Pencil Mode modifier pop-up menu (see Figure 3.7).

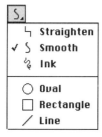

Figure 3.7
The Smooth option selected in the Pencil Mode modifier menu.

3. From the Line Color modifier pop-up menu, choose a color.

4. Choose a thickness of **8** from the Line Thickness modifier pop-up menu.

5. In the Line Style pop-up menu, choose **Custom**.

6. In the Line Style dialog box, check **Sharp Corners** (see Figure 3.8). This option affects how Flash handles corners when the line's direction changes abruptly.

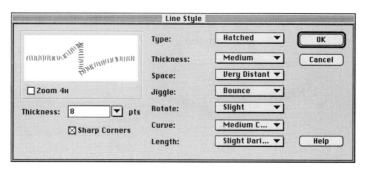

Figure 3.8
The Line Style dialog box with Sharp Corners checked.

7. Choose **Hatched** from the Type pop-up menu. The Hatched option creates a line composed of numerous short strokes, placed perpendicular to the direction of the line.

   When you choose Hatched, several options display that you can use to further define the style:

   - Choose a **Medium** Thickness to control the thickness of the strokes.

   - Choose the **Very Distant** Space option to determine the spacing between each of the perpendicular strokes.

   - The **Jiggle** option randomizes the placement of the center point of each stroke to the right or left of the line. Choose **Bounce** from the Jiggle pop-up menu.

   - Choosing **Slight** for the Rotate option varies each stroke from its perpendicular position with respect to the line.

   - Choose **Medium Curve** from the Curve options to give each stroke a slight bend.

   - Choose **Slight Variation** for Length to give each stroke a different length.

8. Click **OK** to set these choices.

TIP *As you create a custom line style, you can view it close up by checking the Zoom 4x checkbox underneath the preview area in the upper left corner of the Line Style dialog box.*

To draw a curve with the style you've defined:

1. Click on the canvas.

2. Hold down the mouse button and drag to draw your line (see Figure 3.9).

Figure 3.9
The pencil tool in the process of drawing a custom line.

The Smooth option (set in step 2 above when you defined a curved line) evens out line irregularities that may result from drawing with your mouse (see Figure 3.10).

Figure 3.10
The custom line after Flash renders it to the screen.

Drawing shapes with the pencil

Drawing shapes with the pencil tool is easy. Flash can recognize (within limits!) attempts to draw ovals, triangles, and rectangles. There are also Pencil Mode options that give you the ability to draw ovals and rectangles using the more traditional drawing program methods.

To draw an oval:

1. In a new Flash movie, choose the pencil tool.

2. Choose **Oval** from the Pencil Mode modifier pop-up menu (see Figure 3.11).

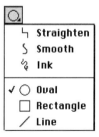

Figure 3.11
The Oval option selected in the Pencil Mode modifier pop-up menu.

3. Click and drag in the drawing area to create an oval outline (see Figure 3.12). The oval grows in size as you move the cursor away from its original position. Release the mouse button.

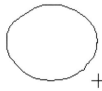

Figure 3.12
The pencil tool (in Oval mode) in the process of drawing an oval.

To draw a rectangle:

1. Choose **Rectangle** from the Pencil Mode modifier pop-up menu (see Figure 3.13).

Figure 3.13
The Rectangle option selected in the Pencil Mode modifier menu.

2. Click and drag in the drawing area to create a rectangular outline (see Figure 3.14). The rectangle grows in size as you move the cursor away from its original position.

Figure 3.14
The pencil tool (in Rectangle mode) in the process of drawing an rectangle.

3. Release the mouse button.

There are two ways to draw triangles in Flash. You can use shape recognition or Flash's snap to grid feature.

To draw shapes using shape recognition:

1. Choose **Straighten** from the Pencil Mode modifier pop-up menu (see Figure 3.15).

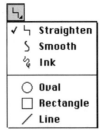

Figure 3.15
The Straighten option selected in the Pencil Mode modifier menu.

2. Click in the drawing area where you want to place one corner of a triangle. Without releasing the mouse button, draw a triangular shape from your original starting point (see Figure 3.16).

Figure 3.16
Using the pencil tool to draw a triangle.

3. Release the mouse button.

4. Repeat the instructions in steps 1 to 3, but draw a rectangle instead (see Figure 3.17).

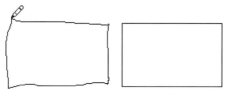

Figure 3.17
The pencil tool (in Straighten mode) used to draw a rectangle, and the resulting rectangle.

5. Draw an oval using the method in steps 1 to 3 (see Figure 3.18).

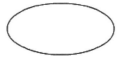

Figure 3.18
The pencil tool (in Straighten mode) used to draw an oval, and the resulting oval.

NOTE *Another option for the Pencil Mode pop-up menu is Ink, which recreates the line you draw as accurately as possible. Sometimes this can result in lines that are more complex than necessary. However, if lines drawn in ink become too complex, you can simplify and optimize them by choosing Modify > Curves.*

Painting shapes with the brush

Another way to draw shapes in Flash is to rough out the shape with the brush tool. Flash creates the shape's outline for you. This technique differs from most vector-based drawing tools and from the pencil tool, which requires that you draw an outline, and then fill it.

Like other programs with brush-type tools, there are a number of shapes you can choose from for your brush tip. If you draw the shape's outside edges with the brush, you can fill the interior with the paint bucket, change the color of the shape, and more.

To define a brush stroke:

1. In a new Flash movie, choose the brush tool (see Figure 3.19).

Figure 3.19
Use the brush tool to create shapes.

2. Set the Brush Mode modifier to **Paint Normal** (see Figure 3.20).

Figure 3.20
The tool palette and Brush Mode modifier pop-up menu with the Paint Normal mode selected.

3. Select a color from the Fill Color palette.

4. Set the Brush Size modifier to the largest brush size (see Figures 3.21 and 3.22).

Figure 3.21
The Brush Size modifier pop-up menu.

Figure 3.22
The same Brush Size setting used to draw two strokes: the one on the left at 100% of canvas size and the other at 200%.

NOTE *Brush size is relative to the Zoom factor. Identical brush settings draw at different sizes—depending on how closely you zoom in the image.*

5. Set the Brush Shape modifier to the round brush (see Figure 3.23).

Figure 3.23
The Brush Shape modifier pop-up menu.

6. Make sure that you have deselected the Lock Fill modifier in the toolbar. The visual differences between the selected and deselected button states are rather subtle, but at this point, you want it off (see Figure 3.24).

Lock Fill deselected (off)   Lock Fill selected (on)

Figure 3.24
The Lock Fill modifier in both selected and deselected states.

NOTE *If you have a pressure-sensitive tablet, you can enable or disable its pressure-sensitive capabilities. Use the Pressure modifier, which appears to the right of the Brush icon in the toolbar, if you have a pressure-sensitive tablet attached to your computer (see Figure 3.25).*

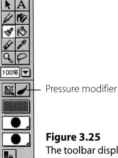

Pressure modifier

Figure 3.25
The toolbar displays the Pressure modifier (deselected in this view), to the right of the Brush modifier.

To paint the brush stroke you've defined:

1. Click on the canvas, draw a closed shape, and leave an unpainted space in the middle.

2. Choose **Outlines** from the **View** menu to display the outlines of the shape you've just drawn (see Figure 3.26).

Figure 3.26
A doughnut-esque shape as created with the brush (left), and displayed with the Outline option (right).

3. Set your View menu option to either **Smooth** or **Fast** to see the shape with or without anti-aliasing.

4. Save this Flash movie. You will use the shape in the following exercises with the brush tool.

To modify the outlines of brush strokes with the ink bottle:

1. Select the ink bottle from the toolbar (see Figure 3.27).

Figure 3.27
Use the ink bottle tool to modify lines.

2. Choose a color from the Line Color modifier that contrasts with your fill .

3. Set the Line Thickness modifier to **4.0** points, and the Line Style modifier to **Solid**.

4. Click anywhere in the colored area of your brush stroke to modify the outline of the brush stroke (see Figure 3.28). You also can use the ink bottle tool to change the line properties of lines and curves drawn with the pencil tool.

Figure 3.28
The doughnut-esque shape with a line modified using the ink bottle tool.

When you use the brush tool to fill enclosed areas, Brush Mode offers several choices for how the tool affects the other shapes.

To use the Brush in normal mode:

1. Select the brush tool again and choose a color from the Fill Color modifier that contrasts with the brush stroke you just created.

2. Make sure that you've set the Brush Mode to **Normal**.

3. Click on the canvas and paint across a small portion of the shape you just created. The stroke covers both the shape's fill and outline (see Figure 3.29).

Figure 3.29
After drawing a brush stroke (with Brush Mode set to Paint Normal) across the shape.

Experiment with other brush modes to see their effects.

To paint over a shape without altering the outline using the brush:

1. Choose the brush tool again and change the Brush Mode modifier to **Paint Fills**. Choose another color from the Fill Color modifier.

2. Starting outside the shape, paint a stroke across the shape (through the open area in the middle of the shape), and out the other side. When you release the mouse, Flash redraws the lines.

   Setting the Brush Mode modifier to **Paint Fills** paints inside and outside the enclosed area but doesn't alter the outline (see Figure 3.30).

Figure 3.30
The shape after drawing a brush stroke with Paint Mode set to Paint Fills (all lines are unaffected).

To paint behind a shape using the brush:

1. Choose another color from the Fill Color modifier and set the Paint Mode modifier to **Paint Behind**.

2. Paint an area that extends from the middle fill area to outside the shape. After you release the mouse, only the previously unpainted area is affected (see Figure 3.31).

Figure 3.31
The shape after drawing a Brush stroke with Brush Mode set to Paint Behind (existing fills and lines are unmodified).

To paint only part of a selected shape using the brush:

1. Choose the arrow tool from the toolbar. Select the upper left corner of the shape by clicking outside the shape and dragging the cursor to the middle of the shape.

2. Choose the brush again and choose yet another color from the Fill Color modifier. Set the Paint Mode modifier to **Paint Selection**.

3. Paint an area that is both inside and outside the selected area. After you've released the mouse button, press the Escape key to deselect everything. Only the areas that you selected are affected by the brush.

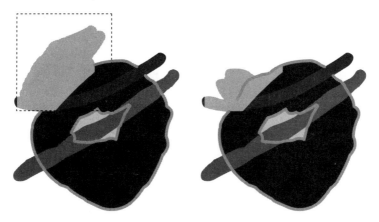

Figure 3.32
The shape on the left shows the area painted with the Brush with Paint Mode set to Paint Selection. The selection area is outlined with a dotted line. The shape on the right shows the results. In Paint Selection mode, only selected fill areas are painted.

To paint only inside an enclosed area using the brush:

1. Choose the brush tool again, select another color from the Fill Color modifier, and set the Brush Mode modifier to **Paint Inside**.

2. Move the cursor so that its center is over a patch of color, and paint anywhere you like. When you release the mouse, only the color patch you started painting is affected. This is similar to what happened when you selected the color patch and used the **Paint Selection** Brush Mode.

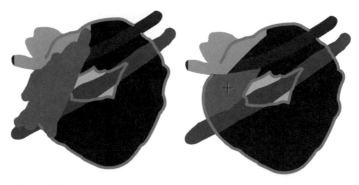

Figure 3.33
The shape at the left shows the area painted with the brush with Paint Mode
set to Paint Inside; then the mouse was clicked over a portion of the darkest
color patch, where the crosshair appears in the right image. The shape at the right
shows the results; in Paint Inside mode, only fill areas that are the same color as the
area you first touched with the brush are painted.

Using these combinations of Brush Modes, you can accomplish
tasks easily and quickly that would require more steps, complex
masks, and filters in other vector drawing programs.

Using the paint bucket, ink bottle, and dropper tools

The Flash paint bucket tool is similar to that found in bitmap editing
programs, except that it modifies vector shapes in addition to filling
an area with color. You can use the paint bucket to add color to
unfilled enclosed areas of the canvas, or to change the color of a filled
area. You can fill separate areas by selecting them, and then clicking
on one area with the paint bucket.

The ink bottle is to lines what the paint bucket is to shapes.
You can use the ink bottle to modify outlines of shapes, fills, or
portions of shapes and lines.

The dropper can determine the line or fill attributes of existing
shapes so that you can apply them to other shapes.

To use the paint bucket:

1. Open the Flash movie *exer03a.fla*. This movie shows you
five empty circles. All have gaps in the outline, except one
(see Figure 3.34).

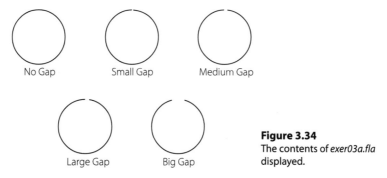

No Gap   Small Gap   Medium Gap

Large Gap   Big Gap

Figure 3.34
The contents of *exer03a.fla*
displayed.

2. Choose **100%** from the View menu. All gaps are relative to the zoom percentage.

SHORTCUT To change the view of the canvas to 100% of the drawing size from the keyboard, press Ctrl-1 (Windows) or Command-1 (Macintosh).

---

3. Choose the paint bucket from the toolbar.

4. Select a color from the Fill Color modifier.

5. Choose **Don't Close Gaps** from the Gap Size modifier pop-up menu.

6. Move the paint bucket over the middle of the first circle at the upper left corner (labeled "No Gap"), and click. The color you selected fills the circle.

7. Move the paint bucket to the next circle (labeled "Small Gap") and click. This circle has a small gap in it that prevents the shape from filling when you have the **Don't Close Gaps** modifier selected.

8. Select **Close Small Gaps** from the Gap Size modifier, and try filling the Small Gap circle again.

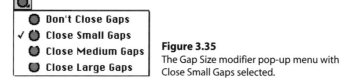

Figure 3.35
The Gap Size modifier pop-up menu with Close Small Gaps selected.

As with several of Flash's settings, the paint bucket tool's interpretation of scale—big gap versus small gap—depends on the current zoom setting.

To test the effect of zooming on the paint bucket's Gap Size setting:

1. Work your way through the other circles, trying different settings for the Gap Size modifier. You should be able to fill all of them except for the one at the lower right (labeled "Big Gap").

2. Use the pop-up menu for the Zoom factor box on the toolbar to view the canvas at 50% of original size.

3. Again, try to fill the circle at the lower right. This time Big Gap fills.

NOTE *Other tools and operations that modify shapes, including the Smooth tool and the Optimize menu selection, also yield different results when used at different Zoom factors.*

Use the ink bottle tool to affect lines attached to shapes. You can use the paint bucket to modify and add fills to shapes.

To alter a graphic using both the ink bottle and paint bucket tools:

1. Open the Flash document named *exer03b.fla* from the CD-ROM. This file is a cartoon face (see Figure 3.36).

Figure 3.36
The contents of *exer03b.fla* displayed.

2. Select **100%** from the View menu.

3. Select the paint bucket from the toolbar, and set the Gap Size modifier to **Don't Close Gaps**.

4. From the Fill Color modifier, choose a color for the face.

5. Fill the white areas inside the lenses of the glasses, the forehead, cheeks, and nose (see Figure 3.37).

Figure 3.37
The face almost completely filled with the paint bucket tool positioned to fill the last area.

6. From the Fill Color modifier, choose the rainbow gradient at the bottom of the palette.

7. Move the cursor over the shape outlining the face, and click to fill the shape with the rainbow gradient (see Figure 3.38).

Figure 3.38
The black area of the face replaced with the rainbow gradient.

8. Choose the ink bottle tool.

9. Choose black from the Line Color modifier. Set the Line Width modifier to **8**, and Line Style to **Solid**.

10. Move the cursor over the rainbow gradient area and click to modify the outline of the shape filled by the gradient.

11. Set the Line Width modifier to **4**, select another color from the Line Color modifier, and click again on the rainbow gradient area to change the attributes of the line assigned to the shape (see Figure 3.39).

Figure 3.39
The face with an 8-point outline applied (left), and after modifying the outline to 4 points (right).

The dropper tool can determine both the fill and line attributes of a shape so you can apply them to other shapes:

To practice using the dropper tool:

1. Open the Flash movie *exer03c.fla* from the CD-ROM. This document is the result of the previous exercise with text added.

2. Select the dropper from the toolbar (see Figure 3.40).

Figure 3.40
You can use the dropper tool to determine a shape's assigned fill and line attributes.

3. Move the cursor over the rainbow-filled shape and click the mouse. The cursor changes to the paint bucket. The rainbow fill from the shape now becomes the selection in the Fill Color modifier.

TIP *When the dropper tool is selected, you can determine if the active portion of the cursor (or "hot spot") is over a fill or a line by looking closely below and to the right of the cursor. A small paint brush icon appears when the cursor is over a fill, and a small pencil icon appears when the cursor is over a line (see Figure 3.41).*

Figure 3.41
The dropper tool cursor in four manifestations (from left to right): when it is not over a fill or stroke; over a stroke; over a fill; and with the Shift key held down to determine both line and fill attributes simultaneously.

4. Move the cursor over *F* in the word "Flashback." Click to fill the letter, and then fill the other letters (see Figure 3.42).

Figure 3.42
The canvas after filling all of the letters with the gradient.

NOTE *The lock that appears as part of the cursor indicates that the gradient fill you're applying is "locked" to the canvas (see Figure 3.43); for now, note that the colors of the gradient line up as they pass through both the text and the cartoon.*

 Figure 3.43
The paint bucket cursor with the padlock, which indicates that the Lock Fill option is on.

5. Once you fill all of the letters with the gradient, select the dropper tool again and move it over the outline around the cartoon head. See the small pencil next to the dropper. Click the mouse button to determine the line attributes (see Figure 3.44). The cursor changes to indicate that the ink bottle is now the selected tool.

Figure 3.44
Using the dropper tool to determine the shape's line attributes.

6. Use the ink bottle to modify the outline of all of the letters at the top of the canvas (see Figure 3.45).

Figure 3.45
The completed exercise, with fills and outlines transferred from the cartoon face to the letters.

TIP *Some shapes, particularly letters, may require a little extra care in modifying the shape's outlines. If you click too close to the edge of either the inside or outside of the shape, you may add a line to that edge only. This leaves edges without lines (see Figure 3.46). Using the zoom tool before applying fills and strokes to shapes can make the process easier.*

Figure 3.46
The ink bottle cursor was too close to the outside edge of the letter when the line was applied, and did not add a line to the inside edges of the shape.

In this exercise, you learned how to use the paint bucket and ink bottle tools to apply fills and lines to shapes and how to change those fills and lines. You also learned how to use the dropper tool to determine the fill and line attributes of existing shapes and how to apply them to other shapes. Now it's time to use the Color window to change colors.

Changing Colors

The colors in Flash's default color palettes are commonly known as "browser-safe" colors. You can be reasonably certain that when a Flash movie plays as part of a web page inside a browser, that the browser-safe colors will display as a solid color without dithering. Dithering is a process where the computer approximates a color it can't display by using a mixture of color pixels it *can* display (see Figure 3.47).

Flat   Dithered

Figure 3.47
The two patches of color were created as similar colors. Flat uses a browser-safe color. The color on the right dithered because it doesn't exist on the browser-safe palette.

If you're creating Flash movies for use on the Web, you should stick to the default color palette. Depending on your needs, however, you can modify, add, or delete colors from the palette, as well as create or modify gradients.

To modify the Flash color palette:

1. Choose the pencil or ink bottle, or the brush or paint bucket tool. The pencil and ink bottle share one set of colors. The brush and paint bucket share another set of colors.

2. With any one of these tools chosen, click the **Fill Color** or **Line Color** modifiers and choose the Color button at the bottom of the pop-up menu (see Figure 3.48). Alternatively, you can choose **Windows > Colors**. Both methods open the Color window.

Figure 3.48
The Color button appears at the bottom of both the Fill Color and Line Color modifiers pop-up menus.

The Color window has two modes: one for editing colors used for solid fills and lines, and one for editing gradients to be used for fills. Invoke the mode you want by selecting either the Solid or Gradient tabs at the top of the window.

Creating a solid color

The Color window enables you to extend and organize solid colors and gradients used in Flash movies.

To create a solid color:

1. Open the Color window by clicking the color button at the bottom of a pop-up color palette, or by choosing **Windows > Colors**. Click the tab labeled "Solid" at the top of the window (see Figure 3.49).

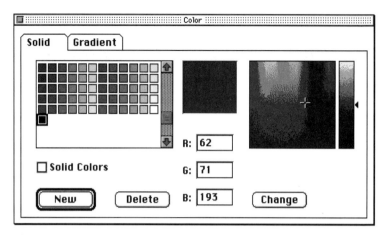

Figure 3.49
The Color window in the Solid color mode.

2. To add a new color, click the **New** button at the lower left corner of the window. If you want to modify a color, simply click on an existing color position.

TIP *The default color palette actually has 228 colors; the first row across the top contains color duplicates from the 216-color, browser-safe palette. If you need to add colors to the palette, it is recommended that you modify one of the colors in the first row, or add new colors at the bottom of the palette, avoiding the browser-safe colors.*

3. You can assign a color to the selected position by using the crosshair to choose a hue and saturation combined with the slider to select a lightness, or by entering values from 0 to 255 for red, green, and blue in the fields R, G, and B. You can view the color you've created or chosen in the color preview area at the top of the window.

4. If you want to ensure that the color you choose can display within a browser (or on an 8-bit monitor) without dithering, you can check the **Solid Colors** box in the Color window. This converts the chosen color to the closest color in the browser-safe palette. It also is a good way to find out the browser-safe equivalent of any given color. It's best to check this button only after you've chosen your color.

NOTE *The browser-safe palette is made up of all possible combinations of the three visible-light color components (red, green, and blue) at multiples of 20 percent (0, 20, 40, 60, 80, and 100%). Zero percent of all three colors is black; 100 percent is white. One hundred percent of one color with 0 percent of the other two colors yields that color by itself (100% red, 0% blue and green = red). Because computers keep track of most things using values from 0 to 255, the browser-safe colors are represented numerically by multiples of the number 51 (20% of 255 = 51). When preparing artwork in other programs to import into Flash, use these values for colors.*

5. Once you've determined the color, click the **Change** button at the bottom right to confirm the addition or modification to the color list.

To delete a color, choose the color from the color list and click the **Delete** button.

Creating a gradient

The Color window is also used to create or edit a gradient or blend.

To create a gradient:

1. Open the Color window by clicking on the color button at the bottom of a pop-up color palette, or by choosing **Windows > Colors**. Click the Gradient tab at the top of the window.

2. Choose the white-to-black gradient and click the **New** button to duplicate the fill in a new position (see Figure 3.50).

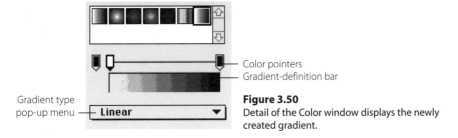

Color pointers
Gradient-definition bar

Gradient type pop-up menu — Linear

Figure 3.50
Detail of the Color window displays the newly created gradient.

The Gradient mode of the Color window is similar to the Solid mode (see Figure 3.51). It uses the same color selection tools in the upper right corner of the window, allowing you to visually determine colors. It also has a numerical entry area in the central portion of the window. One addition to the window is a color pop-up menu just above the Change button.

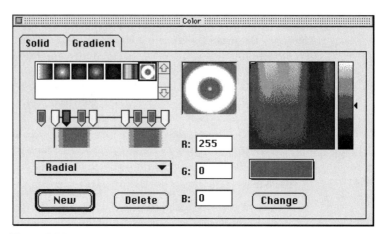

Figure 3.51
The Color window in Gradient mode after defining a new radial gradient.

To define a radial fill:

1. Change the Gradient Type from Linear to **Radial** using the pop-up menu.

2. Use the gradient-definition bar to assign color positions along the gradient. There can be anywhere from two to eight color pointers positioned along the bar (there must always be at least two). Each color pointer can have a different assigned color.

TIP *You can move or adjust color pointers at any time; however, this does not affect shapes that already have gradient fills. Remove pointers by clicking on them and dragging them away from the gradient-definition bar.*

To edit the radial fill gradient to start and end with white:

1. Click the color pointer on the right end of the gradient-definition bar to select it.

2. Type the value **255** in each of the fields labeled R, G, and B, or select white from the Color pop-up menu.

   You can assign a color to a color pointer by either clicking on it after it is in place and using the Color pop-up menu or R, G, B entry fields to choose a color for that pointer; or, by changing the color of the master pointer to the left of the gradient-definition bar. This only changes pointers that you add.

3. Select the master pointer and change its value to white as you did with the other pointer in step 2 above. For this example, you need several white pointers. If you need several pointers with the same color, you can assign the color to the master pointer. Then each new pointer you create has that color as the default.

4. Add a new white pointer to the gradient-definition bar by clicking on the master pointer and dragging it to the line above the bar. Release the mouse button about two-thirds of the distance from the left side of the bar.

5. Position another white pointer on the bar about a third of the distance from the left side.

6. Select the master pointer again and change its color to red by selecting a color from the Color pop-up menu or typing **0** into the G and B fields.

7. Position a new red pointer on the gradient-definition bar just to the right of the pointer at the far left (see Figure 3.52). This creates a red band between the first and second white pointers.

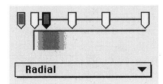

Figure 3.52
Detail of the Color window, which shows the gradient-definition bar after the addition of a red color pointer.

8. Position another new red pointer to the right of the third white pointer (counting from the left). This creates a red band between the third and fourth white pointers. You can preview the changes in the color preview area at the top center of the Color window.

If you look closely at the gradient, you see that the red area is fairly narrow. This is because each blended area in a gradient begins at one color pointer (with the color assigned to that pointer) and ends at the next pointer (and color). This means that as soon as the red pointer is reached, the blend starts back toward white on the other side of the gradient.

There is a blend between the two white pointers at the center of the gradient-definition bar; however, it is a blend between white and white. You can use the same technique to make the red bands wider.

To edit the width of the bands in the gradient:

1. Drag a new red pointer to the space between the first red pointer and the second white pointer. The blend drawn between the red pointers results in a wide red band.

2. Drag another red pointer from the master pointer to just be-fore the end of the bar to make a second red band. Click the **Change** button to confirm your modification to the gradient palette.

Selecting and Reshaping Lines and Fills

Once you've drawn, filled, and added lines on shapes to the Flash canvas, you can move and modify elements that you have created. To do that, you need to select the items you want to change.

Selecting items in Flash is different from most other drawing programs. Flash combines the capability to select fills and lines with the capability to select portions of shapes. Selections are made with two tools: the arrow and the lasso.

Selecting with the arrow tool

The arrow tool is a powerful tool that enables you to select filled objects, line segments, entire lines, and multiple lines, and objects. You can use the arrow tool to move selected portions of objects, as well as to modify lines and outlines (see Figures 3.53 and 3.54). Additionally, you can select part of a filled object or a line by clicking and dragging a rectangular selection marquee.

Figure 3.53
Use the arrow tool for selecting, moving, and modifying objects.

Figure 3.54
The arrow tool cursor in its four states.

No Selection   Move Selection   Reshape Corner   Reshape Curve

To move a fill:

1. Open the Flash document named *exer03d.fla* from the CD-ROM. This document contains shapes that spell the word *FLASH*.

Figure 3.55
The contents of *exer03d.fla* displayed.

2. The *H* is a little higher than the other letters. You need to lower it to the same level as the other characters. Select the arrow tool and move the cursor over the letter *H*.

   The arrow tool enables you to move a filled object without first selecting it. You can tell when your cursor is in the correct position when it displays the move selection cursor (see Figure 3.56).

Figure 3.56
The cursor indicates that it is in the move selection mode.

3. When the cursor is in the move selection mode and you haven't selected an object, you can move the object directly under the cursor when you click the mouse. Select the *H* and move it down so that it's in line with the other letters (see Figure 3.57). The shape is selected when you release the mouse button.

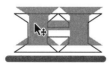

Figure 3.57
The outline indicates where the shape will move.

4. To deselect the shape, press the **Escape** key.

SHORTCUT Deselect all objects by pressing the Escape key, Shift-Ctrl-A (Windows) or Shift-Command-A (Macintosh); click outside all selected objects with the arrow or lasso tool; or choose Deselect All from the Edit menu.

Lines are simple strokes with no fill; you must select lines before you can move or duplicate them.

To duplicate the line below the letter shapes:

1. Move the cursor on top of the line and click to select it (see Figure 3.58).

Figure 3.58
The coarse check pattern indicates that you have selected the line.

2. Press the **Ctrl** (Windows) or **Option** (Macintosh) key as you click and drag the line to a new location (see Figure 3.59). This enables you to create a duplicate of the selected item (or items).

Figure 3.59
Duplicating a line by selecting it and click-dragging.

3. Click on the selected line and drag it down to create a second line underneath the first line. When you're satisfied with the position, release the mouse. The line remains selected.

To add to a selection in Flash:

1. Click with the arrow tool. Each item you click is added to the selection. Click on the upper line to add it to your selection.

   Now you can duplicate both selected lines.

2. Hold down the **Ctrl** (Windows) or **Option** (Macintosh) key, position the cursor over either of the two selected lines, and drag copies of them to the area above the letter shapes to duplicate multiple selections (see Figure 3.60).

Figure 3.60
Duplicating multiple items in a selection by click-dragging.

3. Before proceeding, deselect the lines.

Another method for selecting items allows you to drag a marquee around the elements you want to select. This also allows you to select just part of a shape or line.

To marquee-select elements:

1. Click on the canvas above and to the left of the items on the canvas.

2. Drag the outline so that the right edge lines up with the center of the letter *A* (see Figure 3.61). When you release the mouse button and if you have selected the left half of the lines, the letters *FL*, and half of the letter *A* are selected.

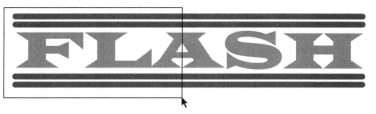

Figure 3.61
Dragging a selection over portions of lines and shapes.

Using the paint bucket on a selection affects only the selected filled shapes.

To fill selected shapes or portions of shapes with the paint bucket:

1. Choose the paint bucket tool and choose a color from the Color modifier list that contrasts with the gray of the type.

2. Move the paint bucket over any part of the selected letters and click to fill the letters with your color choice.

TIP *If you deselect everything (Escape key), you can see your changes better. An Undo (Ctrl-Z on Windows, Command-Z on Macintosh) reselects the items you've deselected without undoing your change.*

Changing the fill color of part of a shape converts the original shape into two shapes: one in which the original color remains, and the other with the new fill. Look at the canvas with the Outlines option selected in the View menu, you'll see that the *A* shape has a line through the middle, indicating there are now two shapes (see Figure 3.62). You also may notice that the *L* and the *A* are actually one shape.

Fast view mode  Outline view mode

Figure 3.62
The "A" shape after filling the left side with a different color.

Applying line styles and colors to selected elements affects an individual shape or all selected lines.

To apply line styles and colors to selected elements:

1. Choose the ink bottle tool.

2. Choose a color from the Color modifier.

3. Use the Line Thickness pop-up menu to set the line width to 2 points.

4. Move the ink bottle over the selected line parts and click to apply your color choice. The line style you select is applied to the selected portions of all four lines (see Figure 3.63); the shapes are not affected.

Figure 3.63
After applying a fill to the selected lines.

To use the ink bottle to make changes:

1. Click with the ink bottle on the *F* shape. Flash applies an outline to the shape, but not to the rest of the selected shapes. The outline on the shape is not selected.

2. Apply an outline to the *L* shape and to the left half of the *A* by clicking on the selected shape with the ink bottle tool.

3. With the arrow tool, double-click any portion of the outlines you've modified. Double-clicking selects all connected outlines of the same color, width, and style.

   When selected, they display the same coarse, checked pattern that the other lines show. Switch back to the ink bottle tool, choose another color from the Line Color modifier, and click anywhere on the selected items. This time, all of the lines and outlines change to match the new line style.

4. Deselect everything by pressing the **Escape** key.

Selections made with the arrow tool are determined by color and outline intersections (for shapes) and line intersections and corners (for lines with no fills).

To practice Flash's selection techniques:

1. Select one of the lines.

2. Ctrl-drag (Windows) or Option-drag (Macintosh) the line to make a duplicate that is centered horizontally on the letter shapes (see Figure 3.64).

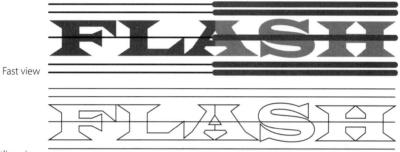

Fast view

Outline view

Figure 3.64
A fifth line is centered on the letters.

3. Deselect the line by pressing **Escape**.

4. Click with the arrow tool on the portions of the line between the letters *A* and *S*, and between *S* and *H*. Only the portions of the line between the edges of the letters are selected.

5. Choose the dropper tool and click on the outline of the letter shapes on the left to determine their line attributes. Flash automatically selects the ink bottle tool.

6. Move the cursor over the selected parts of the middle line and change those parts of the line by clicking them with the ink bottle (see Figure 3.65).

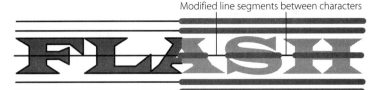
Modified line segments between characters

Figure 3.65
After modifying portions of the line between letters.

7. Before proceeding, deselect by pressing the **Escape** key.

Selecting any part of a line selects all of the lines and outlines of the same weight and color that are connected to the selected line segment.

To change one or more lines in a selection:

1. With the arrow tool, double-click on any portion of the outline around the letter shapes on the left (see Figure 3.66). This selects all of the lines and outlines with the same color and weight.

Marquee indicates that the lines are selected

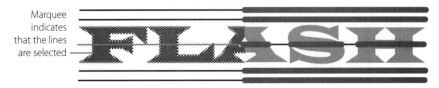

Figure 3.66
A selection of the outlines of the letters on the left and the left half of the middle line.

2. Switch back to the ink bottle tool, and set the Line Width modifier to **1** point.

3. Change the selected lines by clicking on them. Before proceeding, deselect by pressing the **Escape** key.

4. Use the arrow tool to select an outline segment of the *L* above the line (see Figure 3.67). All that selects is the portion between the line and the first sharp corner.

Marquee shows selected line segment

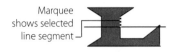

Figure 3.67
Selecting a segment of the outline of the *L* between the middle line and a corner selects just a portion of the line.

5. Deselect the line by pressing the **Escape** key.

6. Select the segments of the middle line on the left side of the illustration (see Figure 3.68) and drag it down below the bottom lines.

Figure 3.68
Selecting the left portion of the line.

3. Use the Arrow key again to select the segment of the *L* outline pictured in Figure 3.67 above. This time, the entire segment from corner to corner is selected (see Figure 3.69). Although it seems to be cut in two parts when the line runs across it, it now selects as a single segment. Deselect the line by pressing the **Escape** key.

Figure 3.69
The outline segment selected after moving the line.

Another selection tool—the lasso—enables you to select objects on a non-rectangular area of the canvas.

Selecting with the lasso

If you need to select an irregular part of an object, or a number of objects that aren't grouped together, the lasso tool can be very useful.

The Lasso allows you to draw a selection outline around or through objects to select all or part of those objects.

To use the lasso:

1. Open the Flash file *exer03e.fla* from the CD-ROM. This document contains shapes that spell out the words *Atomic City Apartments*.

2. Choose the lasso from the toolbar, click outside the letters, and carefully draw a selection shape between the top of the word *Apartments* and the bottom of the words *Atomic City* (see Figure 3.70). (Note the small gaps between some of the letters.) Draw back through the middle of the word *Apartments*. This selects the top portion of the letter shapes.

Figure 3.70
Drawing a selection with the lasso tool.

Use the lasso to add the top half of the words *Atomic City* to the selection by holding down the **Shift** key, clicking the cursor outside the letters, and then dragging a selection shape around the area you want to add to the selection.

NOTE *When you drag-select with the arrow or use the lasso to make a selection, previously selected items are automatically deselected. You can, however, add to a selection using either method by holding down the Shift key as you make the selection.*

3. Choose the paint bucket and choose a color from the Fill Color palette. Click on the selected portions of the letters to fill with your color. When used on a selection containing two or more non-contiguous shapes, the paint bucket fills all the selected shapes (see Figure 3.71).

Atomic City Apartments

Figure 3.71
Flash fills the top halves of the letter forms with a different color.

With the lasso tool, you can select part of the letter forms along an irregular path. The selection of the top halves of the letters in the word *Apartment* is very difficult—if not impossible—without the lasso.

Altering Shapes and Lines

So far you've looked at ways to paint, draw, change, select, and delete shapes and lines. Now it is time to explore altering their shapes.

Using the eraser

Flash shows its kinship to pixel-based paint programs once again with the eraser tool. The eraser enables you to delete portions of shapes and lines by simply dragging the cursor over the object (see Figure 3.72).

Figure 3.72
Use the eraser tool to delete portions of lines and shapes.

To use the smooth, straighten, and optimize features:

1. Open a new Flash file and draw a rectangle with the pencil tool. Use either the **Straighten** or the **Rectangle** mode, and set the Line Width modifier to 4 points before you draw it.

2. Choose the paint bucket tool and fill the rectangle with a color different from that used for the outline.

3. Choose the eraser tool. Select the largest square from the Eraser Size menu and set the Eraser Mode modifier to **Erase Normal**; make sure that you have deselected the Faucet modifier (see Figures 3.73, 3.74, and 3.75).

✓ Erase Normal
Erase Fills
Erase Lines
Erase Selected Fills
Erase Inside

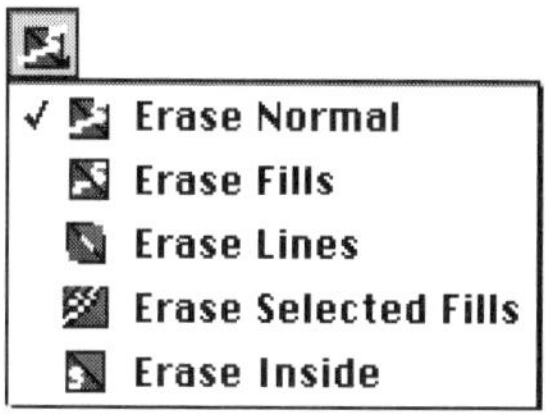

Figure 3.74
The Eraser Mode modifier pop-up menu with Erase Normal selected.

Figure 3.75
The Faucet modifier button (deselected) located above the Eraser Mode modifier pop-up menu.

Figure 3.73
The Eraser Size modifier pop-up menu displayed.

TIP *When selected, the Faucet modifier enables you to erase (or wash away) an entire line or fill with a single click—effectively selecting the object and deleting it in one step.*

4. Use the eraser to cut a swath through a corner of the rectangle, and then take a look at the result with the **Outline** setting from the View menu (see Figures 3.76 and 3.77). The eraser has altered the shape of the rectangle you created, deleting both the line and fill from the affected area.

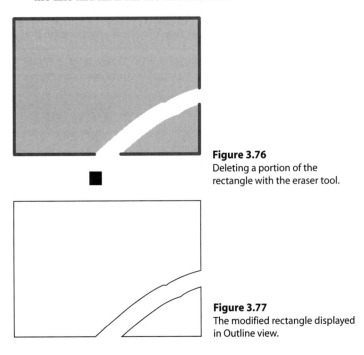

Figure 3.76
Deleting a portion of the rectangle with the eraser tool.

Figure 3.77
The modified rectangle displayed in Outline view.

Reshaping objects

The eraser isn't your only option when modifying a line or shape. As you learned earlier in the chapter, simply drawing an object on top of another can change both objects. With the arrow tool, you can move single corners and modify individual curves. With the Smooth and Straighten modifier buttons, you can modify entire selections (see Figure 3.78). Also available is the powerful Optimize command.

Figure 3.78
Use the arrow tool's Smooth and Straighten modifiers
to modify entire selections.

 TIP *The Optimize command is on the Curves submenu of the Modify menu. The same submenu also houses commands for Smooth and Straighten, which duplicate the function of the modifier buttons.*

To modify lines and shapes using the Smooth, Straighten and Optimize Curves commands:

1. Open the Flash file named *exer03f.fla* from the CD-ROM.

2. Move the arrow tool over a portion of the curves on the right, until you see the cursor change to the Reshape Curve mode.

3. Click and drag on a portion of the curve to reshape it (see Figure 3.79). Move the curve to the right, past the corners of the shape. After you release the mouse button, the shape's outline updates to reflect the change.

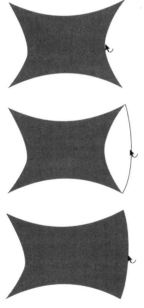

Figure 3.79
The arrow tool encounters the curve and switches
to the reshape curve mode (top). Click-dragging
the curve to reshape it (center). The object after
reshaping (bottom).

4. Perform the same operation on the left side.

5. Select the shape with the arrow tool by clicking in its interior. This activates the Smooth and Straighten modifier buttons.

6. Click the **Smooth** modifier button several times to make the curves of the shape more even. The Smooth operation turns each curve section into a smooth arc section.

7. Click the **Straighten** modifier button several times. Depending on how you modified the curves, the shape eventually turns into a rectangle or an ellipse.

Transforming shapes and gradients

By modifying elements you have created already, you can reduce the number of drawings you have to make. Flash gives you tools that can alter not only the object's shape, but also its relationship to the canvas and other objects.

To alter shapes and change their relationship to the canvas and other objects:

1. Create a new Flash movie.

2. Choose the pencil tool, and set the Pencil Mode modifier to **Oval**.

3. In the View menu, choose both **Grid** and **Snap**.

4. From the Modify menu, choose **Movie** to display the dialog box, and set the Grid Spacing to **18 px** (18 pixels). Close the dialog box.

5. Set the **Line Width** modifier to **2** points, and draw an oval on the canvas that is 1 grid box high by 12 boxes wide.

6. Draw a circle on the canvas that is 8 boxes wide and 8 boxes high.

7. Choose the paint bucket tool and fill the circle with a radial gradient (see Figure 3.80).

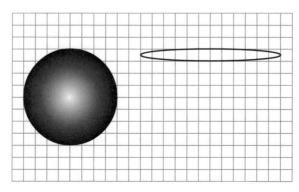

Figure 3.80
The filled circle and the unfilled oval.

8. Choose the eraser tool, select the **Faucet** modifier, and click on the outline around the circle to remove it, leaving only the fill.

9. Choose the paint bucket tool, and then choose the **Transform Fill** modifier at the bottom of the tool palette (see Figure 3 81).

Figure 3.81
The Transform Fill modifier located on the tool palette.

10. Click on the circle with the cursor to reshape the gradient. The radial gradient selection and handles appear (see Figure 3.82).

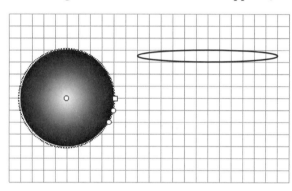

Figure 3.82
The radial gradient selection and handles.

11. Click on the handle at the center of the gradient to move the starting point of the radial gradient. Drag the handle up toward the top half of the circle to give it the appearance of a sphere, lit from above.

12. With the arrow tool, click on the oval shape to select it. Hold down the **Ctrl** key (Windows) or the **Option** key (Macintosh), and drag the selection to make a duplicate of the shape. Be sure that you leave a little extra room between this shape and the others.

13. Choose the Rotate modifier, or choose **Rotate** from the Transform submenu of the Modify menu (see Figure 3.83). Turn off the grid snap option by deselecting the Snap modifier (see Figure 3.84).

Figure 3.83
The arrow tool's Rotate modifier accessed via the toolbar.

Figure 3.84
The arrow tool's Snap modifier accessed via the toolbar.

14. Move the cursor over one of the corner handles. Click and drag to rotate the oval about 15 degrees clockwise (see Figure 3.85).

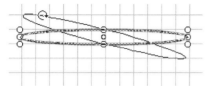

Figure 3.85
Rotating the oval.

15. Duplicate the rotated oval by moving the cursor over the selected oval and dragging it to a new location while holding down the **Ctrl** (Windows) or **Option** (Macintosh) key. You now have three ovals: the original and two rotated ovals.

16. Choose **Flip Horizontal** from the Transform submenu of the Modify menu. This makes the currently selected oval a mirror image of the one you rotated.

17. Deselect the Rotate modifier. The oval you just flipped remains selected, but the rotation handles disappear.

18. Add the other two ovals to the selection by clicking on them with the arrow tool.

19. From the Modify menu, choose **Align**. In the Align dialog box, select the **Center** mode for the Vertical and Horizontal Align options (see Figure 3.86). Click **OK**. This centers all three ovals on the same point of the canvas.

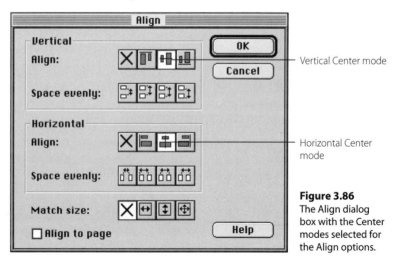

Vertical Center mode

Horizontal Center mode

Figure 3.86
The Align dialog box with the Center modes selected for the Align options.

20. Move the shape made by the ovals over the circle with the
arrow tool. Deselect by pressing the **Escape** key.

21. Use the arrow tool to select the upper portions of the ovals
where they intersect with the circle (see Figure 3.87). Because
Flash selects line segments depending on where they intersect
with other lines and shapes, this is relatively easy. Delete these
lines to make it look like the ovals are behind the circle.

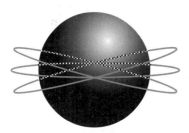

Figure 3.87
The selected portions of the ovals to be
deleted to make the lines appear to go
behind the sphere.

22. Delete the selected portions of the ovals by pressing the
Delete key.

23. Select all of the objects using the **Select All** command from
the Edit menu.

24. Copy the selected items by selecting the **Copy** command from
the Edit menu.

25. Paste the items onto the canvas with the **Paste** command from
the Edit menu.

26. Select the arrow tool's Scale modifier, move the cursor over
one of the corner handles of the selected shapes, click and drag
the handle to make the items smaller (see Figure 3.88).

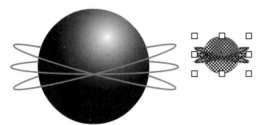

Figure 3.88
The duplicated shapes, resized by the Scale modifier.

27. Deselect by pressing the **Escape** key (see Figure 3.89).

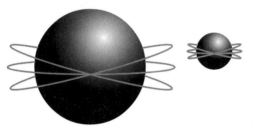

Figure 3.89
The final illustration.

You now have two copies of the circle and ovals, creating what appears to be a sphere and three orbital rings. The amount of time it takes to create this is probably less than it takes to read this paragraph.

Moving On...

By now you've seen how easy it is to create complex artwork using Flash's drawing tools, and we haven't even gotten into animation or interactivity yet! Some of the tools used in this chapter will appear with even more uses in later chapters, so be prepared as we head into the world above the canvas level, one of text, bitmaps, and symbols.

CHAPTER 4

Overlays & Symbols

What you'll learn…

How the overlay level works

How text, bitmaps, and groups work

How to use and create symbols

In front of the lines and

shapes on the canvas level is another level of objects: the *overlay* level, which contains text, bitmaps, grouped items, and *symbols*— objects that are stored in the Library and used repeatedly. All objects on the overlay level appear in front of shapes on the canvas level.

On the canvas level objects interact with each other. Flash evaluates each line and curve in each object to find lines and curves that touch each other, and then joins them. Overlay objects work differently. You can't modify the outlines of overlay objects as freely as those on the canvas level. However, you can move overlay objects without affecting other objects.

Overlay objects don't force Flash to recalculate the position of each line and curve when you move them, and so animations created with overlay objects require less processing. As a result, you can use overlay objects to create movies that download and play faster.

The Overlay Level

It may be useful to think of Flash as having a canvas level at the back of what you see on the screen, with a number of overlay levels in front of it. Overlay objects—text, groups, bitmaps, and symbols—each have their own order within the overlay level and appear in front of each other in an order that you can determine and change (see Figure 4.1).

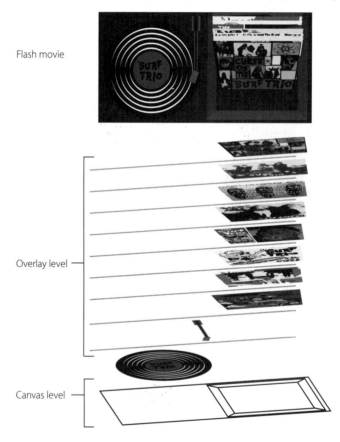

Flash movie

Overlay level

Canvas level

Figure 4.1
The canvas level and various objects on the overlay level illustrated.

NOTE *Be careful not to confuse layers and levels. Each layer in Flash's timeline has its own canvas level and set of overlay levels. (For more about layers, see Chapter 5, "Layers.")*

Although you can move, rotate, and scale overlay objects, you can't modify their outlines unless you open them for editing by double-clicking them or by choosing Edit Selected or Edit Symbol from the Edit menu. Alternately, you can return overlay objects to the canvas level by selecting them and choosing Break Apart from the Modify menu. (For more information about breaking apart objects, see "Breaking apart bitmaps," below.)

NOTE *Breaking apart an overlay object positioned over a graphic on the canvas layer can cause pieces of the graphic on the canvas layer to join or segment each other when you deselect the graphic.*

Text Objects

While examples in earlier chapters included text, for the most part that text was represented by shapes on the canvas level. You can edit text objects—that is, text that exists on the overlay level—throughout the movie creation process by modifying the font, the letter spacing, the line spacing, or even by editing the text itself.

With text objects, you can create highly styled and formatted blocks of letters that you can animate just like any other element in Flash. You have control over kerning, paragraph formatting, and line breaks.

NOTE *Breaking apart text objects into their outlines and modifying them as shapes on the canvas level allows you to create specialized looks for letters and text effects. However, text that you break apart into a graphic is no longer editable as a text object. Even if you break apart text and convert it back into a symbol, you can no longer apply font, kerning, or paragraph modifiers.*

Creating labels and text blocks

Use the text tool to create text objects. You also use the text tool when editing text objects. Flash places text objects into edit mode when you click on them with the text tool (shown in Figure 4.2), or when you double-click text objects with the arrow tool.

Figure 4.2
The text tool found in the tool palette.

There are two types of text objects in Flash: labels and text blocks. Where you place a line break determines the width of a label. Use label text objects when you need to end a line with a particular word. Flash automatically wraps a text block to fit the size of the box you create. You can create a text block by clicking and dragging a box to the desired width. Clicking on the canvas to create a text object automatically creates a label. Label text objects can be converted into text blocks and vice versa.

TIP *You can tell labels and text blocks apart by putting the text object into edit mode and looking at the upper right corner of the selection box. Labels have a handle in the shape of a circle. Text blocks have a handle in the shape of a square.*

To create a text label:

1. Open a new movie in Flash.

2. Choose the text tool and click anywhere in the scene.

   Although all drawing and object creation takes place on the canvas level, text is an exception. Flash always creates text as an overlay object.

3. Choose a typeface from the Font modifier menu (shown in Figure 4.3). Set the Font Size modifier menu to **24** points, and choose a color from the Font Color modifier menu.

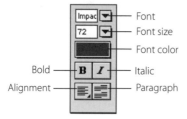

Figure 4.3
The text tool modifiers apply text styles.

4. Type in: **My first word is one of apology for my impossible English.** Depending on where you started typing and the size of the type, you may not see the right edge of the text object.

5. Move the cursor over one of the edges of the text object until you see the move-selection cursor mode, as shown in Figure 4.4. Moving the cursor over the edge of the object allows you to move the object within the level. Move it until you can see the upper right corner of the object.

My first word is one of apolo

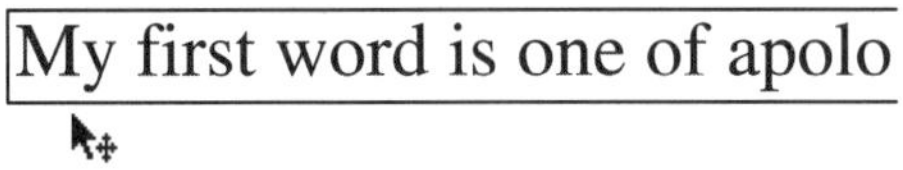

Figure 4.4
Preparing to move the text overlay object with the move-selection cursor in move selection mode.

By default, Flash creates all text as label text. Flash creates a single line of text, unless you press the Return or Enter key to create a line break. In one step, you can type in all the text. Then you can decide how or where you want to place it in the scene. By entering text as label text first, and then converting it to block text, you can place it onto any button or into any space in the scene. The text block automatically wraps to conform to the area.

To convert label text to block text:

1. Find the circle handle at the upper right corner of the object, and move the cursor over the handle until you see the double-ended arrow cursor. This indicates that you can modify the text object's width, which changes how the text wraps. Narrow the width of the box by dragging to the left, as shown in Figure 4.5. When you release the mouse button, the square handle indicates that the text object is now a text block, in which the width of the object determines how the text wraps from line to line.

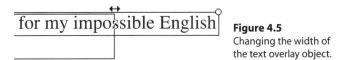

for my impossible English

Figure 4.5
Changing the width of the text overlay object.

NOTE *If you see a thick, checked outline around the object, it is no longer in the text-edit mode. Either double-click the object with the arrow tool or click once with the text tool to return to edit mode.*

2. Experiment with different widths for the text block to see how it affects the text wrap. The height of the object may change depending on how many lines are needed to display the text (see Figure 4.6).

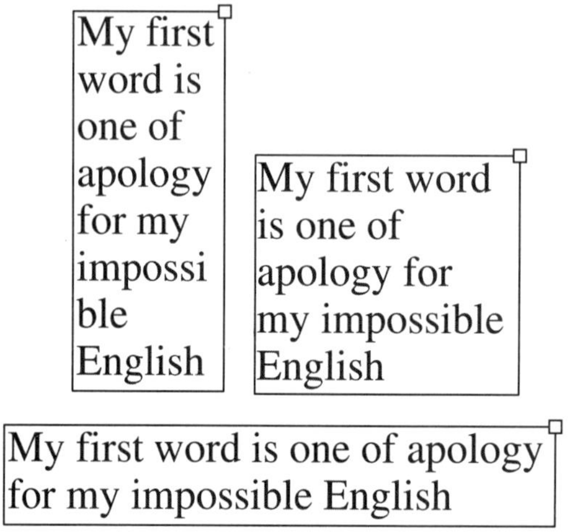

My first word is one of apology for my impossi ble English

My first word is one of apology for my impossible English

My first word is one of apology for my impossible English

Figure 4.6
Text wrapping is determined by the width of the text block.

Sometimes you may want to use a single text object in several differently shaped areas. Or you may decide to place a text object on a button that you want to enlarge, and you want the text to wrap and conform to the new area. In this case, you can convert an existing block of text back to a label text.

To convert block text to label text:

1. Double-click on the handle to convert the text object back to a label. Because the text is all on one line, the width of the object expands to its original size.

2. Click on the text block just before the word "of," and press the **Enter** key (Windows) or the **Return** key (Macintosh) to force a line break and modify the height and width of the box, as shown in Figure 4.7.

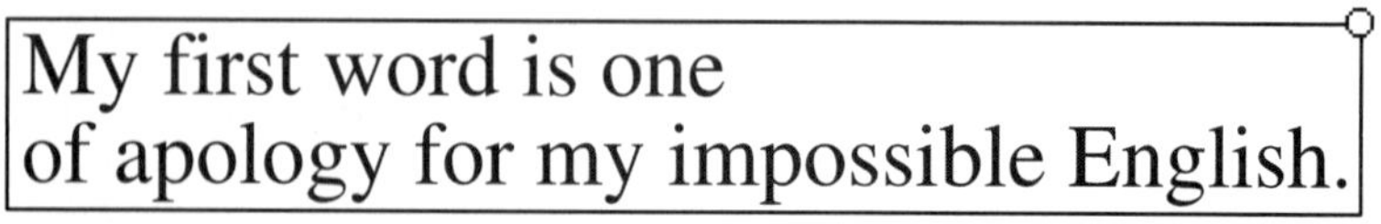

My first word is one of apology for my impossible English.

Figure 4.7
Changing the width of a label by inserting a line break.

3. Click again just before the word "impossible," and press the **Enter** key (Windows) or the Return key (Macintosh) to force a line break. Again, the object's size is modified to indicate the changes in the text.

Flash is not a word-processing program, but it does provide a large degree of control over the appearance of text beyond merely its width. The next exercise explores how you can modify other attributes of a text object.

Styling labels and text blocks

You're not limited to simply placing text in boxes in Flash. You also can modify text by changing its color, font attributes, and alignment within the text box. You can style characters and paragraphs by using the text tool modifiers or (in most cases) through selections from the Modify menu. This exercise demonstrates how to change some of the attributes of individual characters and paragraphs of text blocks and labels.

To modify text style:

1. Open the Flash movie *exer04a.fla*. This movie contains a quotation, which is a text object.

2. Select the text tool, and move the cursor so it's just to the left of the first character of the first line of text. Click and drag to select the first line of text (from the first character to the colon), as shown in Figure 4.8. Flash automatically places the text object in edit mode.

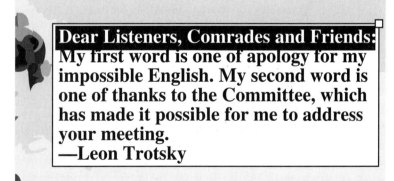

Figure 4.8
The first line of text selected by clicking and dragging with the text tool.

3. Click the **Italic** modifier (shown in Figure 4.9) to italicize the selected text. (The Bold modifier is already activated.)

Figure 4.9
The text tool's Italic modifier italicizes selected text.

To change text alignment:

1. Click anywhere in the last line of the text box.

2. From the **Alignment** modifier, choose **Right**, as shown in Figure 4.10. Because this affects the whole paragraph, there's no need to select the entire line to affect the text.

Figure 4.10
Selecting Right justification from the Alignment modifier.

To modify paragraph properties:

1. Click in the body of the quote (after the first line and before the last line). Modify this paragraph by using the **Paragraph Properties** modifier. Clicking the modifier button displays the Paragraph Properties dialog box.

SHORTCUT Access the Paragraph Properties dialog box by choosing Paragraph from the Modify menu, or by pressing Ctrl-T (Windows) or Command-T (Macintosh).

---

2. The Paragraph Properties dialog box (shown in Figure 4.11) enables you to set values for left and right margins (the minimum amount of space between the sides of the text object and the text characters), indentation (the amount of space that the first line of text is inset from the margin), and line spacing (extra space between lines of text). The values for these entries can be inches, points, millimeters, centimeters, or pixels. Set the Margins and Indentation values to **20 px** (20 pixels), and enter **4 pt** (4 points) for Line Space. Click **OK** to make these changes.

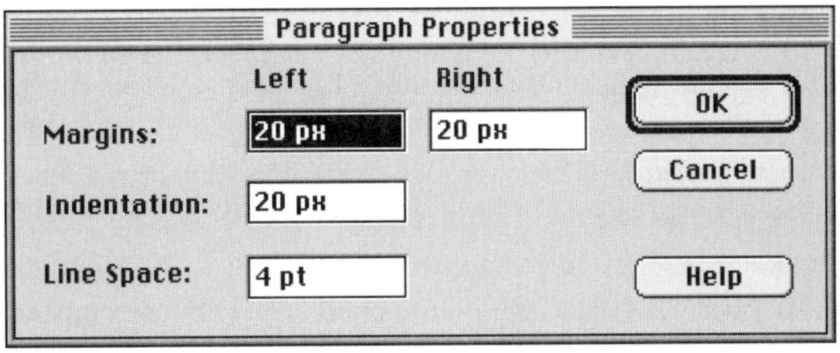

```
┌══════════════ Paragraph Properties ══════════════┐
│                                                    │
│              Left        Right      ╭────────────╮ │
│                                     │     OK     │ │
│  Margins:   │20 px│     │20 px│     ╰────────────╯ │
│                                     ╭────────────╮ │
│  Indentation: │20 px│               │   Cancel   │ │
│                                     ╰────────────╯ │
│  Line Space:  │4 pt│                               │
│                                     ╭────────────╮ │
│                                     │    Help    │ │
│                                     ╰────────────╯ │
└────────────────────────────────────────────────────┘
```

Figure 4.11
Setting attributes in the Paragraph Properties dialog box.

TIP *The default measurement units for all entries—except for Line Space, which always defaults to points—in the Paragraph Properties dialog box are determined by the Ruler Units for the movie, as set in the Movie Properties dialog box. You can use other units at any time by entering the appropriate abbreviation for pixels (px), points (pt), millimeters (mm), centimeters (cm), or inches (") after the number value.*

Bitmap Objects

Although vector images result in smaller, faster movies, there are times when bitmaps are useful. For example, it is easier to scan a recognized logo and import it than to recreate it as vector art in Flash. Or, should you want to include a photo in your movie, using a bitmap is essential. Bitmaps also are useful as illustrative elements, templates for tracing, and fills for other shapes.

NOTE *Take care with bitmaps to keep their number and size to a minimum. Bitmaps take up vastly greater space than vectors and, in most cases, significantly increases the time it takes to download a web file, as well as impacting the speed at which the movie plays.*

TIP *Flash also can export bitmap GIF and JPEG files. Artwork drawn in Flash can be used to create bitmap images at a variety of sizes for cases where objects such as logos, buttons, and other elements need to appear in different forms for multiple purposes.*

You can use bitmaps as part of a Flash movie in several ways: incorporate bitmaps as illustrative elements without any modification; duplicate and modify bitmaps; use bitmaps as fills for shapes drawn in Flash; or you can use them as a reference or template for tracing. Importing the bitmap is a necessary step for all these uses. When you import a bitmap, Flash places it on the overlay level of the current layer and automatically adds it to the Library.

To import a bitmap:

1. Create a new Flash movie.

2. Choose **Import** from the File menu, set the File Type pop-up menu to **JPEG** Image, choose the movie *exer04b.jpg* from the CD-ROM and click Open. This imports the image into the overlay level.

SHORTCUT Invoke the Import command by pressing Ctrl-R (Windows) or Command-R (Macintosh).

---

3. From the Window menu, choose **Library**. This brings the Library window to the front. Flash stores a master copy of every imported bitmap in the Library. (See "Working in the Library" later in this chapter for more information.) The bitmap image is the only item in the Library list at the bottom (see Figure 4.12).

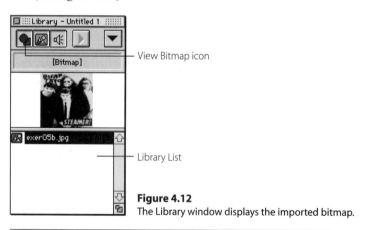

Figure 4.12
The Library window displays the imported bitmap.

SHORTCUT Open the Library window by pressing Ctrl-L (Windows) or Command-L (Macintosh).

If you don't see the image in the Library window, be sure that you have selected the View Bitmap icon at the top of the window (see Figure 4.13).

Figure 4.13
The Library's View Bitmap icon found in the Library window.

After you import a bitmap and store it in the Library, you can use it anywhere in the movie without using much additional memory. This is because you are not creating an additional copy, but simply referencing the original bitmap in the Library.

To move a bitmap from the Library to a scene:

- Click on the thumbnail image of the bitmap in the Library window, and drag it into the scene (see Figure 4.14). Flash creates a link to the master bitmap.

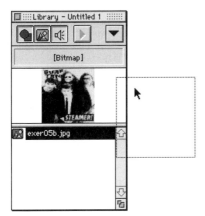

Figure 4.14
Dragging the bitmap image from the Library to the canvas.

Because Flash doesn't save a complete copy of the bitmap and tracks only changes, you can make modifications to the duplicate bitmap without significantly affecting playback performance or file size.

To modify a bitmap:

1. Select the bitmap in the scene.

2. Select the arrow tool and click the button for the **Scale** modifier. Use the handles on the copy of the bitmap to modify the size and proportions of the image.

3. Click the **Rotate** modifier to use the handles for changing the image's orientation (see Figure 4.15).

Figure 4.15
Sizing and rotating the bitmap image using the Scale and Rotate modifiers.

Using an imported bitmap as a fill for shapes drawn in Flash requires an additional step: you must break apart the bitmap. The following section describes this process.

Breaking apart bitmaps

By breaking apart a bitmap, you can use the bitmap as fill inside any shape, just as you would a gradient or solid color. Like a gradient, you can scale, skew, and rotate the bitmap fill just as you can a gradient (see Figure 4.16).

Figure 4.16
Some examples of bitmaps used as fills after being broken apart and transformed.

When you import a bitmap, it's always rectangular in shape. Used as fill, the bitmap is seamlessly tiled if the shape is larger than the bitmap. This gives you a significant advantage when creating a tiled background for a web site because Flash treats the bitmap like a symbol. You then can use the bitmap you broke apart to fill the entire background of a movie. Flash's automatic tiling adds very little size to the movie.

Preparing a bitmap to use as a fill for other shapes begins by moving it from the overlay level to the canvas level with the Modify menu's Break Apart command.

TIP *The Break Apart command isn't used exclusively with bitmaps on the overlay layer. You also can use it to turn text into outlines and to convert symbols into their constituent parts.*

These exercises demonstrate how you can convert a bitmap image on the overlay level to a tiled fill for a shape on the canvas level, how you can modify that shape just like any other shape, and how you can transform the fill's image in size, rotation, and shape.

To convert a bitmap image to a fill:

1. Open the movie *exer04c.fla*. Open the Library window by pressing **Ctrl-L** (Windows) or **Command-L** (Macintosh).

2. Click the image thumbnail and drag it onto the canvas.

3. Choose **Break Apart** from the Modify menu. This converts the bitmap on the overlay level to a fill on the canvas level. Deselect the converted bitmap by pressing the **Escape** key.

SHORTCUT Press Ctrl-B (Windows) or Command-B (Macintosh) to Break Apart an overlay object.

To modify the bitmap fill:

1. Using the arrow tool's curve reshaping capability, tug at the edges of the converted bitmap to make it look more like an ellipse (see Figure 4.17). As the image stretches, Flash tiles it to fill the shape.

Figure 4.17
Using the arrow tool to modify a shape with a bitmap fill.

2. Select the shape by clicking it with the arrow tool.

3. Click the **Straighten** modifier button (or choose **Modify > Curves > Straighten**). Continue clicking until the shape turns into an ellipse.

4. Deselect the shape again.

5. Choose the dropper tool and click the image. In the Fill Color preview area, a thumbnail of the bitmap image appears (see Figure 4.18).

Figure 4.18
The toolbar displays a bitmap image in the Fill Color preview.

6. Select the **Transform Fill** modifier, and click on the shape. Flash places a selection marquee around the original position of the bitmap fill (see Figure 4.19).

Skew fill

Rotate fill

Move fill

Proportional scale

Figure 4.19
The bitmap fill, selected and ready for transforming.

The handles on the bitmap fill allow you to modify how the shape uses the fill:

- The round handle at the center of the selection moves the tile.

- The round handles on the top and right edges of the selection skew the tile.

- The round handle on the top right corner rotates the tile.

- The square handles on the left and bottom edges scale the tile in one dimension.

- The square handle on the bottom scales the tile proportionally.

Play around with the various options for transforming the tile. If you use the Undo command, you must reselect the tile to edit it further.

You can add bitmap fills to other shapes. Different shapes in the same movie can use the same bitmap image with different scaling, rotation, and skew values (see Figure 4.20). Modify the shapes themselves with the Flash drawing tools, including the eraser, paintbrush, and others.

Figure 4.20
Several shapes using various transformations of a single bitmap image as a fill, and as a single movie incorporating all of the shapes.

To apply a bitmap fill to other shapes:

1. Select the dropper tool.

2. Click on the bitmap image with the dropper tool. In the Fill Color preview area, a thumbnail of the bitmap fill appears.

3. Apply the fill to another shape by choosing the paint bucket tool and clicking in the scene, and then on the shape you want to fill.

NOTE *The shape containing the bitmap fill is what is known in other drawing programs as a "clipping path," which shows only a part of the tiled image.*

Tracing bitmaps

Sometimes the advantages and capabilities of vector-based art are more important than absolute fidelity for the bitmap image. Flash can convert bitmaps into vector artwork with a wide range of accuracy using the Trace Bitmap command on the Modify menu.

Converting a bitmap to vector art (by tracing it) differs from using the bitmap image as a bitmap. When you use a bitmap as an overlay element, the image is not modified; and if scaled to a size much larger than the original image, it begins to look grainy or pixellated. Tracing the bitmap by converting it to vectors enables you to scale the image to any size with no loss of resolution.

To convert a bitmap into a vector image:

1. Open the movie *exer04d.fla*. This movie contains a single bitmap image in the overlay level.

2. Select the bitmap image by clicking it with the arrow tool.

3. Choose the **Trace Bitmap** command from the Modify menu to display the Trace Bitmap dialog box (see Figure 4.21).

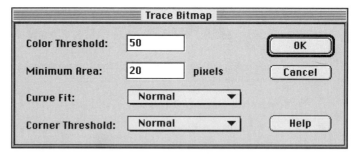

Figure 4.21
Use the Trace Bitmap dialog box to convert bitmap images.

The Trace Bitmap dialog box has four settings that determine how accurately the bitmap reproduces as vector art. Accuracy ranges from individually outlining each pixel to outlining blobs of color that Flash interprets as the same color (see Figure 4.22). The tradeoff for accuracy is file size. For most images, absolute fidelity to the original bitmap makes a vector file that ia larger than the bitmap file.

threshold = 1, area = 1,
curve = pixels,
corners = many

threshold = 50, area = 10,
curve = normal,
corners = normal

threshold = 150, area = 50,
curve = very smooth
corners = few

Figure 4.22
A comparison of the how different settings in the Trace Bitmap dialog box affect the process of tracing a bitmap image.

- The first setting for the Trace Bitmap dialog box is Color Threshold. This value can range from 0 to 500, and determines how much one pixel must vary in color from its neighboring pixel before Flash sees them as different colors. The larger the value, the fewer shapes created.

- The next setting is Minimum Area, which determines the size (in pixels) of each shape created by the trace (at its smallest). This value can range from 1 to 1000. A setting of 1 (depending on the Color Threshold setting) creates very small shapes.

> **NOTE** *One thousand pixels sounds like a large number, but in a 72 dpi image, it's roughly a 1¹/₄-inch square.*

- The Curve Fit pop-up menu has six settings that range from Pixels to Very Smooth, which determine how closely the edges between shapes follow the original bitmap colors. When you use the Pixels option to trace, the program draws many short curves; with Very Smooth, it draws longer curves.

- The final setting is Corner Threshold, which has three settings: Many Corners, Normal, and Few Corners. This setting controls how far a curve must bend before it breaks into two curves with a corner.

4. Set the Color Threshold to **50**, the Minimum Area to **20**, and choose **Normal** for both Curve Fit and Corner Threshold. Then click **OK** to close the dialog box. The Tracing Bitmap progress bar window appears while the process takes place. When finished, Flash removes the bitmap image from the overlay level, and selects the shapes created by the process on the canvas level.

5. Deselect the shapes by pressing **Escape**. Choose **Outline** from the View menu to see the outlines of the shapes.

Once Flash has traced the bitmaps, you can delete them from the Library (see "Working in the Library" later in this chapter).

NOTE *Although the bitmap is deleted from the canvas, it is not removed from the Library; it remains as part of the movie when you save it. You may need to use the Save As command from the File menu to actually remove the bitmap data from your Flash movie, even after it's deleted from the Library.*

Working on the Overlay Level

Using text objects and bitmaps are ways of working on the overlay level. You also can use groups to work with text objects and bitmaps. Groups can combine any type of object, including items drawn on the canvas level, text objects, bitmaps, other groups, and symbols. Objects drawn on the canvas level and combined into a group become part of the overlay level, and are unaffected by any further drawing on the canvas level.

Creating groups

The items in a group need not be adjacent to each other. They can be anywhere on the same layer of a frame. Making a group is as easy as making a selection.

To create a group:

1. Open the movie *exer04e.fla* . This movie contains several objects of varying types, ranging from drawings on the canvas level to text and bitmaps.

2. Using the arrow tool or lasso tool, select any part of the objects on the canvas level or the overlay level (see Figure 4.23).

Figure 4.23
Selecting multiple items before grouping them.

3. Select **Group** from the Modify menu to combine the selected shapes and/or overlay items into a single overlay group. You can resize, rotate, skew, and scale the group.

SHORTCUT Group items by pressing Ctrl-G (Windows) or Command-G (Macintosh). Ungroup items by pressing Ctrl-U (Windows) or Command-U (Macintosh).

The **Ungroup** command (also on the Modify menu) converts the group back to individual items.

As mentioned earlier, overlay objects float in front of the canvas level and don't interact (by deleting part of, or combining) with each other the way that shapes on the canvas level do. This means that some overlay objects sit in front of others. You can control the order, or *stacking* of these overlay objects with the commands on the Arrange submenu of the Modify menu.

Stacking order is arranged in terms of back to front. The canvas level is always the farthest back—behind all of the overlay levels. Objects on the overlay level are opaque, and will hide other objects behind them on the overlay level, as well as any shapes on the canvas level (see Figure 4.24).

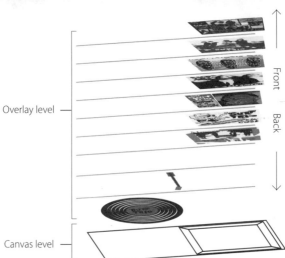

Figure 4.24
The stacking order of overlay objects determines which object is in front (or on top) of others. Overlays always appear in front of objects on the canvas level.

The following exercise demonstrates how you can rearrange the stacking order of the overlay level to bring desired objects to the front, and how to move objects within the stacking order.

To rearrange items in the overlay level:

1. Open the movie *exer04f.fla*. This file contains six grouped objects with numbers that show their original stacking order. The numbers are arranged from the back (1) to the front (6).

2. Select each group and move them so that the pictures are all on top of one another. The group with the number "6" should be in front of all others (see Figure 4.25).

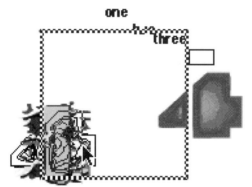

Figure 4.25
Arranging overlays to overlap.

3. Select group 6 and use the **Send to Back** command from the Modify > Arrange submenu to change the stacking order by putting the group behind all others.

SHORTCUT The Arrange commands are invoked by using combinations that include the up and down arrow keys.

---

4. Leave the group selected and move it toward the front, one object at a time using the **Move Ahead** command. Each time you use this command, the selected object moves one place forward in the stacking order toward the front, swapping positions with the object directly in front of it. Continue until the group is once again at the front.

As with most other graphics programs, you can group groups as well as individual objects. If you select all of the items on the canvas—Ctrl-A (Windows), or Command-A (Macintosh)—and choose Group from the Modify menu, you can create a single group from all of the groups in the movie.

You've already had a peek at the Flash Library window, where Flash stores bitmap images. The Library is also the repository for symbols and sounds (see Chapter 9, "Sounds"). Symbols are one of the most important (and most complex) facets of Flash movies. Each symbol can incorporate its own animations, bitmaps and drawn elements, interactivity, and even other symbols. Symbols are stored in the file only once, but Flash can reference them as many times as necessary while the movie plays, without adding significantly to the movie size.

A Flash symbol also can be a sort of movie within a movie. A symbol can have its own animation capabilities. And, most importantly, you can use them over and over without making the Flash file any larger. For example, you could create a symbol of a fish and animate it to swim across the screen. Then you could create a school of fish by duplicating the fish symbol in your movie several times and animating each fish in the movie to enter the scene at a different time. All the fish would inherit the original fish symbol's ability to swim across the screen without adding appreciably to the file size. You size or color each fish distinctly without making your movie bigger. Figure 4.26 illustrates how the repeated use of symbols can reduce the size of Flash files.

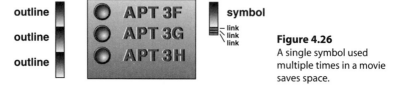

Figure 4.26
A single symbol used multiple times in a movie saves space.

In contrast, you can use duplicated objects or groups multiple times. Each time you make a duplicate object, however, Flash adds a new set of outlines to the file. You also must animate each object separately, adding more data to the final movie. For a complex scene, such as the fish scene described above, that can have quite an impact on your movie's performance and size.

The following exercise demonstrates how to create a simple, non-animated symbol from a selection of objects and shapes.

To examine the Library:

1. Open the movie *exer04g.fla*. This movie contains several items in the Library, as well as some on the canvas and overlay levels.

2. If the Library window is not already open, open it by choosing
Windows > Library (see Figure 4.27 to identify the parts of
the Library Window).

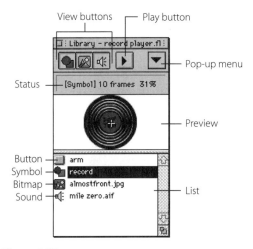

Figure 4.27
The Library window with buttons and parts identified.

3. The Library window features a Preview, where you can see
currently selected items. Directly above the Preview is a line
of text describing the selected item, called Status. The scrolling
list at the bottom shows an icon that identifies whether the
item is a bitmap, sound, symbol, or button, as well as the name
of the item. You can use the buttons at the top left to hide the
various types of Library items to make viewing long lists easier,
as shown in Figure 4.28.

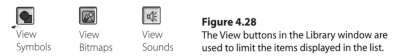

Figure 4.28
The View buttons in the Library window are
used to limit the items displayed in the list.

4. Select one of the sounds in the list (as indicated by the sound
icon next to the name). Click the **Play** button at the top of the
window to listen to the sound. Use the Play button to view
symbols containing animations as well as previewing sounds
in the list.

You can add an item to the Library in two ways. One way is to
import a file into Flash as you've already done with bitmaps. The
process for sounds is much the same. The other method is to select
items on the canvas and overlay levels—instead of making a group—
and create a symbol.

To create a symbol:

1. Select some or all of the items on the canvas, and choose **Create Symbol** from the Insert menu. The Symbol Properties dialog box appears.

SHORTCUT Invoke the Create Symbol command from the keyboard by pressing F8.

---

2. In the Symbol Properties dialog box (see Figure 4.29), enter a name for your symbol. Each item in the Library must have a unique name. Click **OK** to create the symbol.

```
 ═══════════════════ Symbol Properties ═══════════════════

   Name:     ┌─────────────────────────────┐     ┌───────────┐
             │ four                        │     │    OK     │
             └─────────────────────────────┘     └───────────┘

                   ☐ Button Behavior                ┌───────────┐
                                                    │  Cancel   │
                                                    └───────────┘
                                                    ┌───────────┐
                                                    │   Help    │
                                                    └───────────┘
```

Figure 4.29
The Symbol Properties dialog box used to create symbols from selected items.

NOTE *The Button Behavior checkbox means that you can use your symbol as a button to control actions in Flash. Creating buttons is covered in Chapter 7, "Scenes & Actions."*

The items you have selected on the canvas are now represented by the symbol, which—like a group—is one object on the overlay level. You can add another copy of those items to the overlay level simply by dragging the symbol's preview image from the Library window onto the canvas, as shown in Figure 4.30.

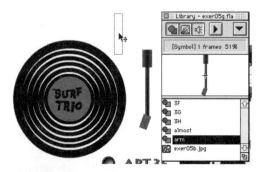

Figure 4.30
Adding another copy of the new symbol to the overlay level by dragging it from the Library.

Each symbol has its own scene for editing, as shown in Figure 4.31. Changes made to the symbol affect every place that symbol appears in the movie.

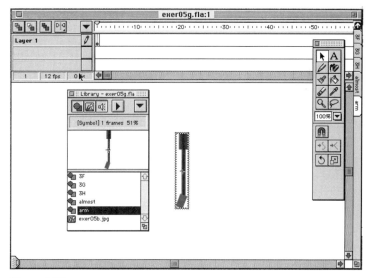

Figure 4.31
A symbol in edit mode ready to modify.

To edit a symbol:

1. Select the symbol in the Library list, and choose **Edit** from the Library window menu.

SHORTCUT You can select a symbol in the overlay level and choose Edit Selected from the Edit menu to edit a symbol. When editing a movie, pressing Ctrl-E (Windows) or Command-E (Macintosh), or selecting Edit Symbols from the Edit menu switches to the symbol editing mode.

---

2. A new scene appears that displays only those items you used to create the symbol. One tab for each of the movie's symbols displays on the scene's right side, as shown in Figure 4.32. At the top of the column of tabs is the **Edit Movie** button that you can use to return you to the movie's scene.

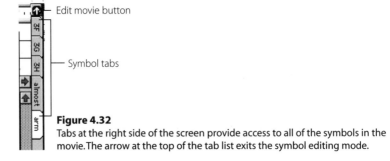

Edit movie button

Symbol tabs

Figure 4.32
Tabs at the right side of the screen provide access to all of the symbols in the movie. The arrow at the top of the tab list exits the symbol editing mode.

SHORTCUT When you are editing symbols, pressing Ctrl-E (Windows) or Command-E (Macintosh) returns to the movie editing mode.

---

3. Use any Flash drawing or painting tool to modify the symbol. When you're satisfied with your results, click on the **Edit Movie** button to return to the movie canvas. Both copies of the symbol in the overlay level reflect the changes you made. Each copy is a *symbol link*. Any changes to a symbol appears in every instance that you have used the symbol as a symbol link.

4. Select just one of the symbol links, and choose **Break Apart** from the Modify menu. The selected shapes are now no longer linked to the symbol. You can edit and modify the selected shapes without editing the symbol, and changes made to the symbol no longer affect the selected shapes.

Symbols are very useful for organizing the elements of your movies. Because you can reuse them without significantly impacting the size of the movie file, they contribute greatly to the portability of Flash movies. As you will learn in the next chapter, symbols can be used to create a single overlay object that animates whenever it appears in a movie.

Moving On...

As the concepts of animation in Flash are further explored in the next chapter, you will learn how to group symbols, text, bitmaps, and groups to create animations and to organize animated elements. The next chapter explores reusing symbols and other Library elements without increasing file size, and your ability to move overlay objects without interacting with other objects or shapes.

CHAPTER 5

Animation

It's what Flash is all about,

really. You can use any illustration program to draw, but they can't make your drawings move.

What you'll learn…

**How to work
with frames**

**Using key frames
and onion skinning**

**Frame-by-frame and
tweened animation
techniques**

Animation techniques are what enable an artist to create the illusion of movement over a period of time. By placing the same object in different places, or by placing different objects in the same place, animators use a sequence of frames and key frames to control what's seen and where it appears.

Flash animation employs techniques familiar to traditional animators such as *frame-by-frame*, in addition to *tweening* (which takes advantage of a computer's capability to calculate change).

This chapter introduces these building blocks of animation and shows you how these techniques can make a movie live up to its name, and *move*.

Each frame of a Flash movie represents one moment in time (usually in the neighborhood of $1/24$ second), depending on the movie's speed. The entire series of frames composing the movie make up the *timeline*.

There are three types of frames: *key frames*, *blank* frames, and *tweened* frames (see Figure 5.1). Key frames indicate points in the movie at which the artwork changes—some element of the artwork moves, changes size or color, or rotates. Blank frames don't contain any visual information so they display the artwork from the previous key frame. *Tweened* frames are derived from two key frames. Flash calculates (*interpolates*) the artwork displayed in a tweened frame by comparing, interpolating, and generating changes between similar elements in the key frame before and the key frame after the tweened frame.

Blank frames
Key frames
Tweened frames

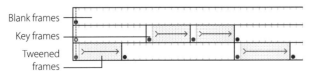

Figure 5.1
The three frame types displayed in the timeline.

You control the speed at which a movie's images change via the Frame Rate setting in the Movie Properties dialog box. (See Chapter 1, "Flash Tour," to review the properties of a movie.) For example, if a movie has a frame rate of 10 fps (frames per second) and contains 100 frames, it will play for 10 seconds from start to end.

NOTE *In Flash, the frame rate defines the upper limit for the movie's playback speed. The size and amount of artwork in the movie, its display quality, and the speed of the playback computer's processor can slow the actual frame rate to below that which you set. Actions assigned to frames and buttons also affect playback speed.*

Adding frames to a movie

At any point in the timeline, you can add frames to a movie to any layer of any scene. Adding frames to a movie (even blank frames) lengthens the potential playing time of the movie. Initially, when you add frames to a movie they appear as blank frames.

To add frames to a movie:

1. Create a new movie in Flash. A new movie always appears with a single, empty key frame (an unfilled circle in the first frame of the timeline). The black line after frame 1 indicates that the movie ends at frame 1 (see Figure 5.2).

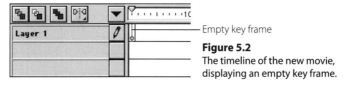

— Empty key frame

Figure 5.2
The timeline of the new movie, displaying an empty key frame.

2. Use the drawing tools to create something on screen. Flash then replaces the empty key frame indicator with a filled circle to indicate that the frame now contains some visual element (see Figure 5.3).

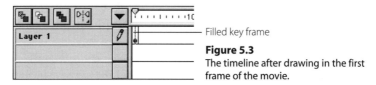

— Filled key frame

Figure 5.3
The timeline after drawing in the first frame of the movie.

3. Click at frame 10 to place the Modify Frames indicator at frame 10 (see Figure 5.4). The Modify Frames indicator appears slightly to the left of the number 10.

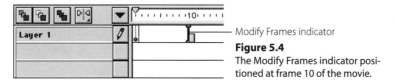

— Modify Frames indicator

Figure 5.4
The Modify Frames indicator positioned at frame 10 of the movie.

4. Click the Modify Frames indicator (the gray tab) to display the Modify Frames pop-up menu, and choose **Insert Frame**. The black line that indicates the last frame now appears after frame 10. Frames 2 through 10 are blank frames.

SHORTCUT Use the F5 key to insert frames.

NOTE *The number of frames inserted depends on the placement of the Modify Frames indicator and whether or not you have selected other frames.*

5. Click the current frame indicator and drag it from frame 1 to frame 10 (see Figure 5.5). You now have blank frames in frames 2 through 10. Because they are blank, the artwork you drew in frame 1 appears unchanged in all of the frames of the movie. The blank frames (frames 2–10) display the same artwork contained in the key frame (frame 1). Keep this movie open for the next exercise.

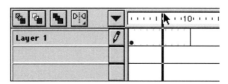

Figure 5.5
Moving the current frame indicator to view other frames of the movie.

The current frame indicator controls which frame displays. It automatically moves through the movie when the movie plays. Clicking on the numbers above the timeline or dragging the current frame indicator to a new position displays a different frame.

NOTE *Editing the artwork on screen affects the most recent key frame if the current frame indicator is not in a key frame. When creating animations, make sure that the current frame indicator points to a key frame, or changes may occur where not expected.*

Adding key frames to a movie

After you have added frames to a movie, you can convert an individual frame, or range of frames, to a key frame. Key frames keep track of where the graphics are on screen and how they change.

To convert a frame to a key frame:

1. Use the movie you began in the previous exercise or open *exer05a.fla*. Click on the timeline in one of the frames between the key frame (frame 1) and the last frame indicator (frame 10) to place the Modify Frames indicator. Move the current frame indicator to the same frame.

2. Choose **Insert Key Frame** from the Modify Frames pop-up menu attached to the Modify Frames indicator. This creates a new key frame at the position indicated (see Figure 5.6), but does not make the movie longer. Note that there is now a black line *before* the new key frame, indicating the end of the previous key frame's influence.

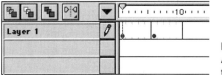

Figure 5.6
A second key frame added
to the movie.

TIP *Select a range of frames and choose Insert Key Frame
to add key frames to make each selected frame a key frame
and copy the artwork of the previous key frame into each new
key frame.*

3. With the current frame indicator in the new key frame, select
the graphic and move it.

4. Now, move the current frame indicator back and forth between
the frames on either side of your new key frame. Because you
moved the artwork in the new key frame, the artwork appears
to jump when the current frame indicator moves to it from the
previous frame.

When you want to determine which frame you are looking at in a
Flash movie, you have two choices: one way is to locate the current
frame indicator on the top edge of the timeline. The dotted line
extending down from the current frame indicator through all the
layers of the timeline determines which frame of the Flash movie
displays. When you are working with movies that contain many frames
on screen, the current frame indicator may scroll off one side of the
timeline. When this occurs, use the numeric readout at the lower left
corner of the timeline; it displays the current frame number (see
Figure 5.7).

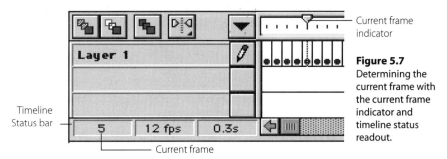

Current frame
indicator

Timeline
Status bar

Current frame

Figure 5.7
Determining the
current frame with
the current frame
indicator and
timeline status
readout.

Dating back to the first days of cartooning, *frame-by-frame* animation represents movement in a scene by modifying a piece of the picture little by little from one frame to the next throughout a scene. For example, to create the illusion of a ball moving from one side of the screen to the other, an animator uses a sequence of still frames with the ball moving a short distance along its path in each frame until it reaches its destination.

This technique gives you control over the movement of an element and is useful for adding variety and personality to the animation. You can introduce or remove items from frame-by-frame animations by simply drawing them in or removing them from the picture at any frame.

Creating frame-by-frame animation

When you create frame-by-frame animations in Flash, each frame in which change to the picture occurs is a key frame. So the first task is to create a sequence of key frames that contain the art you want to manipulate. The second task is to modify the artwork in each frame to achieve the effect you want.

To create a sequence of key frames containing artwork:

1. Open the movie *exer05b.fla* in Flash. This movie is a picture of a caution sign with a flashing light on top. The movie is already 10 frames long. In its current state, nothing in the movie changes. Choose **Loop Playback** from the Control menu, and then **Play** to see that as the current frame indicator moves through the timeline, nothing happens.

SHORTCUT Pressing Enter (Windows or Macintosh) or Return (Macintosh) starts and stops the movie.

---

2. Click in frame 1 of the timeline and drag to select all 10 frames of the movie. Choose **Key Frame** from the Insert menu or **Insert Key Frame** from the Modify Frames pop-up menu that appears at the end of the selected frames. Either action results in Flash adding identical key frames to all of the selected frames (see Figure 5.8).

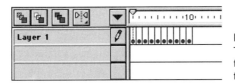

Figure 5.8
The timeline with key frames inserted at each frame of the movie

---

SHORTCUT Use the F6 key to add a key frame to the selected frame or frames.

---

3. Move the current frame indicator to frame 2.

SHORTCUT Use the > and < keys to move the current frame indicator forward and backward. (You do not need to press the Shift key.)

---

4. Deselect all of the art by pressing the **Esc** key, or use the arrow tool to select an area outside of the artwork.

5. Select the paint bucket tool, and then select a Fill Color that's a dark gray. Move the paint bucket tool over the yellow flashing light and fill it with the dark gray. Congratulations, you've just created your first frame-by-frame animation in Flash! Move the current frame indicator into the frame before or after frame 2, and back again to see the light flash.

6. Repeat Steps 3 through 5 for frames 4, 6, 8, and 10. When you have finished, be sure that you set the **Loop Playback** option in the Control menu and play the movie. The light appears to flash on and off in every other frame. If you vary the Frame Rate of the movie in the Movie Properties window, you can see how the frame rate affects the flashing light's speed.

Onion-skinning

Often it is difficult to judge just how far to move objects in each frame of a frame-by-frame animation sequence. Smooth-looking motion isn't always easy to achieve. To make it easier, you can view simultaneously multiple frames of a movie through a process called *onion-skinning* (a name derived from a thin, semi-transparent paper that was employed in hand-drawn animation sequences). In Flash, onion-skinning enables you to make adjustments to the position of the art in a single frame, while displaying the artwork in the frames both before and after the current frame.

To adjust a frame-by-frame animation through onion-skinning:

1. Open the movie *exer05c.fla*. This movie contains a picture of a man. The man's left arm is a separate symbol shape, which you can rotate to simulate a waving motion.

NOTE *The left arm was converted into a group, and the Edit Center command from the Transform submenu of the Modify menu was used to move the center point to the shoulder area. Because a symbol or group moves around its center point when you rotate it, placing the center point at the shoulder gives the impression that the arm is waving from the shoulder.*

2. Eight key frames for this sequence have been created already. Move the current frame indicator to frame 2, and select just the right arm (see Figure 5.9). Use the Rotate modifier of the arrow tool to rotate the art up slightly. Repeat this process for frames 3 through 8, approximating the arm movements in Figure 5.9.

Select this arm

| Frame 1 | Frame 2 | Frame 3 | Frame 4 |
| Frame 5 | Frame 6 | Frame 7 | Frame 8 |

Figure 5.9
Arm positions for frames 1 to 8.

After you've moved the arm in each of the key frames, play the movie and watch how the arm moves.

3. Move the current frame indicator to frame 1, and click the Onion Skin button. Choose Onion All from the Modify Onion Markers menu (see Figure 5.10). The Onion Skin button toggles the display of frames (other than the current frame). The Onion All setting indicates that all of the frames of the movie display. Artwork in frames other than the current frame display in

lighter tones than those of the artwork in the current frame. The first frame to display is lightest, and the last frame to display is darkest (except for the current frame). Moving the Start Onion Skin and End Onion Skin markers in the timeline controls which frames display.

Onion skin

Onion skin outlines

Edit multiple frames

Modify Onion markers

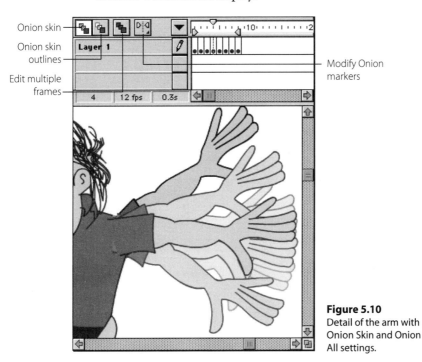

Figure 5.10
Detail of the arm with Onion Skin and Onion All settings.

4. Click the **Onion Skin Outlines** button. What appears on the screen is similar to what you see when you choose Onion Skin. However, with **Onion Skin Outlines**, the artwork in frames other than the current frame appear as outlines only. Flash shades the outlines—just as Flash shades the filled shapes in the Onion Skin view. Select the arm in the current frame with the arrow tool and use the Rotate modifier to adjust its position. The Onion Skin and Onion Skin Outlines views allow only editing of the current frame.

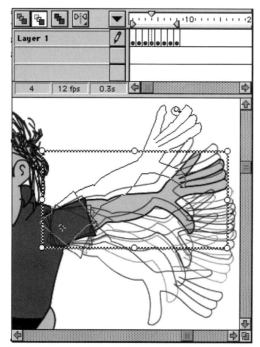

Figure 5.11
Rotating the arm with
Onion Skin Outlines and
Onion All settings.

5. Click the **Edit Multiple Frames** button. This onion-skinning
   option enables you to edit of all of the visible frames. Each
   piece of artwork displays at its full color value. With the **Rotate**
   modifier of the arrow tool, select each arm and adjust it so that
   the distance between each of the arms is equal. When the
   movie plays now, the animation appears smoother.

   Keep this movie open for the next exercise.

Viewing animations as filmstrips

When you are working with frame-by-frame animation, you may find
the timeline's view choices give you a better sense of the movement
than the default symbolic view. There are two options in the Modify
Frame View menu that display a thumbnail view of each key frame
in the timeline (see Figure 5.12). Although it can be time-consuming
to view the timeline this way when there are many key frames, it can
be helpful when looking for a specific movie frame.

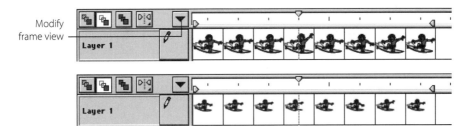

Modify
frame view

Figure 5.12
Two options for viewing the timeline: Preview option for the timeline (above),
and Preview in Context option (below).

■ With the finished movie from the previous exercise open,
  choose **Preview** from the Modify Frame View menu. The
  artwork for each of the key frames in the movie displays,
  scaled to fit the small size of the timeline frame.

■ After the previews have been scaled, choose **Preview in
  Context** from the Modify Frame View menu. The same
  frames display, but Flash scales each picture to show its
  size relative to the entire movie frame.

Tweened Animation

By now you are probably asking yourself if there isn't a better way to
create smooth animation sequences than incrementally moving parts
of a picture. There is a better method and it's called *tweening* (short
for "in-betweening"). The computer does the tweening by calculating
the positions for artwork between two key frames.

Using the frame-by-frame method, you must position a shape
that moves from one position to another in every single frame of the
animation, each of which needs to be a key frame. With tweening, you
can create a key frame for the beginning of the movement and another
for the end of the movement, and then let the computer calculate (or
interpolate) the changes in the artwork for the intermediate frames.

Tweened animations are easier to modify than frame-by-frame
animations. A change in a tweened animation requires a change in
just one of the two key frames; a modification to a frame-by-frame
sequence, like the one in the previous exercise, might require eight.
On the other hand, because the computer calculates tweened animation, you don't get the quirkiness that frame-by-frame animation can
sometimes impart.

NOTE *Unlike frame-by-frame animations, tweened animations require the use of overlay objects (groups, text, bitmaps, or symbols). You cannot animate shapes and lines on the canvas level with tweening.*

Creating tweened animation

A tweened animation starts with just two key frames. First, you copy the artwork in the first key frame into the last key frame where you move, scale, rotate, or recolorize the artwork. Flash then calculates movement, scaling, and rotation for the frames between the first key frame and the last key frame in even steps to create the illusion of a smooth animation.

To create a simple tweened animation:

1. Open the movie *exer05d.fla*. The movie contains a single picture of a car, composed of shapes on the canvas level.

2. Select the artwork and turn it into a symbol by choosing **Create Symbol** from the Insert menu.

3. Add frames to the movie by moving the cursor over frame 10 of the timeline, clicking to place the Modify Frames indicator, and then choosing **Frame** from the Insert menu.

4. Create a key frame in frame 10 by choosing **Key Frame** from the Insert menu. Flash places the key frame in frame 10.

5. Set the Modify Frames indicator at frame 1 by clicking on the timeline at the beginning of the movie. Choose **Tweening** from the Modify Frames pop-up menu to display the Tweening dialog box

6. Choose **Motion** from the Tweening dialog box, and be sure that you have checked the **Tween scaling** and **Tween rotation** boxes (see Figure 5.13). Move the **Easing** slider to the middle, if it is in any other position. The Tweening dialog box enables you to set the options that control the artwork generated between key frames. Click **OK** to tween the graphic.

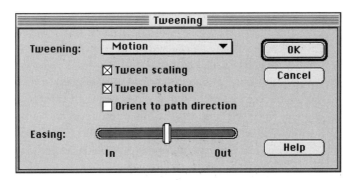

Figure 5.13
The Tweening dialog box.

After the graphic tweens, a red arrow appears in the frames between the two key frames, and the backgrounds of the tweened frames turn a light gray. If you play the movie right now, nothing appears to happen. This is because there's no difference between the key frames, and the movie is tweening between two identical frames, which makes the tweened frames identical as well. Changing one or the other of the key frames also changes the tweened frames.

7. With the current frame indicator in either one of the key frames, select the car with the arrow tool and move it. Use the **Rotate** and **Scale** modifiers to transform it, and then drag the current frame indicator across the length of the movie. Each change you make to one of the key frames changes the tweened frames (see Figure 5.14).

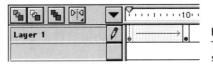

Figure 5.14
The tweened frames of the movie, shown between two key frames.

Tweening is a very powerful tool for creating animation sequences that you may want to change or modify before finishing the movie.

Not every movement takes place at an even, steady speed. An essential part of natural-looking animation (if that's your goal) is acceleration and deceleration. If you create a 20-frame animation and move the car across the screen and tween it, you get a steady movement across the screen, with the car moving an equal amount every frame. To accelerate and decelerate the movement, use easing.

In this exercise, you make the car speed up and slow down using the Ease In and Ease Out controls of the Tweening dialog box.

To accelerate and decelerate an object:

1. Open the movie *exer05e.fla*. The movie is similar to the previous movie file, except that the artwork for the car already has been grouped.

2. For this animation, you use 20 frames: 10 for the car to speed up and 10 for the car to slow down. To begin, add 19 frames, then set a key frame at frame 20.

3. Move the current frame indicator to the frame 20 and drag the car across the screen to the left side of the frame.

4. Click anywhere in the timeline between frame 1 and frame 19 to place the Modify Frames indicator before the key frame at frame 20. Choose **Tweening** from the Modify Frames pop-up menu.

TIP *It isn't necessary to place the Modify Frames indicator directly on a key frame to tween the frames. Tweening automatically tweens the key frames on each side of the Modify Frames indicator. This happens no matter where on the timeline the Modify Frames indicator is when used to open the Tweening dialog box.*

5. In the Tweening dialog box, choose **Motion** from the Tweening pop-up menu. Be sure that you have checked the **Tween scaling** and **Tween rotation** boxes. Move the **Easing** slider to the middle, as you're not ready to use it yet. Click **OK** to tween the graphic in frames 1 to 20.

6. Put the Modify Frames indicator at frame 10, and create a new key frame by choosing **Insert Key Frame** from the Modify Frames pop-up menu. This key frame is the halfway point between the beginning and the end of the animation—where the car stops accelerating and begins decelerating (see Figure 5.15).Move the current frame indicator to frame 10 to see the car in the halfway position.

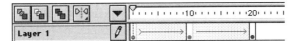

Figure 5.15
A new key frame inserted into a tweened sequence uses the attributes of the object at that frame.

TIP *Tweening is a handy way to begin frame-by-frame animation sequences. By using the interpolated positions of the tweened frames, you get a good idea where you want the animated object positioned; you then can make key frames where you want to adjust the course of the object.*

7. Put the Modify Frames indicator in one of the frames preceding frame 10 and choose **Tweening** from the Modify Frames menu to open the Tweening dialog box again. This time, move the **Easing** slider all the way over to **In** (see Figure 5.16). The Easing slider controls how quickly the car begins to move. Click **OK**.

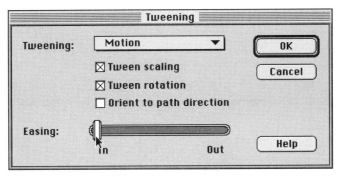

Figure 5.16
Easing in the animation at the beginning of the movie

8. Put the Modify Frames indicator in one of the frames following frame 10, and choose **Tweening** from the frame insertion menu to open the Tweening dialog box. Move the Easing slider way over to **Out**. In this section of the movie, the car begins to accelerate, and then slows down as it approaches frame 20. Click **OK**.

9. Move the current frame indicator to frame 20, and select the car. Choose **Transform** from the Modify menu and select Scale and Rotate. Type **90** in the Rotate box and click **OK** to rotate the car 90° clockwise (see Figure 5.17). Move the car so that its edge just touches the outside edge of the frame.

SHORTCUT Press Shift-Ctrl-S (Windows) or Shift-Command-S (Macintosh) to open the Scale and Rotate dialog box.

Figure 5.17
The rotated car in frame 20.

10. Play the movie.

When you play the movie back, the car speeds up, reaches the midpoint of the frame, and then screeches to a halt before it runs off the edge. (It only screeches metaphorically—you haven't added sound yet.)

TIP *If you're having trouble seeing the acceleration effect, try changing the speed of the movie to a slower frame rate in the Movie Properties dialog box.*

Altering a tweened animation

Inevitably, you will need to make changes to your movies. As mentioned before, tweened animations have some significant advantages when it comes to making alterations. The previous exercise showed you how changing something like the rotation of an object affects the tweened frames. If you try to make the same change in a frame-by-frame animation, you might have to start over.

Not so with a tweened animation. You can move key frames back and forth; insert or delete frames from ranges of tweened frames; and add new key frames to alter the course of the animation.

To alter a tweened animation sequence:

1. Open the movie *exer05f.fla*. The movie is the end result of the previous exercise. Play the movie a couple of times to get a feel for how it flows. The first change to make is to tighten the tension as the car approaches the edge by slowing the deceleration process. To do that, the key frame in frame 10 needs to be moved closer to frame 20.

2. To move the key frame, press the **Ctrl** (Windows) or **Command** (Macintosh) key and move the cursor over the black line just before frame 10 in the timeline. The cursor displays a pair of vertical lines with arrows pointing left and right, indicating that you can move the key frame. Click and drag the key frame to the right, until it is in frame 12 (see Figure 5.18). Both tweening sequences adjust to fit the new position of the key frame. Play the movie now to see the car speed up quickly, reach the middle of the scene in frame 6 of the movie, and then slide to a stop ever so slowly.

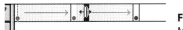

Figure 5.18
Moving an existing key frame.

3. The car is moving equal distances before and after frame 12, which doesn't look very natural. Put the current frame indicator in frame 12, select the car, and move it until it's about two-thirds of the distance across the screen.

4. Next, you add a fishtailing effect to the car before it slides to a stop. Use the Modify Frames indicator to add a new key frame at frame 4. Move the current frame indicator to frame 4, and then select the car with the arrow tool. Rotate the car slightly clockwise. Repeat this process at frame 8, rotating the car slightly counter-clockwise. Now, when the movie plays, the car swerves back and forth, then slides dramatically to a stop (see Figure 5.19).

Figure 5.19
The entire car sequence, shown with Onion Skin and Onion All settings.

Advanced Animation

In addition to the frame-by-frame and tweening techniques described above, there are a few other basic techniques that are important building blocks for complex animations. Color animation, animating symbols, and tweening on paths are three advanced animation techniques used in some variation for nearly every type of animation created in Flash.

Color animation

You can use frame-by-frame animation techniques to animate color as well as motion (shown in the frame-by-frame animation of the sign with the flashing light). Color animation is not limited to just changing a color, nor is it limited to frame-by-frame animation. You can modify the color of an entire symbol by using the Element command in the Modify menu, and then choosing either the tweening or frame-by-frame techniques.

To modify the color of a symbol:

1. Open the movie *exer05g.fla*. The movie contains the surfer dude from our earlier exercise. He's a symbol now, and an extra key frame was created in frame 10.

2. Make sure the current frame indicator is in frame 1, and then select the surfer.

3. Choose **Element** from the Modify menu to open the Link Properties: Symbol dialog box. This dialog box controls several symbol attributes. To fade in the surfer from the movie's white background, drag the slider to the right until the Brightness percentage field dislays the number 100 (see Figure 5.20). Typing 100 in the field also works. Click **OK**.

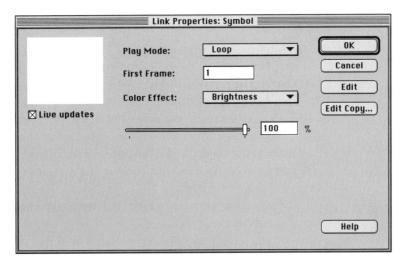

Figure 5.20
The Link Properties: Symbol dialog box with the Brightness setting selected for Color Effect.

The Color Effect menu gives you several options for applying overall color modifications to the selected symbol. Brightness shifts the colors toward black when you drag the slider to the left and toward white when dragged to the right. To fade the surfer in from the white background of the movie, drag the slider to the right and click **OK**.

4. Place the frame insertion marker in any of the frames from 1 to 9, and choose **Tweening** from the pop-up menu. In the Tweening dialog box, select **Motion** from the Tweening menu. Click **OK** to close the dialog box. Tweening the frames between the first frame (where the image's colors shift to white) and the last frame (where its colors are unmodified) causes a fade-in effect.

This same color effect created using frame-by-frame animation means that you must manually set a slightly different color for each frame, one at a time, using the Element dialog box. By tweening, as you did in the above exercise, you can achieve a more refined version of this effect in much less time.

So far, you have used symbols only as a grouping with a name that you store in the Library. Symbols also have a much more powerful use. They can be animated elements in and of themselves.

Each symbol has its own timeline, allowing it to be animated separately from the rest of the movie. When you place an animated symbol into a movie, you can synchronize the frames of its timeline with those of the movie, so that the first time the current frame indicator moves into a frame that contains the animated symbol, frame 1 of the symbol displays.

The process of animating a symbol is virtually identical to that of animating a movie.

To animate a symbol:

1. Open the *exer05e.fla* movie again.

2. Select the car and convert it to a symbol. Name it **car**.

3. Choose **Edit Symbols** from the Edit menu. In symbol editing mode, you see a timeline specifically for the symbol.

SHORTCUT Toggle between symbol-editing and movie-editing modes by pressing Ctrl-E (Windows), Command-E (Macintosh), or double-clicking the symbol.

---

4. Insert a frame, and then insert a key frame at frame 10 of the symbol's timeline.

SHORTCUT To quickly insert a new frame and make it a key frame, position the Modify Frames indicator in the timeline where you want the new key frame, press F5, and then press F6.

---

5. Move the current frame indicator to frame 10 of the symbol's timeline.

SHORTCUT Clicking on the frame numbers in the timeline moves the current frame indicator to the position on which you clicked.

---

6. Drag the car to the left side of the screen with the arrow tool and tween frames 1 to 9. If you play the movie (press the **Enter** key), you see the car drive from right to left.

7. Return to movie editing mode by choosing **Edit Movie** from the Edit menu.

8. Insert a frame in the movie's timeline at frame 10 and play the movie. The animated symbol moves across the stage—even though it wasn't tweened or animated in the movie timeline (see Figure 5.21).

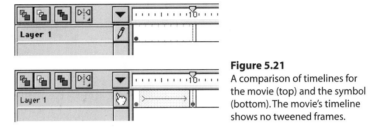

Figure 5.21
A comparison of timelines for the movie (top) and the symbol (bottom). The movie's timeline shows no tweened frames.

9. Rewind the movie, open the Library, and drag another copy of the car symbol into the movie. Place it next to the first car and play the movie to see them race (see Figure 5.22).

Figure 5.22
The two animated car symbols, viewed with the Onion Skin and Onion All options.

If you're feeling adventurous, try using the Element command from the Modify menu to alter the color of the second car (using the Color Effects as described above in "Color animation"). The Element command can affect one copy of a symbol without affecting others.

Tweening on paths

One of the most powerful features of Flash is its capability to create animations that follow irregular paths. Sometimes key frames, tweening, and frame-by-frame animation just isn't enough for a desired effect. In those cases, with Flash, you have the ability to draw the exact path you want the object to follow as it moves between key frames.

Tweening an object on a path makes use of a special layer called a motion guide. A motion guide layer contains a line that you draw on its canvas level, and then use to define the movement of an overlay object. The motion guide layer always is associated with the layer directly above it in the layer list. Only objects on the associated layer can use the motion guide's path.

To create a motion guide:

1. Open the *exer05b.fla* movie. This is the end result of the previous exercise.

2. Enter Symbol Edit mode by opening the Library and double-clicking on the preview for the car symbol. This is an alternative method of entering symbol editing mode.

3. Scroll the editing window so that the car is on the right side of the screen. (The editing window centers the artwork by default.)

4. Click the layer button for Layer 1 and choose **Add Motion Guide** from the Modify Layers menu in the timeline. This adds a motion guide layer to the layer that contains the car and makes that layer the current drawing layer (see Figure 5.23). A motion guide layer displays part of an oval shape with a sphere on it, next to its name in the layer list.

Motion
guide layer

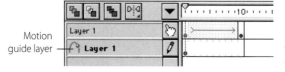

Figure 5.23
The motion guide added to the timeline of the car symbol.

5. Select the pencil tool from the toolbar, and choose **Smooth** modifier.

6. Draw a curvy line across the editing window, either beginning or ending near the position of the car **(see Figure 5.24).**

Figure 5.24
A line drawn across the edit window for the car to follow.

To define an object's motion using the motion guide:

1. Select **Snap** from the View menu (if it's not already selected).

2. Move the current frame indicator to frame 1 of the symbol's timeline. Click on the center of the car (near the small crosshair icon, which indicates the symbol's reference point) and use the arrow tool to drag the car to the end of the motion path. It snaps into place (see Figure 5.25). Click the arrow tool's **Rotate** modifier to align it with the angle of the line.

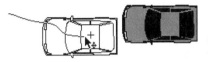

Figure 5.25
Snapping the car into place on the right end of the line.

3. Move the current frame indicator to frame 10 of the symbol's timeline and drag the car to the left end of the line. Click the arrow tool's **Rotate** modifier to align the car with the angle of the line there as well. If you play the movie at this point, the car moves along the line, but it doesn't turn with the curves.

4. Place the Modify Frames indicator in the tweened section of frames in the symbol's timeline. Click to display the Modify Frames pop-up menu and choose **Tweening**. In the Tweening dialog box that appears, check the box for **Orient to path direction**, and click **OK** (see Figure 5.26). Play the movie again, and the car turns as it moves along the line.

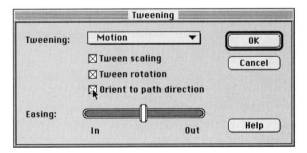

Figure 5.26
Checking the Orient to path direction box in the Tweening dialog box.

5. Choose **Edit Movie** from the Edit menu to exit symbol editing mode. Playing the entire movie demonstrates how changes to a single symbol can affect all instances of the symbol, as both of the cars move and turn along the same path (see Figure 5.28).

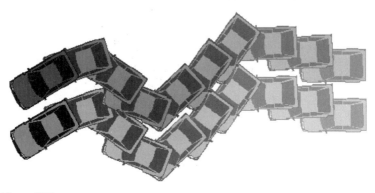

Figure 5.28
The entire animated car sequence with both cars following the curved path, shown with Onion Skin and Onion All settings.

You can edit and modify a motion path with all of the same tools you use to create any other Flash artwork.

Moving On...

The movies and animations created so far have been simple, one-layer projects, intended to introduce basic drawing and animation techniques. Groups and symbols have been introduced as organizational tools for artwork, and now for animation sequences. The next chapter introduces another organizational technique that makes a big difference in the performance of Flash movies: layers.

Layers

CHAPTER 6

What you'll learn...

What layers are

How to work with layers while editing movies

How to use layers to speed movie playback

Layers add a new dimension
to Flash movies—*depth*. Because artwork on the first layer appears closer to the viewer than artwork on subsequent layers, you can create scenes that have perspective, and scenes with objects moving in front of other objects.

In addition to letting you simulate perspective, layers are useful in creating and organizing complex scenes. You can name layers to help you easily remember what's on each layer. You can hide and show layers—one layer at a time, or all layers simultaneously. You can quickly change a layer's order in relation to other layers. And, because each layer contains its own separate canvas level and overlay level, you can draw shapes on the canvas level of one layer without affecting another layer's canvas level.

Layers also can help you optimize the movie's playback. By putting art elements that don't change on one layer and each piece of animated artwork on its own layer, you can constrain the total area of change in each frame. This decreases the time it takes Flash to calculate the changes between frames, and consequently increases the playback speed of your movie.

Each scene of a movie, each symbol in a movie, and every button of a movie has layers. You can use these layers to create a sense of depth in a scene, symbol, or button. (For more on scenes and buttons, see Chapter 7, "Scenes & Actions.") Any portion of a layer that is not artwork is transparent; all artwork is opaque. In a movie containing several layers, transparent portions of a layer allow the other layers behind (or underneath) them to be seen while the artwork on a layer hides artwork on the layers beneath it (see Figure 6.1). By taking advantage of these aspects of layers, you can create the illusion of depth.

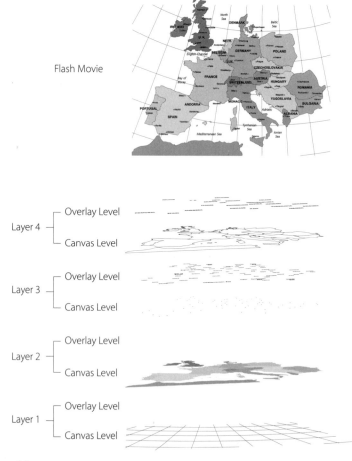

Figure 6.1
Layers are transparent where there are no objects, shapes, or lines.
Each layer has a separate canvas level and overlay level.

Each layer has its own canvas and overlay levels. Shapes drawn on the canvas level of a single layer automatically modify (or are modified by) the outlines of other shapes when they intersect. Shapes drawn on the canvas level of different layers, however, do not interact.

Typically, each animated element should have its own layer, particularly in tweened animation in which only one overlay object should occupy each layer. No canvas-level shapes should be on the same layer of a tweened animation. You can move layers forward and backward (in front of or behind other layers), while editing the movie—although they remain in place once you save the movie for viewing.

Layers also appear in the timeline of a scene or symbol. Each scene and symbol can have its own set of layers (see Figure 6.2). Layers are not universal throughout the movie. Symbols created with layers do not affect the layers of the scenes in which the symbol appears. The symbol simply appears as a single object on the layer on which you place it.

Layers —

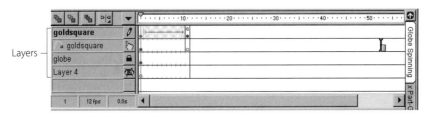

Figure 6.2
A symbol has its own set of layers in its timeline.

One layer is always created when you create a new movie scene, symbol, or button. Each new layer always has one frame, a key frame. The process for creating a new layer is similar for all timelines.

The following exercises illustrate two basic principles of using layers: creating new layers, and moving artwork from one layer to another.

To add layers to a movie:

1. Open the movie *exer06a.fla*. This movie contains two layers: top menu (which is in front), and display (which has four objects on its overlay level). In this step, a layer will be added to the movie (behind the existing layers) to hold the movie's static elements (the legend at the bottom of the scene)

To add a layer in back of the others, find the first unused layer toward the bottom of the timeline. An unused layer has a blank Modify Layers button (see Figure 6.3 for the iconcs that appear in the Modify Layers button). Choose **Insert Layer** from the Modify Layer pop-up menu (see Figure 6.4) to display the Layer Properties dialog box.

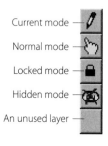

Current mode

Normal mode

Locked mode

Hidden mode

An unused layer

Figure 6.3
Modify Layers button displays icons showing the current mode of the adjoining layer. An unused layer has no icon.

Figure 6.4
The Modify Layers pop-up menu provides an alternative method of accessing layer-related commands like Insert Layer.

2. Name the layer **legend** in the Layer Properties dialog box (see Figure 6.5), and click **OK**. When a new layer is created, it appears in the timeline with an empty key frame in frame 1. The newly created layer is the current layer, as indicated by the pencil icon in its Modify Layers button.

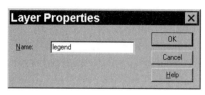

Figure 6.5
The Layer Properties dialog box.

3. Next, add a layer between the top menu and display layers. Select the **Modify Layers** button of the display layer, and choose **Insert Layer** from the button's pop-up menu. When you use the Modify Layers button of an existing layer to insert a new layer, Flash places the new layer in front of the existing layer, and above the name of the existing layer in the layer list. Enter the name **bottom menu** in the Layer Properties dialog box, and click **OK**.

Now that you have a movie with multiple layers, you can experiment with different effects by arranging your artwork on different layers.

To move art from one layer to another:

1. Normally, you can select and modify all of the objects in the current frame of the movie, even if they are not on the current layer. The current layer determines where Flash places new artwork when you draw or import it. However, it is not necessary to make a layer the current layer to copy or move objects. Next, you copy objects from the display layer.

The artwork in the movie is currently all in the display layer. The only layer with anything other than an empty key frame in it is the display layer. Therefore, everything visible in the movie must be in that layer. Select the group object at the lower left containing the words: *Typeface Terminology*. This group is on the display layer. Choose **Edit > Cut** to remove the group from the display layer.

2. Make the legend layer the current layer by selecting **Current** from the layer's Modify Layer button. By doing so, the legend layer becomes the default drawing layer, and the previous current layer becomes a normal layer, enabling you to select it. A layer is editable when it is the current layer (indicated by the pencil on the layer's Modify Layers button), or when it is in the Normal mode (indicated by the hand with the pointing finger).

SHORTCUT Double-clicking on a layer name or a Modify Layer button makes a layer the current layer.

3. Paste the copied group into place on the legend layer by using the **Edit > Paste In Place** command to put the box into the same position on the new layer. (If you use the standard Paste command, Flash centers the box in the drawing area in the center of the screen.)

4. Perform steps 1 to 3 again with the line of text above the large characters and the line below, putting them on the top menu and bottom menu layers, respectively. Now, each of the four items resides on its own layer. You can test this by hiding and showing the layers with the settings from the Modify Layers menu.

5. The movie's artwork should now be distributed among the layers as seen in Figure 6.6. Identify the layer's contents by choosing the **Hide Others** option in the Modify Layers pop-up menu. Hide Others displays only the artwork on the selected layer. To once again view all the artwork in the current frame, choose **Show All** from the Modify Layers pop-up menu.

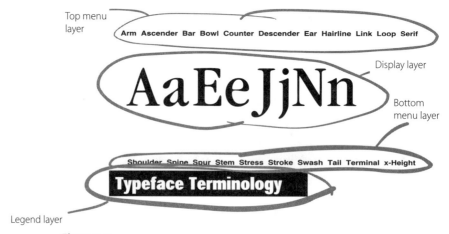

Figure 6.6
Each of the four layers contains a different graphical element.

Working with Artwork and Layers

Understanding how to manipulate layers can make working with complex artwork much easier. You can lock layers to keep the objects on a given layer from being selected; and, you can hide layers to temporarily simplify a complex scene, or facilitate selecting or moving artwork.

The following exercises demonstrate some of the techniques that make using layers an effective tool for creating complex scenes. You've already used the Hide Others command in the previous exercise; in this exercise, you'll use Lock Others.

To lock, name, hide, show, and delete layers:

1. Open the movie *exer06b.fla*. The top eight layers of this movie contain album covers. Because the artwork is stacked closely on top of each other, selecting any particular album's artwork can be somewhat difficult. The first task for this exercise is to move one of the album covers forward and shift its position in the scene.

   Select Layer 1, and choose **Lock Others** from the Modify Layers pop-up menu. This makes Layer 1 the current layer and sets all of the other layers to the Locked mode (see Figure 6.7), preventing you from selecting the artwork on those layers.

TIP *You can lock and hide layers separately by choosing Locked and Hidden from each layer's Modify Layers pop-up menu.*

Figure 6.7
Lock the other layers with the Lock Others command.

2. With all of the other layers locked, selecting and moving the artwork for Layer 1 is simple. Click on the stack of album artwork and make a selection. Because you have locked all of the other layers, the only object that you can select is on Layer 1.

TIP *Another quick method of selecting the elements on a layer when you have locked all of the other layers is to use the Edit > Select All command.*

3. Click and drag the selection until the bottom edge of the album is slightly lower than the artwork for the topmost album cover, as in Figure 6.8. This demonstrates an advantage to locking layers as opposed to hiding them. When you lock a layer, it's still visible and you can use it as a guide for movement or alignment.

Figure 6.8
The heavy marquee shows the original position of the object being moved; the outlines show the object's current position.

4. Next, name the layer something that represents what's on the layer. Naming your layers isn't essential—the default letter/number combinations work just fine. However, in a large project, naming layers makes identifying which layer contains what portion of the movie easier.

   To change the name of Layer 1, choose **Properties** from the layer's Modify Layers pop-up menu. The Properties dialog box appears. Use it to name the layer **unreleased**, and click **OK**.

5. Using layers enables you to easily move artwork in front of or behind other artwork. To move the "unreleased" layer to the front of all other layers, click on its name in the layer list and drag it to the top of the timeline. A heavy dotted line indicates that Flash has placed this layer in front of the "curse" layer (see Figure 6.9). Release the mouse and the "unreleased" layer is in front.

Layer insertion marquee —

Figure 6.9
A layer insertion marquee shows where a layer dragged vertically in the timeline will be placed in the layer stacking order.

6. Now that you have isolated and edited the layer, it's time to unlock the other layers. You can set layers that are Hidden or Locked to the Normal mode individually, or use the **Show All** command in the Modify Level pop-up menu.

   Show All sets to Current Mode the layer whose Modify Layers button you use. All other layers are set to Normal mode, even if they're Hidden or Locked. Use **Show All** now to unlock all of the locked layers.

7. Deleting a layer is simple. From the Modify Layer pop-up menu for the "unreleased" layer, choose **Delete Layer**. Flash removes the layer from the timeline, along with any artwork on the layer.

When you create a new layer, Flash automatically gives it as many frames as the longest frame sequence in an existing movie scene. You can add frames to layers individually or as a group. Continue using the previous movie to practice inserting layers.

To insert frames into multiple layers simultaneously:

1. Add 9 frames to all of the layers by clicking in frame 10 of the top layer and dragging straight down to the bottom layer (see Figure 6.10). If you cannot view the entire timeline in your window, make the timeline portion of the window larger by dragging on the border between the frame window and the timeline; or click in frame 10 of the top layer, scroll the timeline so the bottom layer is visible, and click in frame 10 of the bottom layer while holding down the Shift key to select all the layers in between. The length of each of the selected layers becomes 10 frames after the new frames are inserted. Choose the **Insert Frame** command from the Modify Frames pop-up menu.

Figure 6.10
The frame selection indicator
stretches across layers.

2. Play the movie at this point to see the animated record-spinning symbol, and watch the current frame indicator move through the 10 frames.

When you're working with a lot of artwork, you can speed the redraw of the screen during the creation process by using View > Outlines to view the shapes and lines of the artwork. With more complex artwork, however, it becomes difficult to tell what's what. By displaying the artwork from each layer as different colored outlines, you can tell at a glance which art is on what layer.

The following exercise demonstrates the use of color coding to help organize and manipulate artwork on different layers.

To color-code layers:

1. Select the box layer's **Modify Layer** pop-up menu and choose **Green Outlines**. The four trapezoid shapes around the album covers display in green.

2. Choose **Red Outlines** for the record layer.

3. Choose **Blue Outlines** for the arm layer (see Figure 6.11).
   As with the standard Outlines view, the outlines display when you play the movie.

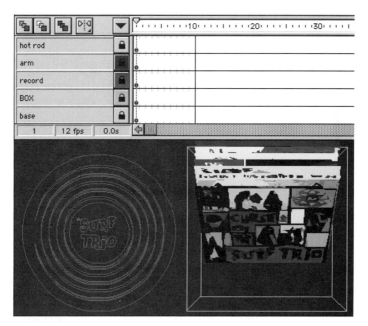

Figure 6.11
Viewing the scene with color outlines turned on for some layers.

Animating with Layers

One reason to use layers is to organize your art. A far less prosaic reason to use layers is to make movies run faster.

Many factors determine a movie's speed. But speed depends, in large part, on how much of the picture changes from frame to frame. If artwork all over the screen changes from frame to frame, then Flash has to check every element of the scene (all of the outlines), and every frame to see if the picture needs updating.

By putting immobile parts of the movie—backgrounds, for instance—on one layer, and the parts that change on other layers, Flash checks and updates only the elements on the changing layers.

Flash registers change with key frames and tweened frames (see Figure 6.12). Key frames contain all artwork that appears in a movie. Tweening indicates changes to the artwork's position, color, size, etc., from its appearance in the previous key frame. Key frames and tweened frames appear in a single layer and indicate change on that layer only. The same frame of two different layers can each contain a key frame, but the artwork represented in each layer is different.

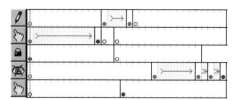

Figure 6.12
Key frames indicate changes in a layer's artwork. Tweened frames indicate that information about the artwork (position in the frame, color effects, transformations) is interpolated between key frames.

The opposite, of course, is also true. A blank frame (not an empty key frame containing no artwork, but a frame with no key frame or tweening) indicates to Flash that there are no changes in the layer's artwork for that particular frame. Flash doesn't need to check the artwork on that layer to see if there's a change.

The flashing light animation from Chapter 5, ("Creating Frame-by-Frame Animation," *exer05b.fla*) provides a good example of how you can create an animated element on its own layer to speed an animation. Open the *exer06c.fla* movie file. This is the single-layer method for building a flashing light animation. Because there's only one layer, all of the artwork is reproduced in every key frame (see Figure 6.13). Flash checks all of the outlines of all of the shapes and lines, and draws each of them on screen—each and every frame of the movie. The movie's frame rate is set at 12 frames per second, but on slower computers, it runs at only 2 or 3 fps.

Figure 6.13
This version of the flashing light duplicates all of the artwork in every key frame.

The *exer06d.fla* movie is identical to *exer06c.fla* movie, except for one little detail. The flashing light has been moved onto its own layer—the one with 8 key frames—and the sign has its own layer with only one key frame (see Figure 6.14). This movie plays significantly faster (12 fps or better, even on slower computers) than its predecessor, because in this movie only a portion of the artwork—the flashing light—is updated in each key frame.

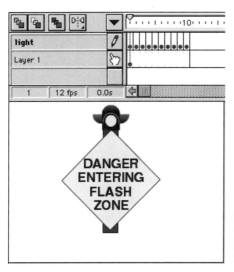

Figure 6.14
This version of the flashing light doesn't duplicate any portion of the sign itself.

Two other considerations also can help you determine how to use and organize layers. The first is file size. This information repeats in every key frame. Therefore, complex artwork quickly increases file size.

NOTE *Symbols are also an improvement over canvas-level artwork—or even groups—for reducing file size. Flash requires a much smaller amount of data to store a symbol in a key frame than to store outline data.*

Performance is the second consideration that can help you determine how and when to use layers. In a networked environment, where Flash movies are used as objects in web pages, Flash delivers the data in the movie sequentially, from the beginning of the file to the end.

If the same data repeats in multiple key frames, it not only makes the file larger, but it also increases the transmission time for the movie (see Figure 6.15). When you separate the changing portions of the movie from unchanging artwork using layers, the size of the file and the time it takes to transmit the file are reduced (see Figure 6.16).

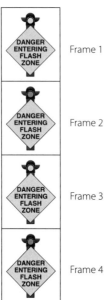

Frame 1

Frame 2

Frame 3

Frame 4

Figure 6.15
An illustration of the
file data structure for
the movie in Figure 6.13.

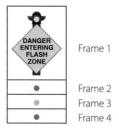

Frame 1

Frame 2
Frame 3
Frame 4

Figure 6.16
An illustration of the file
data structure for the
movie in Figure 6.14.

Keeping file sizes, data structures, and transmission times in mind during the planning stages of a movie can save you hours of time in the development of larger projects and tracking down performance problems in all movies.

Moving On...

The transparency of layers add depth and lushness to your movies. Organizing with layers can help increase your productivity. And the proper use of layers can make a world of difference in the performance of a movie, its file size, and the speed at which it streams across a network.

The next chapter introduces interactivity. The concept of multiple scenes in Flash movies, frame actions, and buttons are explored as well.

CHAPTER 7

Scenes & Actions

What you'll learn...

**How to use scenes
to organize Flash
movies**

**How to use
frame actions**

**How to make
interactive buttons**

Flash movies contain *scenes*

(multiple timelines), which you can use to break a movie into logical chunks. Rather than organizing an entire animation in a single timeline, you can give each part of a movie its own scene. As a movie plays, Flash automatically moves from the end of one scene to the beginning of the next.

Actions let you modify Flash's automatic behavior. Using actions you can, for example, control the playback of a movie by jumping from the end of one scene to the middle of another or back to the beginning of the same scene. Actions attached to a frame are called, naturally, *frame actions*. You can also use *buttons*, a special type of symbol, to trigger actions. You can animate buttons to react to the cursor's position or the click of a mouse button. They can start and stop a movie, as well as control which scene and frame display.

This chapter explores creating scenes and buttons, and shows how to make Flash movies interactive by attaching actions to frames and buttons.

Without scenes, complex movies would have timelines that stretched for thousands of frames; scrolling to find a particular portion of such a movie would be a nightmare. Use scenes for portions of a movie that perform different functions. Each scene is like a movie itself with its own timeline, layers, and artwork. Scenes can share any of the symbols, sounds, and bitmaps (as well as buttons) used in other scenes of the same movie.

Scenes are largely an organizational aid. Each movie scene requires a small addition of file size overhead to keep track of the scene's artwork and symbols. Copying artwork from the canvas level of a layer in one scene to another scene results in a duplication of the artwork; as with layers, it's best to use symbols when sharing artwork between scenes.

Creating a scene

There's always at least one scene in a Flash movie. Flash automatically names the scenes, Scene 1, Scene 2, and so forth. For reference purposes, you can give scenes more descriptive names.

To change the name of an existing scene:

1. Open the Flash movie file *exer07a.fla*. This movie has a single scene, currently named Scene 1.

2. Select **View > Tabs** to display the names of each scene in the movie (as tabs on the right side of the screen). In this movie, there is only one scene.

3. Choose **Modify > Scene** to display the Scene Properties dialog box, and change the scene's name to something descriptive. Type in **roll right**, and click **OK**.

To create a new scene:

1. Choose **Insert > Scene** to add a new scene to the movie, with the default name, Scene 2. New scenes have one layer and a single frame and are completely empty.

2. Double-click the tab for the new scene (Scene 2), to display the Scene Properties dialog box (you also can use the **Modify > Scene** menu selection). Name this scene **roll left** and click **OK**. The tabs now display both scene names: roll right and roll left (see Figure 7.1).

Figure 7.1
The tabs after both scenes have been named.

To copy frames from one scene to another:

1. Change the current scene by clicking the roll right tab. Selecting a tab displays that scene and its timeline in the Flash window.

2. Select the five frames of Layer 1 in the timeline, and use the Modify Frames pop-up menu to choose **Copy Frames**.

3. Click the roll left tab to make it the current scene. Select Layer 1, and select frame 1 (see Figure 7.2). If you merely place the Modify Frames indicator before frame 1, rather than selecting the entire frame, an empty frame appears after the pasted frames. Then choose **Paste Frames** from the Modify Frames pop-up menu to duplicate the frames from the roll right scene into the roll left scene.

Figure 7.2
Selecting frame 1 of the timeline.

4. Select all five frames of the timeline in the roll left scene. The pictures in this scene animate from right to left, instead of left to right (as in the roll right scene). This is easy to do by reversing the sequence of frames. Select **Reverse Frames** from the Modify Frames pop-up menu (see Figure 7.3).

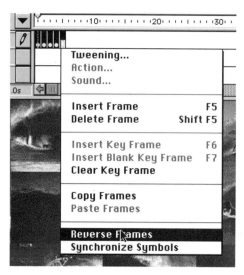

Figure 7.3
Reversing the frame sequence.

5. If the movie played right now, you would see only one scene. To play both scenes of the movie, check the Play All Scenes option in the Control menu. If you also have checked the Loop Playback option, the movie plays through each scene (beginning with the topmost tab) and returns to the first scene after the last scene (the bottommost tab) plays. (The Shockwave Flash Player automatically plays all of the scenes of a movie.) Watch the tabs as the movie plays to see which scene displays.

You can reorder scenes in a movie by clicking and dragging a scene's tab up and down, along the side of the Flash window.

Frame Actions

Everything you have done so far has relied on the default actions of Flash: opening movies with the Player (movies don't play automatically) with each scene in a movie playing from its first frame to its last frame. The first scene of a movie plays first; the second scene of a movie plays next, and so forth.

Actions change all that. Actions can start and stop a movie, jump from one frame of a scene to another frame of another scene, and more.

Actions attached to a specific frame of a movie are frame actions. You typically use actions to control the position of the current frame indicator. This includes starting and stopping the movie as well as changing scenes. Flash executes a frame action when the frame indicator reaches a frame with an attached action.

When the current frame indicator encounters a frame with an action attached to it, the artwork for the frame displays, then the action executes. Actions can be somewhat more limiting than buttons, but, in certain instances, they're very useful. There are fewer actions that can be assigned to frames than can be assigned to buttons. Frame actions are automatically executed when the current frame indicator reaches a specific frame, and don't require the user to take any action. For example, if you want to make sure that your movie stops long enough for the user to read text, you might use a Stop action on the frame containing the text. Or you could combine buttons and actions using buttons to go to specific frames of a movie and frame actions to play only a few frames of the animation.

Adding a Play **action**

One simple action plays a movie when the Shockwave Flash Player opens it. Normally, a movie doesn't play until the user chooses the *Play* option from the Play menu. To automatically play the movie when it opens, you can add a Play action to the first frame of the movie.

To add a Play **action:**

1. Open the Flash movie file *exer07b.fla*. This movie has four scenes, and is similar to the movie in the previous exercise. A Shockwave Flash movie made from this movie, if opened in the Player, does not begin playing automatically.

2. Place the Modify Frames indicator in frame 1 of the first scene. Choose the **Action** item on the Modify Frames pop-up menu to display the Action dialog box (see Figure 7.4).

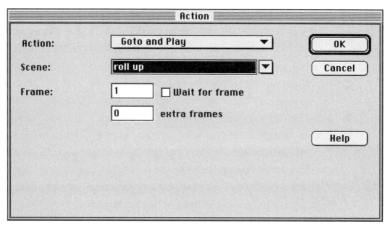

Figure 7.4
The Action dialog box displaying options available after the Goto and Play action has been chosen from the Action pop-up menu.

3. Choose **Play** from the Action pop-up menu, and click **OK**. A small *a* appears in the key frame in which you applied an action, indicating that this frame has an action associated with it.

4. Choose **File > Export Movie** to display the Export Movie dialog box. Set the movie as a **Shockwave Flash** type. Name the file and save it to disk.

5. The Shockwave Flash file can now be opened in the Player application. When the current frame indicator encounters the Play action in the first frame of the movie, Flash initiates the action and the movie starts.

Using Goto and Play actions

The Goto and Play action combines two actions: Play, which initiates playback of the movie, and Goto, which sends the current frame indicator to a specific frame within the movie. A Goto action by itself moves the current frame indicator, but stops the playback of the movie (if it is indeed playing). The Goto and Play action moves the current frame indicator and starts playback of the movie, or continues it if the movie is playing.

With no actions applied to any frames, this movie simply plays the scenes in the order in which they appear in the tabs at the right of the Flash window. You can modify the playback order by changing the order of the tabs, or by adding frame actions that change the next scene to display.

The Goto and Play action moves the current frame indicator to the scene whose name you enter in the Scene field and to the frame of the scene you specified. Goto and Play also can control how the movie displays the new frames by using the Wait for Frame and Extra Frame options.

To modify the playback of a movie with a Goto and Play **action:**

1. Open the Flash movie *exer07b.fla* again.

2. Place the Modify Frames indicator in the last frame of the roll right scene (the first scene of the movie), and choose **Action** from the Modify Frames pop-up menu to display the Action dialog box.

3. Choose **Goto and Play** from the Action pop-up menu to display the options for this action. Type **roll up** (the third scene of the movie) into the Scene field, or choose it from the pop-up menu to the right of the entry field. Leave the **Frame** value set at 1 and click OK.

NOTE *The Scene pop-up menu contains all of the movie's current scene names in alphabetical order, not in the same order the tabs appear on the right side of the Flash window.*

4. Select the **Enable Frame Actions** option from the **Control** menu.

   This option executes actions when a movie plays back in Flash. You can turn the Enable Frame Actions option on or off to test animations.

5. Play the movie. Now the current frame indicator skips over the second scene (roll left) going directly from the roll right scene to the roll up scene because of the frame action in the last frame of the first scene.

TIP *To remove an action from a frame, use the Modify Frames pop-up menu to set the action to None.*

You can place frame actions in any key frame of a movie, not just the first and last frames. If you place actions into two or more layers in the same frame, only the action in the topmost layer executes.

TIP *A simple method of keeping track and preventing different layers from containing conflicting frame actions is to create a separate layer in each scene that contains the frame actions.*

It's not enough to be able to start a movie with actions, or to go from one frame to another. You also need to stop and start a movie, and to choose which frame to go to. In other words, you need buttons.

Buttons

When you build a movie in Flash, it just plays the file from beginning to end. And if it runs across frame actions, Flash does what they tell it to do. Flash always does the same thing, in the same order, every single time the movie plays.

Buttons provide a means for the viewer to interact with and control a movie.

In Flash, a button is a type of symbol with four special frames (see Figure 7.5). The four frames (Up, Over, Down, and Hit), control the normal appearance of the button (Up), its appearance when the cursor is over the button (Over), its appearance when the user clicks the button (Down), and the area where the button responds to the cursor (Hit).

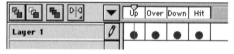

Figure 7.5
The four frames of a button symbol control a button's appearance.

You can make the artwork for your Flash buttons simple or complex. For example, the Over state of a button can reveal instructions; or you can use a Hit area that is larger or smaller than the artwork for the button. And, similar to frame actions, you can attach actions to buttons to perform tasks.

Stopping and starting a movie

This exercise adds some control to the movie used previously in this chapter, providing buttons that enable the viewer to stop and start the animation at will.

To make buttons from artwork:

1. Open the Flash movie *exer07c.fla*. It is similar to the movies in the previous exercises, but this movie has a new layer added to all scenes, and artwork for two buttons added to the new layer in the first scene.

2. Select the artwork for the Play button with the arrow tool (be sure that you haven't selected any other artwork). This artwork is grouped for easy selection.

3. Choose **Insert > Create Symbol** to turn the selection into a symbol. Name the symbol **play button** in the Symbol Properties dialog box, and check the **Button Behavior** checkbox. Click the **OK** button to close the dialog box.

4. Deselect the Play button artwork, and select the Stop button artwork. Repeat step 3 for this button, naming the symbol **stop button**. Open the Library window to display the two button symbols along with the bitmap images used in the movie (see Figure 7.6).

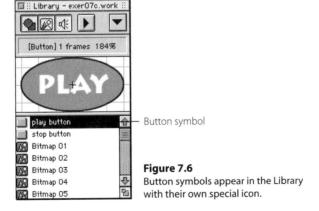

— Button symbol

Figure 7.6
Button symbols appear in the Library with their own special icon.

To create button states for a button:

1. Choose **Edit > Edit Symbols** to shift to the Symbol Editing mode. The first symbol—play button—should display, showing a single key frame (Up) with artwork in its timeline (see Figure 7.7), and nothing in the other three frames. Place the Modify Frames indicator in the frame labeled Hit, and use the Modify Frames pop-up menu to **Insert Frame**.

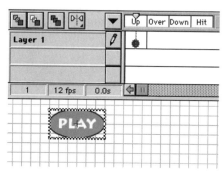

Figure 7.7
A button symbol being edited

2. Use the Modify Frames indicator to select the Over, Down, and Hit frames. Then use the Modify Frames pop-up menu to **Insert Key Frame**. This duplicates the artwork from the Up frame into each of the other three frames.

3. Move the current frame indicator to the frame Over, and double-click on the grouped artwork with the arrow tool to make it editable (alternatively, you can ungroup the artwork).

4. Repeat step 3 for the Down frame. Leave the Hit frame alone.

TIP *Any artwork that appears in the Hit frame defines the button's active or hit area. You can use the Hit frame to make buttons respond to an area larger then the visual portion of button, or even to an area of the scene different from the area covered by the button's visual portion.*

5. Repeat steps 1 through 4 for the stop button symbol.

To assign an action to a button:

1. Choose **Edit > Edit Movie** to shift into movie editing mode. No actions have been assigned to the buttons yet, but selecting **Control > Enable Buttons** shows the changes in the buttons as the cursor rolls over them or as the user clicks them. Deselect the Enable Buttons option before continuing this exercise.

2. Use the arrow tool to select the Play button (be sure that you have not selected anything else). Choose **Modify > Element** to open the Link Properties: Button dialog box (see Figure 7.8). This dialog box is used to assign actions to buttons and shares many of the options of the frame Action dialog box. Select **Play** from the Action pop-up menu and click **OK** to close the dialog box. This assigns a Play action to the Play button.

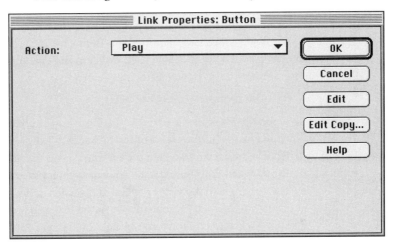

Figure 7.8
The Link Properties: Button dialog box assigns button attributes.

3. Repeat step 2 for the Stop button and assign it a Stop action. Enabling the buttons and playing the movie at this point displays the buttons only in the first scene—they disappear in the other three scenes because they haven't been placed there yet—but you can start and stop the movie during the first scene. Be sure to disable the buttons before continuing.

To use buttons in multiple scenes:

1. Select both of the buttons and copy them with the **Edit > Copy** command.

2. Move to the roll left scene by clicking on its tab. Make the buttons layer the current layer by selecting **Current Layer** from the Modify Layers pop-up menu for the layer. Choose **Edit > Paste in Place** to duplicate the buttons into the current layer. Repeat this step for the roll up and roll down layers.

3. Choose **Control > Enable Buttons** and play the movie.

Try it out as a Shockwave Flash movie in the Player. Remember, if you want the movie to start automatically in the Player, put a Play action in the first frame.

Exercise greater control over the playback of a movie by assigning actions to buttons. Goto can target individual frames, movies can step through a series of frames like a slideshow, or skip from scene to scene using buttons and frame actions. In this exercise, several buttons have been added to the movie used earlier in the chapter, to provide more options to the viewer as the movie plays.

To add a looping action to each scene:

1. Open the Flash movie *exer07d.fla*. More buttons have been added to the buttons layer of the first scene. The pictures layer is locked to make selecting the buttons easier. In addition to the Play and Stop buttons, four buttons around the edges (see Figure 7.9) take the viewer to the four scenes in the movie. The arrow-shaped buttons (between the Play and Stop buttons) step backward and forward through the frames of the movie (using single arrows), or jump backward and forward through the movie's scenes (using double arrows).

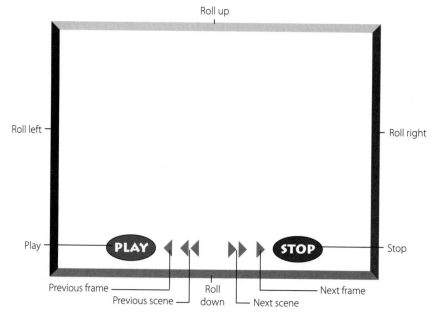

Figure 7.9
The buttons used in the exercise.

2. Place the Modify Frames indicator in the last frame of the pictures layer of the first scene (roll right). Choose **Action** from the Modify Frames pop-up menu and set a `Goto and Play` frame action in the Action dialog box. Leave the Scene field empty (so the `Play` action applies to the current scene), and enter **1** in the Frame field. Click **OK**.

3. Repeat step 2 for each of the other movie scenes. If the movie played now (with Enable Frame Actions on), it would loop in the current scene.

To add an action to one of the additional buttons:

1. In the roll right scene (where the buttons have been added to the buttons layer), play the movie with Enable Frame Actions and Enable Buttons on to see what's enabled. All of the buttons have been created with Over and Down states, but only the Play and Stop buttons have been assigned actions. The scene itself loops back to the first frame of the scene each time the scene finishes playing.

2. Stop the movie and deselect the Enable Buttons option. Disabling the Enable Buttons option makes it easier to select the button for editing.

3. Select the yellow bar at the top of the frame and choose **Modify > Element** to open the Link Properties: Button dialog box. Choose **Goto and Play** from the Action pop-up menu, and choose roll up from the Scene pop-up menu. Click **OK**.

4. Play the movie. When you press the button, the current frame indicatorjumps to the first frame of the roll up scene. Don't forget to enable the buttons.

To add actions to the other buttons:

1. Deselect the yellow button by pressing the **Escape** key. Select the red button at the right side of the frame, and choose **Modify > Element**. Choose **Goto and Play** from the Action pop-up menu, and choose **roll right** from the Scene pop-up menu. Click **OK**.

2. Deselect the red button. Select the blue button at the left side of the frame, and choose **Modify > Element**. Choose **Goto and Play** from the Action pop-up menu, and **roll left** from the Scene pop-up menu. Click **OK**.

3. Deselect the blue button. Select the green button at the bottom of the frame, and choose **Modify > Element**.
Choose **Goto and Play** from the Action pop-up menu, and **roll down** from the Scene pop-up menu. Click **OK**.

   At this point, if you play the movie with the Enable Buttons option on, it rotates through the first scene repeatedly until you click the Stop button or one of the other buttons. Then the movie jumps to a different scene and loops until the movie stops. (Clicking the red button doesn't change scenes, but jumps to the first frame of the roll right scene.)

4. Deselect everything. Select the single green arrow pointing to the left, and choose **Modify > Element**. Choose **Previous Frame** from the Action pop-up menu. Click **OK**. When you click the button, the current frame indicator moves back one frame and the movie stops.

5. Deselect everything. Select the double green arrow pointing to the left, and choose **Modify > Element**. Choose **Previous Page** from the Action pop-up menu. Click **OK**. When you click the button, the current frame indicator moves to the first frame of the scene preceding the current scene (according to the tabs at the right of the Flash window) and the movie stops.

6. Deselect everything. Select the single green arrow pointing to the right, and choose **Modify > Element**. Choose **Next Frame** from the Action pop-up menu. Click **OK**. When you click the button, the current frame indicator moves forward one frame and the movie stops.

7. Deselect everything. Select the double green arrow pointing to the right, and choose **Modify > Element**. Choose **Next Page** from the Action pop-up menu. Click **OK**. When you click the button, the current frame indicator moves to the first frame of the scene following the current scene (according to the tabs at the right of the Flash window) and the movie stops.

To add all the buttons to a new scene:

1. Now that you have created all of the buttons in the first scene, you can add them to the other scenes. Select all of the buttons by choosing **Edit > Select All**. Then choose **Edit > Copy** to copy the buttons.

2. Click the tab for the roll left scene to make it the current scene. Make the buttons layer the current layer (it should be empty). Paste the copied buttons into the buttons layer by choosing **Edit > Paste in Place**. This puts the buttons in the same positions they occupied in the roll right scene, and copies the actions assigned to the buttons as well.

TIP *You can copy multiple key frames by selecting the frames and using the Copy Frames and Paste Frames commands in the Modify Frames pop-up menu.*

3. Choose **Edit > Paste in Place** to add the buttons to the other two scenes of the movie.

4. The movie is now complete. Play the movie and test the buttons. The four buttons on the perimeter of the screen take the viewer to a different animated sequence that loops due to frame actions. The start and stop buttons control the playback of the movie; using the arrow buttons allows you to step through the frames and scenes one-by-one. The playback speed of a movie in the Player is typically faster than the playback speed from the Flash application. Testing the movie in the setting for which it is intended is essential.

Button actions and frame actions make Flash more than a simple animation tool by enabling movies to interact with the viewer. A few simple commands such as: `Play`, `Stop`, `Goto`, `Goto and Play`, `Next Frame`, `Previous Frame`, `Next Page`, and `Previous Page` can be combined with your animation to create movies that capture the eyes of your viewing public.

The next chapter introduces actions that provide Flash with access to the World Wide Web. The basics of HTML (Hypertext Markup Language) and URLs (Uniform Resource Locators) are described, and the relationships between web pages and Shockwave Flash movies are explored.

You will also learn how to make a single button perform multiple tasks, with a technique called *complex actions*.

Actions

You've already learned some

of Flash's frame and button actions.
In the previous exercises, they for the most
part modified the movie's playing status and enabled you
to move through the frames; however, they were limited
to a single movie file.

Actions and buttons can do more. A Flash movie
displayed in a web browser or embedded in an HTML
(HyperText Markup Language) document can use buttons
and actions to interact with the web page. For example,
you can assign actions to frames and buttons to specify
what displays in a web browser. This requires some
knowledge of how to build HTML pages and Internet
addresses. It's not specific to Flash, but it's important.

This chapter shows you how to use buttons as more
than something to click. You'll also learn what to do
when you need more than one event to occur as a
consequence of a frame action or button click. And,
it explores the limitations of actions and some tricks
to get around them.

For Shockwave Flash movies to play in most browsers, the Shockwave Flash Player must be installed on the user's machine as a plug-in or an ActiveX control. Newer versions of browsers may include the Flash plug-in or ActiveX control as part of their default installation. ActiveX browsers can automatically install the control, or link to the installer download page on the Macromedia Web site.

Flash has three actions: `Get URL`; `Get URL and Goto`; and `Get URL, Goto and Play`. These powerful actions are available only when a Shockwave Flash movie plays within a web browser such as Netscape Navigator, Microsoft Internet Explorer, or the America Online Web browser and others.

The following are Flash actions specific to web browsers:

- **Get URL**
  Replaces a frame in the current browser window, or creates a new browser window, with the document specified by the URL.

- **Get URL and Goto**
  Replaces a frame in the current browser window, or creates a new browser window, with the document specified by the URL; *and* then sends the open movie's current frame indicator to the specified frame.

- **Get URL, Goto and Play**
  Replaces a frame in the current browser window, or creates a new browser window, with the document specified by the URL; *and* sends the open movie's current frame indicator to the specified frame; *and* then plays the movie from that point.

To understand how to use these actions, you need some background in the how the World Wide Web works.

The URL

The URL is an address for a document on the Internet. It identifies the method used to access a file, the computer (or server) that stores the file, the path to the file server, and the file's name (see Figure 8.1).

http://www.macromedia.com/shockzone/ssod/index.html

| | | | |
Protocol   Machine.Domain   Directory path   Document

Figure 8.1
The parts of a URL.

You see URLs everywhere now: in articles, advertising, on TV, and so forth. There are many different types of URLs. On the Web, they typically start with the characters "http://". The "http" stands for HyperText Transfer Protocol, and the "://" characters separate the protocol from the rest of the address. HTTP is the standard method of communicating with a web server, and indicates to a browser that it's talking to a web server—and not, for example, a FTP (File Transfer Protocol) server. Files from a web server typically display in a web browser; files from a FTP server usually are saved to disk.

The next part of a URL indicates a specific computer attached to the Internet. This can be two or more words representing a domain and usually a specific machine within the domain. *Top-level domains*, such as .com (commerical), .edu (education), .mx (Mexico), .jp (Japan), and .de (Germany) indicate the type of organization or geographic location. *Secondary domains* identify specific organizations within a top-level domain. Macromedia's domain is, naturally enough, macromedia.com. The Macromedia Japan domain is macromedia.co.jp, which indicates that macromedia is a commercial business (co) in Japan (jp).

A domain name or a machine name can be combined with one or more subdomain names. In the address www.macromedia.com, www is the name of a computer in the macromedia.com domain.

NOTE *In larger networks, two or more actual computers may share the same name, splitting duties such as web serving among multiple computers. For this discussion, however, one computer per name is assumed.*

The path to the document follows the server name. The folder names are separated from the machine name, each other, and the document name by slashes (/); each slash indicates a new sublevel of folders.

Finally, the specific document name follows the protocol, machine, and path. The document name should end with a period, and then an extension, which indicates the file type (e.g., .swf for a Shockwave Flash file, or .html for an HTML file, etc.).

File names, path names, machine and domain names should include only alphanumeric characters, hyphens, or underscores. Periods (.) should only be used in file names and to separate machine and domain names. Use slashes only to separate names in a path from machine names, document names, and each other.

When you type a URL into your browser's Open Location field, your computer (the *client*) sends a message to the machine named in the URL (the *server*). Software on the server reads the URL, finds the file in the named directory, and sends it back to the client, where the browser decides what to do with it.

NOTE *Browsers also can open files from the hard drive. The URL then begins with "file:///", the name of the hard drive, and the folder names in the file's path.*

HTML

Web pages are plain text files that contain codes (*tags*) that define each part of the document and affect its layout. The tags make up the HyperText Markup Language (HTML). Browsers interpret tags to display text in different sizes and colors, create tables, insert pictures, and much, much more.

HTML tags are set off from the rest of the text in the file with the bracket (< >) characters. The browser knows that anything between the brackets is a tag, so the tag itself doesn't display. Text outside the brackets displays in the browser window (although it can be modified by the tags).

Tags frequently come in pairs with one tag indicating the beginning of a tag's effect, and another showing the end of the affected text. These are *delimiters* usually indicated by a slash character after the first bracket (see chart below).

This chart displays a very simple HTML page (on the left), which contains a Shockwave Flash movie, some text, and a GIF image. Descriptions of the tags appear on the right. See Figure 8.2 for an example of how this page would appear in a browser.

`<HTML>`	*Indicates beginning of HTML document.*
`<HEAD>`	*Indicates this section contains web page information.*
`<TITLE>`	*Text following this tag displays in browser title bar.*
`Atomic City Apartments`	*Actual text that displays in the browser title bar.*
`</TITLE>`	*Delimiter for <TITLE> tag.*
`</HEAD>`	*Delimiter for <HEAD> tag.*
`<BODY>`	*Indicates beginning of the document that displays in the browser window.*
`<OBJECT CLASSID="clsid:D27CDB6E-AE6D-11cf-96B8-444553540000" CODEBASE= "http://active.macromedia.com/ flash2/cabs/swflash.cab#version= 2,0,0,0" WIDTH="100%" HEIGHT="100%">`	*Identifies a Shockwave Flash movie ("menu.swf") and provides information to ActiveX browsers about the movie's display and play.*
`<PARAM NAME="Movie" VALUE="menu.swf">`	*Provides the browser with a relative URL to the Shockwave Flash movie.*
`<EMBED SRC="menu.swf" WIDTH="100%" HEIGHT="70%" pluginspage= "http://www.macromedia.com/ shockwave/download/ index.cgi?P1_Prod_Version= ShockwaveFlash2">`	*Identifies a Shockwave Flash movie ("menu.swf") and provides information to browsers using plug-ins about the movie's display and play. SRC= "menu.swf" provides the browser with a relative URL to the Shockwave Flash movie.*
`</EMBED>    </OBJECT>`	*Delimiters for the <EMBED> and <OBJECT> tags.*
`<H1>`	*Text following this tag displays in browser's largest headline style.*
`"22nd Century Living: NOW"`	*Actual text that displays as a headline.*

`</H1>`	*Delimiter for the <H1> tag.*
`<IMG SRC="graphics/acafoot.gif"` `    WIDTH=100% HEIGHT=15%>`	*Inserts a GIF image into the page. The parameters inside the tag indicate which image to use, and the image's size. The parameter SRC="graphics/ acafoot.gif" is the relative URL to the image. The <IMG> tag needs no delimiter.*
`</BODY>`	*Marks the end of the material that displays in the browser window.*
`</HTML>`	*Marks the end of the document.*

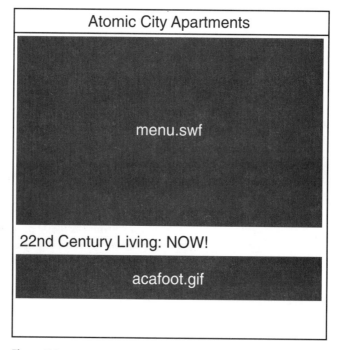

Figure 8.2
A schematic of the web page described in the HTML document above.

A web page could refer to Shockwave Flash movies, graphics, or other pages (in links), or a number of other media types. Shockwave Flash movies can link to pages, other movies, and other media. You can embed URLs in Shockwave Flash movies, web pages, and other file types to refer to other files.

It's not always necessary to use a URL in its complete form, as shown in the previous section. URLs that include a protocol (e.g., http://) are *complete* URLs. But once a web page is retrieved from a server, it can refer to other items on the same server with *relative* URLs. A relative URL uses the original web page URL, subtracts the document name, and then adds the relative URL. In the example above, the relative URL to the Shockwave Flash movie is "menu.swf". To determine the complete URL for the Shockwave Flash file, the browser performs the following calculations:

`http://www.atomiccityapts.com/` `   index.html`	*The complete web page URL.*
`- index.html`	*The document name of the web page.*
`= http://www.atomiccityapts.com/`	*The complete URL after the document name is subtracted.*
`+ menu.swf`	*The relative URL to the Shockwave Flash file.*
`= http://www.atomiccityapts.` `   com/menu.swf`	*The complete URL for the Shockwave Flash movie.*

In this example, the "index.html" and "menu.swf" files are in the same folder on the server.

If a file is in a folder other than the web page, the relative URL needs to contain a file path. In the `<IMG>` tag in the HTML page above, the "acafoot.gif" image is in the "graphics" folder. The "graphics" folder itself is in the same folder as the "index.html" document. Using the calculation above:

`http://www.atomiccityapts.com/` `   index.html`	*The complete web page URL.*
`- index.html`	*The document name of the web page.*
`= http://www.atomiccityapts.com/`	*The complete URL after the document name is subtracted.*
`+ graphics/acafoot.gif`	*The relative URL to the GIF file.*
`= http://www.atomiccityapts.` `   com/graphics/acafoot.gif`	*The complete URL for the GIF file.*

You also can delete portions of a URL path by using two periods (..) instead of a folder name in a relative URL. The relative URL "../upone.gif" refers to a GIF image in the folder that contains the folder in which the current document resides.

NOTE *A less-used URL type is the* absolute URL, *which contains the entire path and file name. Relative URLs can make locating a file somewhat confusing in larger sites—absolute URLs are less ambiguous. The original document determines the protocol and machine/domain name information. Absolute URLs always begin with a slash and are identical—no matter which document on the server refers them.*

This chart compares the complete, absolute, and relative URLs for the elements of the web page described in Figure 8.2.

Complete URL	Absolute URL	Relative URL
http://www.atomiccityapts.com/index.html	N/A —the HTML document URL establishes the server the absolute URL resides on	N/A —the HTML document URL establishes the location the relative URL is relative to
http://www.atomiccityapts.com/menu.swf	/menu.swf	menu.swf
http://www.atomiccityapts.com/graphics/acafoot.gif	/graphics/acafoot.gif	graphics/acafoot.gif

Framesets

An HTML document that contains *framesets* is particularly useful for Shockwave Flash movies. Framesets provide instructions that divide the browser window into individual frames. Each frame has a name (for reference), and an URL for the document that displays in the frame.

Frames can have borders and/or scrollbars, or they can be entirely transparent to the viewer. The HTML document describes whether borders or scrollbars appear, what color the borders should be, etc.

Each frameset divides a portion of the window into two or more columns or rows. You also can nest framesets inside one another, splitting a frame into smaller subframes. In Figure 8.3, the browser window is first split horizontally into two frames—top and bottom— then the top frame and bottom frame are themselves split vertically into left and right frames, resulting in four frames—any one of which you can modify or change.

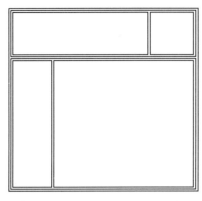

Figure 8.3
A four-frame browser window, using three framesets. The first frameset divides the window vertically into two frames. The other two framesets each divide the frames horizontally into two frames.

When a browser opens a frameset document, the window divides according to the instructions in the frameset, and then the appropriate HTML document (and any accompanying graphics or movies) fills each frame.

The HTML document on the left side of the following table outlines a frameset that is similar to that in Figure 8.3.

`<HTML>`	*Indicates beginning of HTML document.*
`<HEAD>`	*Indicates beginning HTML document information.*
`<TITLE>Sample Frameset</TITLE>`	*Indicates that the text between <TITLE> and its delimiter displays in the browser title bar.*
`</HEAD>`	*Delimiter for the <HEAD> tag.*
`<FRAMESET ROWS="110,*">`	*Beginning of first frameset, which splits the browser window horizontally into two rows. The first row from the top will be 110 pixels tall, the "*" indicates that the other row will fill the remainder of the* window.

`<FRAMESET COLS="*,150">`	*Beginning of second frameset, which splits the top row of the first frameset into two columns. The left column fills the space the second column, set to 150 pixels wide, doesn't use.*
`<FRAME SRC="top_left.html"` `  NAME="top_left" SCROLLING=NO>`	*Identifies the first frame from the left in the top row. It gives the window's top-left frame a name, provides a content URL, and specifies that no scrollbar display if the frame content is larger than the frame (to display the frame's content, the window would need to be made larger).*
`<FRAME SRC="top_right.html"` `  NAME="top_right" SCROLLING=NO>`	*Identifies the second frame from the left in the top row. Names the top-right window frame, provides a content URL, and specifies that no scroll bar display, if the content for the frame is larger than the frame.*
`</FRAMESET>`	*Delimiter for the second frameset. The first frameset remains unclosed.*
`<FRAMESET COLS="78%,22%">`	*Beginning of the third frame set, which splits the bottom row of the first frameset into two columns. The first column from the left is set to fill 78% of the row's width, the next column is set to fill 22%. (You could use a "*" to specify that the second column fill the remainder.)*

`<FRAME SRC="bottom_left.html"`
`  NAME="bottom_left "`
`  SCROLLING=YES`
	Identifies the first frame from the left in the bottom row. Names bottom-left window frame, provides a content URL, specifies that a scroll bar display, and prevents the user from resizing the frame.

`<FRAME SRC="bottom_right "`
`  NAME="bottom_right "`
`  SCROLLING=NO>`
	Identifies the second frame from the left in the bottom row. Names the bottom-right window frame, provides a content URL, and specifies that no scroll bar display, if the frame's content is larger than the frame.

`</FRAMESET>`	*Delimiter for the third frameset. The first frameset remains unclosed.*
`<NOFRAMES>`	*Indicates that the text between <NOFRAMES> and its delimiter is ignored by browsers capable of displaying frames.*
`<BODY>`	*Indicates the beginning of document that displays to non-frame browsers.*
`Viewing this page requires a browser capable of displaying frames.`	*Text that displays to non-frame browsers.*
`</BODY>`	*Delimiter for the <BODY> tag.*
`</NOFRAMES>`	*Delimiter for <NOFRAMES>. Marks the end of text designed specifically for browsers unable to display frames.*
`</FRAMESET>`	*Delimiter of the first frameset.*
`</HTML>`	*Indicates end of the HTML document.*

Flash movies work well with framesets because several Flash actions can go to frames other than the one in which the movie resides. A Flash movie designed as a menu bar or navigation aid, for example, can reside in one frame and control what displays in other frames.

To create an HTML frameset for a Shockwave Flash menu bar:

1. Use an HTML or text editor (e.g., Notepad or SimpleText) to open the HTML file *exer08a.htm*. This is a template for a two-frame document. You can use it for any frameset you create. The file contains the following:

```
<HTML>
<HEAD>
 <TITLE>Frameset Title</TITLE>
</HEAD>
<FRAMESET ROWS="100,*" BORDER=0 FRAMESPACING=0
FRAMEBORDER=NO>
 <FRAME SRC="top.htm" NAME="my_top"
MARGINHEIGHT=0 MARGINWIDTH=0 SCROLLING=NO
NORESIZE>
 <FRAME SRC="body.htm" NAME="my_body"
MARGINHEIGHT=0 MARGINWIDTH=0>
 <NOFRAMES>
```

```
   <BODY>
    Frame-less browsers see this
   </BODY>
  </NOFRAMES>
 </FRAMESET>
</HTML>
```

2. Replace the text **Frameset Title** with **Atomic City Apartments**.

   The `<FRAMESET>` tag shows that the window is divided into two rows. The first (counted from the top of the window) is set to be 100 pixels tall (pixels are the default), and the lower row fills what remains of the window. The BORDER parameter controls how the spaces between frames appear in Netscape Navigator, the FRAMESPACING and FRAMEBORDER parameters control Microsoft Internet Explorer's display of borders between frames. In this case, the spacing is set to **0**, and no border displays.

3. Change the SRC parameter value of the first `<FRAME>` tag "top.htm" so that it reads **menu.htm**. This URL controls the HTML page that displays in the top frame. Because there is no "http://" or "/" character at the beginning of the URL, it is treated as a relative URL; and, because there is a document name for the URL, it is assumed to be in the same folder as the frameset document.

4. Change the NAME parameter value from "my_top" to **ac_menu**. This is how the frame refers to a URL that targets the frame. The MARGINHEIGHT and MARGINWIDTH control the top/bottom and left/right margins between the edges of the frame and the contents. The scrollbars are turned off for the frame, and the user cannot resize the frame.

   TIP *Choosing something simple (like "top" or "bottom") for* `<FRAME>` *tag NAME values can cause unexpected results if other pages in the same browser attempt to change their frames with the same name.*

5. Change the value of the SRC parameter from "body.htm" to **home.htm**, and change the NAME parameter value to **ac_body**. This frame is similar to the previous one, but the lack of a SCROLLING parameter means that if the size of the content exceeds the size of the frame in either dimension, the appropriate scrollbar(s) appear.

6. Save the file as **index.htm**.

TIP *When a URL supplies only the machine name or machine and path (as in "http://www.macromedia.com/" or "http://www. macromedia.com/shockzone/ssod/"), most web servers look for a default document name. For most Unix and Macintosh servers, the default file name is "index.html". Many Windows servers use "index.htm" or "default.htm". If the main document in each web site folder uses the default file name, you can omit the file name when referencing the file (as in the examples above). This makes the URL shorter and easier to remember. This does not work when reading files from the hard drive.*

Now that you have finished the frameset file, you need to create other web pages to place in the frames. The top frame ("ac_menu") holds a menu bar; the bottom frame ("ac_body") shows the current selection from the menu. You will need one HTML page for the top frame (named "menu.htm", the file referenced in the first <FRAME> tag), and three others for the lower frame. The three possible selections for the lower frame are "home.htm", which displays at the time the frameset first opens; "amen.htm", which displays the goodies that come with the apartment when the user selects "Amenities" from the menu; and "hood.htm" for the map that displays the location of the apartment.

The HTML file that displays in the top frame, "menu.htm" holds a Shockwave Flash movie that controls the HTML file that displays in the lower frame. The frameset automatically displays the file defined in a <FRAME> tag for that frame, but the file can be changed a number of ways, including a Shockwave Flash movie.

To create a Shockwave Flash movie that controls a frame in a frameset:

1. Use Flash to open the file *exer08b.fla*. This is a single-frame movie with artwork and buttons already in place.

2. Deselect **Enable Buttons** in the **Options** menu.

3. Use the arrow tool to select the button under the word "home."

4. Choose **Modify > Element** in the menu bar to display the Link Properties: Button dialog box (see Figure 8.4). Choose **Get URL** from the **Action** pop-up menu.

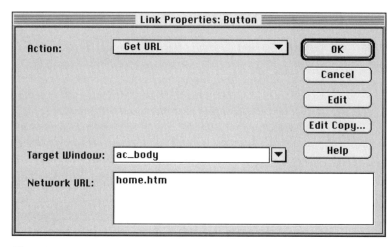

Figure 8.4
The Get URL action selected in the Link Properties: Button dialog box.

5. Type the NAME of the lower frame, **ac_body**, in the Target Window field. This field's content determines which frame is replaced by the URL that's retrieved.

6. Enter the relative Network URL of the file that will display in the frame when the button is clicked: **home.htm**. This file doesn't exist yet, but it will reside in the same folder as the "index.htm" file. Click **OK**.

TIP *In Shockwave Flash, relative URLs are based on the URL of the HTML file in which you have embedded the movie. This differs from some other types of embedded multimedia types (Shockwave for Director, for instance). In Director, the HTML file and the embedded movie are stored in different folders and use relative URLs based on the location of the movie rather than the web page.*

7. Repeat steps 4 to 6 for the other two buttons. This chart shows the values that you should assign to each button:

	home	*amenities*	*'hood*
Target Window	ac_body	ac_body	ac_body
Network URL	home.htm	amen.htm	hood.htm

8. Use the **File > Export Movie** menu command to create a Shockwave Flash movie from the file. Name the movie **acity.swf** and save it to the same folder as the "index.htm" file created in the previous exercise.

This movie is relatively simple with no animation other than the buttons (which are already created). Moreover, you could have an animation looping in the background while waiting for the user to make a move.

The next step in adding Flash movies to the frameset is to create an HTML file for the Shockwave Flash movie. The movie could be displayed in the frame without an HTML file, but it would have a gray border between the edges of the movie and the browser window when displayed.

To create the HTML file that holds the Shockwave Flash file and matches the page color and movie background color:

1. Use a text editor to open *exer08c.txt*. You can use this text file as a template for the `<OBJECT>` `<EMBED>` tags that insert a Shockwave Flash movie into a web page. (See Appendix C, "`<OBJECT>`/`<EMBED>` Tag References," for detailed explanations of the `<OBJECT>` and `<EMBED>` tags parameters.)

2. Edit the document so the first three lines are:

   ```
   <HTML>
    <BODY BGCOLOR=#0000CC>
    <OBJECT>
   ```

   The first tag indicates the beginning of an HTML document. The second shows the beginning of the main body of the document, with a parameter—BGCOLOR—that matches the background of the document to the color of the movie background. This creates the effect of a seamless frame all the way to the edge of the browser window.

3. At the end of the document, after all other characters, add the following two lines:

   ```
   </BODY>
    </HTML>
   ```

   These tags close the `<BODY>` and `<HTML>` tags added in step 2.

4. Change the value after WIDTH in the fourth line of the `<OBJECT>` tag to **100%** Change the HEIGHT value to **100%**.

5. On the line with <PARAM NAME="Movie", change the value between quotes after VALUE= to **acity.swf**. This relative URL tells the browser to insert the Shockwave Flash movie created in the last exercise into the page.

6. Delete the seven lines following <PARAM NAME="Movie", which read:

```
<PARAM NAME="Loop" Value="True">
<PARAM NAME="Play" Value="True">
<PARAM NAME="BGColor" Value="ffffff">
<PARAM NAME="Quality" Value="AutoHigh">
<PARAM NAME="Scale" Value="ShowALL">
<PARAM NAME="SALign" Value="L">
<PARAM NAME="Base" Value="http://www.server.com/
    base/">
```

These lines control attributes of the movie that aren't required for the task at hand.

7. Change the VALUE parameter after <PARAM NAME="Menu" to **False**. This prevents the user from zooming in on the menu bar in this movie.

8. Change the first two lines of the <EMBED> tag to read:

```
<EMBED SRC="acity.swf" WIDTH=100% HEIGHT=100%
    SCALE="ShowALL" MENU="FALSE"
```

Delete the lines:

```
QUALITY="AutoHigh" SCALE="ShowALL" SALIGN="L"
BASE="http://www.server.com/base/ MENU="True"
```

They are not essential for the operation of the Shockwave Flash movie.

9. Save the file as **menu.htm** in the same folder as "index.htm" and "acity.swf."

The frameset and the contents of the "ac_menu" frame won't change, but the "ac_body" frame will be controlled by the Shockwave Flash movie "acity.swf." There are three pages that can display in the frame, the names of pages are the values used for the Network URL fields in the Get URL actions assigned to the buttons.

Now it's time to start creating the pages for the lower frame. First, you need to create a Flash movie and HTML document for the default page ("home.htm"), which displays when the frameset opens, and when the user clicks the "home" button.

To create a Flash movie for an HTML document:

1. Use Flash to open *exer08d.fla*. This movie has the elements that display in the lower frame. In the following steps you will automate the word "NOW!" to appear from the background in red as the animation plays.

2. Select frame 20 of the timeline in all three layers. Use the Modify Frames pop-up menu to **Insert Frame**, making the movie 20 frames long.

3. Use the arrow tool to select the word "NOW!". It's already a symbol.

4. Choose **Modify > Element** to display the **Link Properties: Symbol** dialog box (see Figure 8.5.). Choose **Tint** from the Color Effect pop-up menu, set the Color Effect slider to **100%**, and choose the first color on the sixth row from the top of the color palette. Alternatively, type **0** for R, **0** for G, and **204** for B. These settings change the color of the selected symbol to match that of the background. Click **OK**.

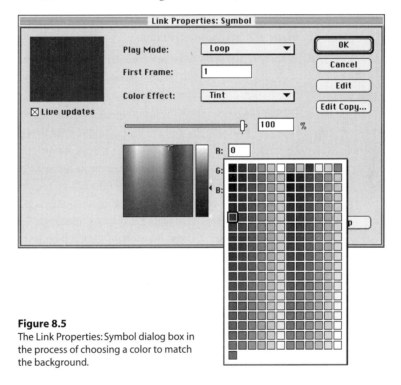

Figure 8.5
The Link Properties: Symbol dialog box in the process of choosing a color to match the background.

TIP *To determine the palette position of an unknown background color, look at the palette in the Modify > Movie dialog box.*

5. The text is always in the frame, but in the first and last frames it appears to be invisible because the color of the text matches the background exactly. The key frame in frame 1 supplies the initial color, another key frame at the end of the movie indicates its final color. The symbol is on a separate layer because it's the only animated object in the movie. Place the Modify Frames indicator in frame 20 of the "now" layer and choose **Insert Key Frame** from the Modify Frames pop-up menu to add a key frame in frame 20.

6. Place the Modify Frames indicator in frame 8 of the "now" layer and add another key frame by choosing **Insert Key Frame** from the Modify Frames pop-up menu.

7. Move the current frame indicator to frame 8. This is the frame where the text appears in red.

8. Make sure that you have selected the symbol with the word "NOW!" (although the word is invisible, the selection marquee should display). Choose **Modify > Element** to display the Link Properties: Symbol dialog box again. It should appear with the settings from step 4. Change only the color assigned to the symbol, pick a bright red, and click **OK**.

9. Place the Modify Frames indicator in frame 12 and choose **Insert Key Frame** to set the end of the frame sequence in which the text will appear in red. If you play back the movie right now, the text is invisible in frames 1 through 7, red in frames 8 through 19, and invisible in frame 20. Tweening the frames between the color changes produces a gradual change in color between the key frames.

10. Place the Modify Frames indicator in frame 1 and choose **Tweening** from the Modify Frames pop-up menu to display the Tweening dialog box. Choose **Motion** from the Tweening pop-up menu, and click **OK** to close the dialog box.

11. Repeat step 10 with the key frame in frame 12. There now should be two tweened frame sequences in the "now" layer. The first sequence begins after the key frame in frame 1 and continues to frame 8. The next sequence begins after the key frame in frame 13 and continues to the last frame. These two sequences represent the color animations.

12. Choose **File > Export Movie** from the menu bar and save the movie as a Shockwave Flash file named **home.swf**.

To create an HTML document for this movie:

1. Use the *exer08c.txt* file again, and make the following additions (shown in ***bold italic***), changes (shown in **bold**), and deletions (shown with ~~strikethroughs~~):

```
<HTML>
 <BODY>
  <OBJECT
      classid="clsid:D27CDB6E-AE6D-11cf-96B8-
444553540000"
      codebase="swflash.cab#version=2,0,0,0"
      ID="movie" Width=100% Height=100%>
      <PARAM NAME="Movie" VALUE="home.swf">
      <PARAM NAME="Loop" Value="True">
      <PARAM NAME="Play" Value="True">
      <PARAM NAME="BGColor" Value="ffffff">
      <PARAM NAME="Quality" Value="AutoHigh">
      <PARAM NAME="Scale" Value="ShowAll">
      <PARAM NAME="SAlign" Value="L">
      <PARAM NAME="Base" Value="http://
        www.server.com/base/">
      <PARAM NAME="Menu" Value="True">
     <EMBED SRC="home.swf" WIDTH=100% HEIGHT=100%
     NAME="movie" LOOP="True" PLAY="True"
        BGCOLOR="ffffff"
     QUALITY="AutoLow" SCALE="ShowAll" SALIGN="L"
     BASE="http://www.server.com/base/"
        MENU="True"
      PLUGINSPAGE="http://www.macromedia.com/
      shockwave/download/
      index.cgi?P1_Prod_Version=ShockwaveFlash2">
     </EMBED></OBJECT>
 </BODY>
</HTML>
```

2. Save this file as **home.htm**.

You now have assembled the core elements of the frameset:

- The frameset file itself, "index.htm".

- The HTML file for the menu frame, "menu.htm".

- The Shockwave Flash file embedded in the menu frame's HTML file, "acity.swf".

- The default HTML file for the lower frame, "home.htm".

- And the Shockwave Flash file "home.swf" that appears inside "home.htm".

All of the files should be in the same folder. Opening the "index.htm" file with a browser displays the menu in the top frame and the animation in the lower frame. The "amenities" and "'hood" buttons do not load pages into the lower frame because those pages have not been created yet.

To complete this set of pages, use the following files and resave them (for HTML files), or export them as Shockwave Flash files (for Flash movies). Put all finished files in the same folder as the other files that you have been created for this project.

Original File Name	What To Do	New File Name
exer08e.htm	Save as or change file name	hood.htm
exer08f.fla	Export as Shockwave Flash	hood.swf
exer08g,htm	Save as or change file name	amen.htm
exer08h.fla	Export as Shockwave Flash	amen.swf

With all of the files in the same folder, open "index.htm" with a web browser to view all the pages. The pages displayed in the lower frame (or any other frame in a more complex page) can have any combination of text or graphics, not just Shockwave Flash movies.

TIP *If a gray box appears in the browser window when the pages open, make sure that you have named all of the files correctly— no spaces before or after the file name, etc. On the Macintosh, check to see if an extra ".swf" was added to the name of the file.*

Button Effects

Buttons can do more than just sit there and wait for someone to click them. Buttons already have a certain amount of interactivity built-in through their rollover effect. The "hit" area of a button doesn't need to actually cover the button's area. In fact, it doesn't even need to be anywhere near the button. The ability to have a button affect another area of the screen (and vice versa) gives Flash buttons the capability to emulate pop-up help balloons, or affect other types of onscreen changes through the cursor's position.

Virtual objects

One type of button effect that you can simulate in Flash is that of a virtual object that can rotate around an axis by moving the cursor. This type of effect can use drawings, exports from CAD/CAM (Computer-Aided Design/Machining) systems, or files created with 3D design programs. You begin this effect with a series of images, similar to those shown in Figure 8.6.

Figure 8.6
A series of images exported from a 3D design program.

In this exercise, the movie presents a rotating dollar sign (created from the images in Figure 8.6) when the cursor is not over the movie. When the cursor is over the movie, the viewer can move the dollar sign from side to side, as if examining it.

To simulate a virtual reality object in Flash:

1. Use Flash to open the movie *exer08i.fla*. The movie already contains the artwork. The movie is 10 frames long and contains 10 different views of a rotating dollar sign, each contained as a symbol in the Library.

   The key to creating this type of effect is to have the dollar sign animation linked to the cursor's position. Ten buttons running from left to right across the screen will be used to determine where the cursor is (see Figure 8.7). In order to make the animation seamless, the buttons (also referred to here as zones) will shift horizontally so that one of the buttons is centered on screen (see Figure 8.8).

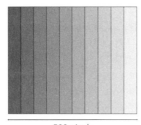

500 pixels

500 pixels

Figure 8.7
The movie frame can be divided into 10 vertical buttons to determine the cursor's position.

Figure 8.8
Shifting the buttons by half the width of a single button results in one centered button, and another button split between the left and right edges.

2. To create the zones, insert a new layer in front of the existing layer by choosing **Insert Layer** in the **Modify Layers** pop-up menu to display the Layer Properties dialog box. Name the layer **overlay** and click **OK**.

3. Choose **Modify > Movie** to display the Movie Properties dialog box, and change the **Grid Spacing** to **25** (pixels). Check the **View Grid** box and click **OK**.

4. Select the **View > Snap** option from the menu bar.

5. Select the pencil tool from the toolbar, and choose the **Rectangle** modifier. With the pencil tool, draw a rectangle from the top left corner of the visible grid to enclose the first column of squares. Draw the next rectangle around the second and third columns. Then make another rectangle around the fourth and fifth columns. Continue until you reach the last column. Draw a rectangle around the last column. There should be a total of 11 rectangles that outline a pattern similar to that shown in Figure 8.8.

6. Deselect any selected items by pressing the **Escape** key. Using the arrow tool, double-click on any portion of the rectangles to select the entire complex of lines (without selecting the animated dollar sign).

7. Choose **Insert > Create Symbol** to display the Symbol Properties dialog box. In the Symbol Properties dialog box, name the new symbol **VR01** and check **Button Behavior**. Click **OK**.

8. Choose **Edit** > **Edit Symbols** to shift into symbol editing mode. Select the symbol **VR01** from the tabs on the right side of the window.

9. Select the paint bucket tool from the toolbox and choose a light gray color from the palette. Starting at the edge of the rectangles, fill every other rectangle with the light gray color. Choose a different gray and fill the remaining rectangles. Double-click with the arrow tool to select the outlines and delete them (see Figure 8.9).

Figure 8.9
Zones filled with alternating colors.

10. Place the Modify Frames indicator in the "Hit" frame of the timeline and choose **Insert Frame** from the Modify Frames pop-up menu. Next, choose **Insert Key Frame** from the Modify Frames pop-up menu to add a key frame to the "Hit" frame. Finally, place the Modify Frames indicator in the "Over" frame and choose **Insert Key Frame** from the Modify Frames pop-up menu to add a key frame to the "Over" frame.

11. Make sure that the current frame indicator is over the "Up" frame. Choose **Edit** > **Select All** and delete everything from the frame. When nothing is in the "Up" frame of a button, the button is invisible when the cursor isn't over its hit zone. For now, put a small dot in the middle of the symbol editing window in this frame to enable you to see the button's location while creating it.

12. Move the current frame indicator to the "Over" frame. Use the paint bucket tool to fill all of the rectangles with white. When the cursor is over the hit zone of the button, it fills the frame with white, obscuring the animated dollar sign that is on a layer behind the button. The "Down" frame is ignored for the purposes of this exercise.

The graphical elements for the 10 buttons of the VR effect are complete now. Each button is transparent in its "Up" phase and has a white background in its "Over" phase.

To create the different buttons that control the VR effect:

1. Open the **Library** window and duplicate the **VR01** button 9 times by choosing **Duplicate** from the Library pop-up menu. Name the duplicates **VR02** to **VR10**.

2. Select the tab for the **VR01** button on the right side of the Flash window, and move the current frame indicator to the "Over" frame.

3. Select the **dollar05** symbol from the Library window and drag it from the preview window to the symbol editing window (see Figure 8.10). The symbol is placed with the top-left corner at the center point of the editing window. Choose the **View > Snap** option, and drag the symbol so that its center point snaps to the center point of the symbol editing window.

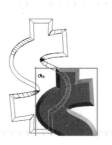

Figure 8.10
Dragging the dollar sign into place at the center of the symbol editing window.

4. Move the current frame indicator to the "Hit" frame. Choose **Edit > Select All**. Then, hold down the **Shift** key and use the arrow key to deselect the center rectangle. Remove the rest of the rectangles by choosing **Edit > Cut**.

5. Choose **Edit > Edit Movie** to shift into movie editing mode.
Move the current frame indicator to frame 1 of the movie.
Select the **VR01** button in the Library window and drag its
preview onto the editing window. Click on the black dot at the
center of the button (created in step 11 of the previous
exercise) and move it to the center of the editing window.
Choosing the **Control > Enable Buttons** option causes the
dollar sign with the white background (the "Over" frame of the
VR01 button) to display when the cursor moves over the center
of the editing window. Deselect the Enable Buttons option
when finished.

Repeat steps 2 to 4 for the other 9 buttons. Use the chart below
to help determine which images to use in the "Over" frame,
and which rectangles to delete in the "Hit" frame.

Button	*Put this symbol in "Over" frame*	*Delete all but shaded rectangle in "Hit" frame (lines are for reference only)*
VR01	dollar05	
VR02	dollar06	
VR03	dollar07	
VR04	dollar08	
VR05	dollar09	

VR06	dollar10	
VR07	dollar01	
VR08	dollar02	
VR09	dollar03	
VR10	dollar04	

7. After you have edited the buttons, add them to the movie, as you did with VR01 in step 5.

8. Center all of the buttons in the middle of the movie window.

9. Once you have placed all the buttons, check their placement by enabling the buttons and moving the cursor across the movie frame. You may need to make adjustments to the alignment of the buttons to prevent jumpy frames.

10. After you have adjusted the buttons, go into each of the "Up" button frames and delete the dot at the center of the frame. When the movie plays now, the buttons remain invisible until the cursor rolls over the movie.

This is an example of how planning ahead can make complex tasks in Flash far simpler than they would be otherwise. Specifically, in this case, creating the alternating colored rectangles and a button that contains all the elements from which you can create other elements, speeds the process of creating complex movies.

Complex Actions

Sometimes, you need more than one task to take place as the result of user interaction. It's possible, with some planning, for a button to trigger a complex action, incorporating two or more individual tasks.

To enable a button to trigger a complex action, it's helpful to break the action into its tasks. Each frame of an animation performs a different task, changing an image on screen; complex actions can do the same thing, executing a different task in each movie frame.

That, in fact, is the essence of creating complex actions. When you need a button to perform multiple tasks with a single click, it's relatively simple to set up a sequence of frames (or a scene) to perform those tasks, with each sequence frame executing a task. Again, it just takes a little planning.

Multi-Frame Update

You've already used buttons to display pages in a frame. What if you want to update more than one frame at the same time?

Figure 8.11 is a schematic of an HTML frameset taken from the Atomic City Apartments example above. The control frame of the frameset contains a Flash movie that displays information about various apartment types in the other two frames. The "floorplan" frame contains another Flash movie that displays a diagram of the apartment layout. The "availability" frame contains up-to-date information about the pricing of the apartment in which the viewer is interested. The HTML for the top-level page actually contains two framesets:

```
<FRAMESET cols="150, *">
  <FRAME name="control" SRC="control.swf">
  <FRAMESET rows="*,150">
    <FRAME name="floorplan"
    SRC="floorplan.html">
    <FRAME name="availability"
    SRC="available.html">
  </FRAMESET>
</FRAMESET>
```

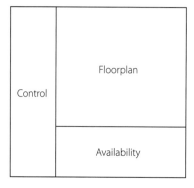

Figure 8.11
Schematic of a three-frame HTML frameset.

The first frame splits the window vertically, sectioning off 150 pixels of the window for the control frame. The Shockwave Flash file occupies the control frame without an HTML file. The second frameset, contained within the first, splits the remaining section of the window horizontally with 150 pixels reserved for the "availability" frame, and the rest used for the "floorplan" frame.

In the Flash file used to create control.swf, there are 7 buttons. Each button needs to load a separate file into the other two frames. Because a button can have only one action attached to it, and because a single action can affect only a single frame, this design requires the creation of a complex action.

The movie in its current state does nothing, it simply has 1 frame with the title and buttons in different layers. To display the layout and availability information for the one bedroom apartment, you need to add a complex action to the top button.

For this complex action there are two primary tasks:

- Load an HTML document that contains another Flash file into the floorplan frame; and

- Load an HTML document into the availability frame.

In this example you'll create a Flash movie that controls two frames of an HTML frameset. As this example develops, you'll find that some minor tasks evolve between the major tasks.

To create the actions to load the upper frames of an HTML frameset:

1. The files for this exercise are contained in the folder *exer08j*. Open the file *control.fla*.

2. The first movie frame needs to wait for user interaction. Place the Modify Frames indicator in the first frame of the timeline and assign a **Stop** action to the frame with the Modify Frames pop-up menu.

3. Select the top button graphic and the grouped-shape that reads "1-bedroom" in the first frame. Choose **Insert > Create Symbol** to display the Symbol Properties dialog box. Name the symbol **1BR**, check **Button Behavior**, and click **OK**. The movie is now ready for you to set up the action that initiates the complex behavior.

4. The method for creating this complex behavior uses a series of frame actions, beginning at frame 5. So the first action is to get from the menu to frame 5. Make sure that the symbol you just created is still selected and choose **Modify > Element** to display the Link Properties: Button dialog box. Choose **Goto** from the Action pop-up menu, and target frame 5 (see Figure 8.12). Click **OK**.

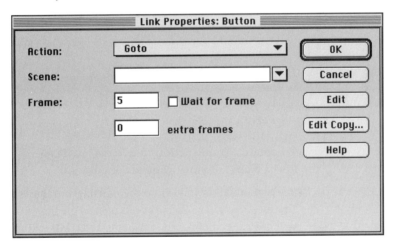

Figure 8.12
Assigning a Goto action to the button.

5. In the timeline, select both layers in frame 10 and choose **Insert Frame** from the Modify Frames pop-up menu.

6. The complex action really begins at frame 5. Place the Modify Frames indicator in frame 5 of the "buttons" layer. Insert a key frame by choosing **Insert Key Frame** from the Modify Frames pop-up menu.

7. The first major task is to load in the floorplan for the 1-bedroom apartments, which is contained in the HTML document floorplan01.htm. In frame 5 of the buttons layer, assign a **Get URL and Goto** action, inserting the relative URL for the HTML document (**floorplan01.htm**) and the name of the target frame (**floorplan**) in the appropriate places. After the Get URL portion of the action is complete, Goto takes the movie to the next major task in frame 6. When you've entered those items (see Figure 8.13), click **OK**. It's time to move on to the next task.

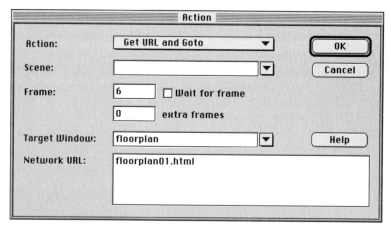

Figure 8.13
Assigning a GetURL and Goto action to a frame.

To create a frame action that loads an HTML page into the lower frame of your frameset document:

1. Insert another key frame into the timeline at frame 6 of the "buttons" layer. This frame accomplishes the next major task of your complex action, loading an HTML page into the lower frame.

2. Add another **Get URL and Goto** action to the new key frame. Load the HTML document **available01.html** into the "availability" frame, and go to frame **7** (see Figure 8.14).

```
┌─────────────────────── Action ───────────────────────┐
│                                                       │
│  Action:      ┌───────────────────────┐              │
│               │ Get URL and Goto    ▼ │  ┌────────┐  │
│                                          │   OK   │  │
│  Scene:       ┌─────────────────────┬─┐  └────────┘  │
│               │                     │▼│  ┌────────┐  │
│                                          │ Cancel │  │
│  Frame:       ┌───┐                       └────────┘  │
│               │ 7 │   □ Wait for frame                │
│               └───┘                                   │
│               ┌───┐                                   │
│               │ 0 │   extra frames                    │
│               └───┘                                   │
│                                          ┌────────┐  │
│  Target Window: ┌───────────────────┬─┐  │  Help  │  │
│                 │ availability      │▼│  └────────┘  │
│                                                       │
│  Network URL:   ┌───────────────────────────────────┐│
│                 │ available01.html                  ││
│                 │                                   ││
│                 │                                   ││
│                 │                                   ││
│                 └───────────────────────────────────┘│
│                                                       │
└───────────────────────────────────────────────────────┘
```

Figure 8.14
The Action dialog box assigning an action to frame 7.

3. In frame 7 of the buttons layer, create a new key frame and
   add a **Goto** action to move back to the main menu in frame 1.
   The timeline for this movie should now look like Figure 8.15.

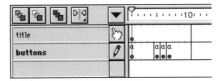

Figure 8.15
The timeline of the movie
after step 3.

You can design each of the other buttons to operate in the same
manner, with just a few frames controlling the complex task for each
button.

The above technique isn't the only way to accomplish this task.
If you're loading a movie into the "floorplan" frame, you can
easily insert a frame action that loads the HTML document for
the "availability" frame. Once you've completed a couple of
variations on this technique, you'll think of even more.

Moving On...

This chapter delved into a number of realms, from the Internet
to buttons that are not buttons, to ways of combining actions that
do more than they can do individually.

The next chapter introduces a new dimension to Flash movies:
the world of sound.

CHAPTER 9

Sound

Flash movies are obviously

a visual medium, but there's more
implied by the word *multimedia* than just
moving pictures. Not only can you watch the action of
a Flash movie, you can *hear* it.

Unfortunately, as in many other multimedia venues,
when designers create Flash movies, they often overlook
sound. There are a number of reasons that sound is
the forgotten child of multimedia—even though most
computers have speakers. Creating digital audio files
requires an additional set of tools and skills that many
web designers do not have.

With Flash, you can incorporate sound in movies.
Sounds can be captured and digitized for a specific
purpose or come from sound-file collections that you
can obtain commercially. Adding sound to a movie can
truly make the movie stand out from the crowd, as well
as adding a level of interaction that goes beyond a
single sense.

What you'll learn...

**The essentials of
digital audio**

**How to attach
sounds to buttons**

**How streaming audio
works in Flash movies**

There are two types of computer sound: sampled and synthesized. Synthesized sounds are computer-generated from a series of instructions that the computer interprets, and then turns into sound waves—in a manner analogous to how Flash draws objects on screen from simple lines and shapes. MIDI sound is perhaps the most well-known synthetic sound file format. Synthetic sound files are very small, but they tend to produce audio without the minute variations that give non-synthetic sounds their realism. Synthetic sounds are not used in Flash movies.

Sampled sounds are the audio equivalent of bitmap images. For every portion of a sampled sound, a measurement—or *sample*—of the sound wave is taken and converted to a number (see Figure 9.1). The numbers derived from the samples approximate the ups and downs of the sound wave. Flash uses sampled sound files. AIFF and WAVE files are common types of sampled sounds.

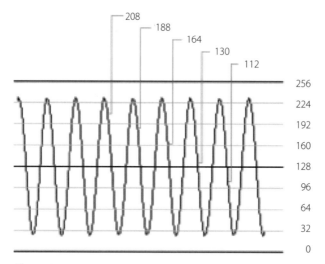

Figure 9.1
A sampled sound file uses numbers to approximate a sound wave.

Digital sound is a time-based medium, unlike digital imaging. When an image displays, the viewer sees all of the image simultaneously. Sound, on the other hand, "displays" one sample at a time. As a sound plays, subsequent portions of the sound file are used to create the sound wave.

A sampled sound file contains data about the sound wave's *amplitude* (volume) at regular intervals. The frequency of those intervals is known as the *sample rate*. The digital audio files on a standard audio compact disc have a sample rate of 44.1kHz (kiloHertz), or 44,100 samples per second. That means the computer uses 44,100 numeric values to approximate a sound wave for every second the sound plays. Other standard rates for sound files are even divisors of 44.1kHz: 22.05kHz and 11.025kHz.

The numbers stored in each sample determine how close the actual amplitude level approximtes the digital sound. This is called the *sample size*. Audio compact discs have a sample size of 16 bits, which allows them to divide the possible amplitude spectrum into over 65,000 possible values. The alternative (in most digital sound systems) is a sample size of 8 bits, which can store 256 possible values.

The higher the digital sound's sample rate and sample size (i.e. the closer the original sound wave is approximated), the better the sound quality. Lower values for the sample rate result in a loss of high-frequency tones; a smaller sample size results in a loss of subtle changes in amplitude. Figure 9.2 illustrates the difference sampling rates can make in the shape of a sound wave. Above, a constant tone is sampled at 44.1kHz (each vertical line represents a single sample). Below, the same sound is sampled at 11.025kHz. For every 4 samples in the 44.1kHz version, there's only 1 sample in the 11.025kHz version.

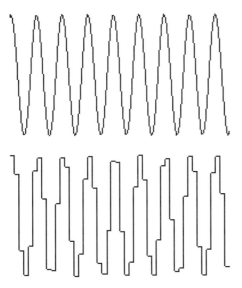

Figure 9.2
A higher sampling rate (above) makes a digitized sound wave a better approximation than the sound sampled at a lower rate.

When a sampled sound plays, its samples reconstruct a sound wave. The accuracy with which the samples record the actual sound wave amplitude reflect the fidelity of the digital file to the original sound. With less fidelity, the overall shape of the sound is retained, but the sound's subtleties and tone are flattened (see Figure 9.3).

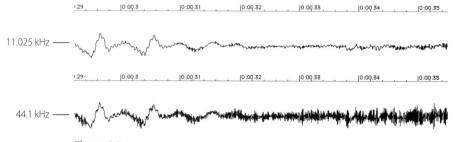

Figure 9.3
Two versions of the same vocal selection, sampled at 11.025kHz (above) and 44.1kHz (below). Fewer samples result in a less-accurate reproduction of the harmonic tones, flattening the sound wave. The extra samples in the 44.1kHz sound wave show a more jagged-looking, "noisy" appearance.

The Sound and the Flash

The current frame indicator or a button triggers sounds in Flash. Sounds are attached to key frames in a movie scene's timeline, or in a button symbol's frame.

Flash sounds can be *event-driven* or *streamed*. Event-driven sounds start (and stop) based on the key frame to which the sound is attached. The data for an event-driven sound is encapsulated in a single frame. This means that once the computer reads the sound, it can play. If the movie slows down for any reason, the sound continues playing.

Streaming sounds are synchronized to the frames of a movie. The streaming sound data is stored in chunks, with each chunk stored with the frame's image data. When the movie plays back, it may skip frames of the animation to keep the sound and animation in synch.

Typically, short sounds work better as event-driven sounds, while longer sounds that have multiple points of coincidence with the visual elements in the movie do better as streaming sounds.

TIP *The time it takes a sound to load from disk or across a network is also a factor in deciding whether to use event-driven or streaming sounds. Event-driven sounds load into memory in their entirety before they play; so if the sound is rather large, it can halt the movie while the sound downloads. Because each frame in which a streaming sound occurs only stores as much of the sound data as the frame uses, the sound can begin playing almost immediately.*

Sounds added to Flash movies can be looped and you can modify and change their amplitudes. A sound's beginning and end can be clipped off as well.

Each sound that you import into Flash is stored inside the movie file. The sound maintains a link to the original sound file and updates if the sound file is modified. The sound also can be replaced everywhere it occurs with a completely different sound.

To import a sound into a Flash movie:

1. Open the Flash movie *exer09a.fla*. This short movie has two layers and a frame action in the last frame that takes it to a previous frame (13) when the movie reaches its end.

2. Choose **Insert Layer** from the **Modify Layers** pop-up menu to add a new layer below the "halloween" layer and open the **Layer Properties** dialog box. Name the layer **sounds** and click **OK** to close the window. Sounds can be placed in the same layers as graphics, but it's often best for clarity's sake to make distinct layers.

3. Choose **File > Import** to open the **Import** dialog box. Import the file **exer09a.wav** (Windows) or **exer09a.aif** (Macintosh) by selecting the file and clicking **Open** to import the file.

The Sound Properties dialog box contains a variety of information and options about an imported sound (see Figure 9.4). At the upper left is a thumbnail of the stereo sound waves, or a single sound wave if the sound has only one channel.

Figure 9.4
The Sound Properties dialog box displays the imported sound's attributes.

To review a sound's attributes:

1. Choose **Window > Library**. The Library window displays a symbol used in the movie as well as the newly imported sound.

2. Select the sound in the Library list and choose **Properties** from the Library pop-up menu to display the **Sound Properties** dialog box

3. Click **OK** to close the Sound Properties dialog box.

Each imported sound can be used more than once in a movie; each time it is used is known as an *instance*. The Sound dialog box controls how each individual instance plays (see Figure 9.5).

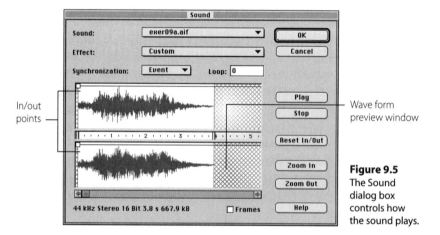

In/out points

Wave form preview window

Figure 9.5
The Sound dialog box controls how the sound plays.

You can change the sound's name by typing in the name field at the top of the dialog box. This name appears in the Library list and in other dialog boxes. Beneath the sound's name is the directory path to the original sound that you imported, its last modification date, and information about the sound's sampling rate, stereo or monaural, the sample size, play time, and file size.

NOTE *The Export Rate and Export Compression pop-up menus can override the default sound export settings. The default settings are determined when the file is exported as a Shockwave Flash movie or digital video file.*

The Update button reads the original file and changes the copy of the sound stored in the movie file, if it finds that the sound has changed. The Import button can import an entirely new sound file, replacing the current sound data. The Test button plays the sound, and the Stop button halts playback of the sound.

The waveform preview window shows the separate waveforms for each channel of a sound. The beginning and end of the sound are controlled by two handles (known as the In/Out points) on the sound's timeline. The timeline displays seconds by default, but can display frames by checking the Frames button below the waveform preview window. Dragging the In or Out handle moves the lines and cross-hatching that indicates the beginning and end of the sound (the cross-hatched areas are not played as a part of this instance of the sound). The In and Out handles can be reset to the beginning and end of the sound file by clicking the Reset In/Out button.

Square handles for each of the channels of the sound control the volume of the sound as it plays. Add handles to the line extending from the amplitude handles (the amplitude envelope) by clicking the line. Additional handles can be used to create fade effects, or to quiet the sound at a particular point in time. Handles can be deleted by selecting them and dragging them out of the window. The default setting for the amplitude envelope and handles doesn't affect the sound. To see some of the ways a sound can be affected by the amplitude, choose one of the items from the Effect pop-up menu.

The Play button previews the changes you apply in the Sound dialog box. Of course, the sound can be stopped with the Stop button.

The Synchronization pop-up menu determines whether the sound is event-driven or streamed.

The value assigned to Loop controls how many times the portion of the sound between the In and Out handles repeats during playback. The Loop value controls the number of times the portion of the waveform between the In and Out handles is repeated. Event sounds will automatically play all of the repetitions before it stops. Because streaming sounds are synchronized to the specific frames in which the sound appears, if the current frame indicator leaves the frames where the sound appears, the sound will stop, regardless of the Loop value.

To play the sound:

1. Place the Modify Frames indicator in the first frame of the "sounds" layer in the timeline. Choose **Sound** from the Modify Frames pop-up menu to display the Sound dialog box.

2. Choose **exer09a.wav** (Windows) or **exer09a.aif** (Macintosh) from the Sound pop-up menu. Click the **Zoom Out** button until the entire sound waveform displays in the waveform preview window.

3. Set the Effect pop-up menu to **None**, and choose **Event** from the Synchronization pop-up menu. Leave the Loop setting at **0**. Click **OK** to close the dialog box. The waveform of the sound displays in the "sounds" layer of the movie's timeline (see Figure 9.6).

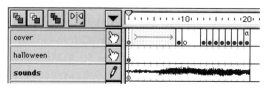

Figure 9.6
Sound waveform thumb-nails are displayed in the layer and key frame to which they are assigned.

TIP *To remove a sound from a key frame, set the Sound pop-up menu to None.*

4. Play the movie. The sound begins with the movie and plays through to the end of the sound. An event-driven sound such as this one always begins play when the current frame indicator reaches the key frame to which the sound is attached.

NOTE *In this example, if the sound is synchronized with the Streaming option, the sound will play as it would with an Event sound until the current frame indicator reaches the end of the movie. When the action in the last frame sends the current frame indicator back to frame 13, an Event sound would continue playing to the end of the sound. A streaming sound will repeat the portion of the sound synchronized to frames 13 and 20.*

More sounds

Multiple sounds play simultaneously in a Flash movie. Each sound can be unique or it can be an instance of the same sound. You can use the same event-driven sound multiple times in a movie without storing it multiple times.

Sounds also can be stopped by assigning Stop synchronizations to frames or by using the Stop All Sounds action as a frame or button action.

To add more sounds to a movie:

1. Open the Flash movie *exer09b.fla*. This movie is the end result of the previous exercises, with an extra sound added to the Library.

2. Put the Modify Frames indicator in frame 13 of the "sounds" layer, which is the beginning of the loop. Choose **Insert Key Frame** from the Modify Frames pop-up menu to add a new key frame to the layer.

3. Choose **Sound** from the Modify Frames pop-up menu to display the Sound dialog box and choose **exer09b.aif** from the Sound pop-up menu to assign the sound to the new key frame. Set the Synchronization pop-up menu to Event and click **OK**.

Playing the movie at this point results in the original sound beginning at frame 1. As the movie reaches frame 13, the new sound (thunder) begins. Each time the movie loops from frame 20 to 13, a new instance of the thunder sound begins, eventually layering several instances of the sound. Each instance eventually ends, but others start up. Stopping the movie allows each of the current instances to end in turn.

To see how the Stop synchronization operates:

1. Put the Modify Frames indicator in frame 19.

2. Choose **Insert Blank Key Frame** from the Modify Frames pop-up menu to create a new key frame in frame 19

3. Choose **Sound** from the Modify Frames pop-up menu to display the Sound dialog box.

4. Choose **exer09a.aif** from the Sound pop-up menu and **Stop** from the Synchronization pop-up menu. Click **OK**.

The Stop setting stops only the sound specified by the Sound pop-up menu. (Multiple instances of the same sound are stopped by a single Stop synchronization). Playing the movie back, the organ music starts as usual in frame 1, the thunder begins in frame 13, but the Stop synchronization prevents the organ music from finishing. The thunder continues as it did before you added the Stop synchronization.

When animation sequences need to synchronize with specific points in longer sounds, some form of synchronization is needed. Thumbnails of the sound waves of event-driven sounds do appear in movie timelines, but they merely indicate how long the sound is if the maximum frame rate is maintained. If the movie slows down for any reason, the sound continues to play—and the sound finishes playing in a frame well before the end of its thumbnail in the timeline.

It's difficult to predict the playback speed of movies; differing conditions in movie complexity, the playback size of the movie, other programs running in the background, etc., can cause variations in the actual frame rate. So if the movie rate is slow and if a synched sound is playing, animation frames are skipped so that what is seen on the screen matches the next chunk of music to play. If a movie takes 3 frames worth of time to draw a frame, the next two frames of the movie are skipped, so that the animation can catch up with the sound.

Testing a movie with a sound can help determine whether synchronization is necessary.

To test a movie with a sound:

1. Open the Flash movie *exer09c.fla*. This movie is a simulation of a record player, with the player arm swinging from the outside of the record to the edge of the label. The player arm is timed to reach the label's edge about the time that a sound ends. Deselect the **View > Smooth** option.

2. Place the frame selection indicator in frame 11 of the "audio" layer. Choose **Sound** from the Modify Frames pop-up menu to display the Sound dialog box. Choose **exer09c.aif** in the Sound pop-up menu, and None from Effects; and, for now, choose Event from the Synchronization menu. Click **OK**.

   The space between key frames in the layer has been made to fit the length of the sound.

3. Play the movie. Playing the movie on most computers at this point, the current frame indicator reaches the end of the sound in the timeline at the same time the sound finishes playing and the arm reaches the edge of the label.

4. Choose **View** > **Show Frame** to enlarge the image of the movie in the window. Select **View** > **Smooth** to improve the quality of the image. Play the movie again, and the sound finishes before the current frame indicator reaches the end of the sound. The movie rate is set to 5 frames per second. Check the frame rate indicator while the movie plays to determine the actual frame rate.

5. Repeat step 2, but choose **Stream** from the Synchronization menu instead of Event. Playing the movie after setting this option forces it to maintain the 5 frame per second rate while the synchronized sound plays.

Adding sounds to buttons

Audio cues can make buttons easier for people to identify. Sounds can be attached to a button symbol's frames, and different sounds can be attached to the individual frames to indicate whether the cursor is rolling over the button, whether the button is clicked, etc.

To attach a sound to the button:

1. Open the *exer09d.fla* movie in Flash. The movie's timeline is empty and two sounds were imported into the Library.

2. Choose **Xtras** > **Libraries** > **Buttons-Geometric** display the Library: Buttons-Geometric window.

3. Select the **Mondrian** button in the Library list. Drag the preview of the button from the Library window to the movie editing window to add the button to the movie.

4. Choose **Edit** > **Edit Symbols** to enter the symbol editing mode. The only editable symbol in the movie is the Mondrian button you dragged from the Library.

5. Place the Modify Frames indicator in the "Over" frame. Adding a sound to the "Over" frame plays the sound when the cursor moves over the button. Choose **Sound** from the Modify Frames pop-up menu to display the Sound dialog box. Select **exer09d2.aif** from the Sound menu and make sure the Synchronization menu is set to **Event**. Click **OK** to assign the sound to the frame.

6. Repeat step 5 for the "Down" frame and assign the sound **exer09d1.aif** to the frame.

7. Choose **Edit > Edit Movie** to enter the movie editing mode. Choose **Control > Enable Buttons** to make the button active. Moving the cursor over the button plays the sound assigned to the "Over" frame. Depressing the mouse button plays the sound assigned to the "Down" frame.

If the cursor is moved on and then off the button, the sound continues to play. Moving the cursor rapidly over the button (without pressing the mouse button) creates multiple instances of the sound assigned to the "Over" frame. While some interesting effects can be created this way, in most cases, the desired effect would be for the sound to stop when the cursor moves off of the button.

8 Choose **Edit > Edit Symbols** to enter the symbol editing mode to edit the button's symbol.

9. Repeat step 5 for the "Up" frame and set the **Synchronize** option to **Stop**. Switch back to the movie editing mode by selecting **Edit > Edit Movie**. Now, when the cursor moves off of the button, the sound assigned to the "Over" frame stops.

Even small snippets of sound can make a difference in the richness of a multimedia presentation. Sounds attached to frames and buttons can provide a variety of audio cues to the viewer that make the movie a true multimedia experience.

Moving On...

Everything up to this point has focused on creating a Flash movie. For the most part, however, the movies created in earlier chapters were playable only with Flash. The next chapter describes the various methods for creating Flash movies that someone can view without Flash, and it explores the options for creating those files.

CHAPTER 10

Delivering Movies

What you'll learn...

Details of the Shockwave Flash Export dialog box

How compression affects bitmaps and sounds

How to use and evaluate Size Reports

You can save the work you

create in Flash as drawings, bitmaps, or digital video to use in whatever application you want. But the program's primary purpose is for creating interactive movies.

As you finish creating your movies there's a last set of considerations for delivering them: Will the movie play from the standalone Shockwave Flash Player or from the Web? How can you make movies smaller? How much should you compress bitmaps and sounds? And so on. This chapter helps you make decisions like these by explaining how Flash saves and compresses data, and by demonstrating how to use the Flash Size Report.

Movies that are exported as a series of individual vector files, bitmaps, or as a single digital video file lose their interactive elements, as well as any sounds (except in digital video files). In most cases, the speed at which the movie plays back or responds to user interaction is not important.

Speed, however, is a concern when you use a Shockwave Flash (*.swf*) file—the compressed, optimized version of the Flash (*.fla*) movie.

While this chapter focuses on the Flash 2.0 format, most of the discussion also applies to files saved in the FutureSplash Player (.spl) format. Files saved by Flash 2.0 for the FutureSplash Player contain sound data that the Shockwave Flash Player can read, but the FutureSplash Player cannot.

The Shockwave Flash movie file format contains all of the necessary data to reproduce the functionality of a Flash movie in a compressed, optimized format. While the original movie file might have pictures, sounds, and symbols that it never uses—if they've been imported or added to the Library, but not actually placed in the timeline—saving a Flash file removes unused Library items from the file. Bitmaps are compressed as JPEG images. Sound is compressed using options set in the Export Shockwave Flash dialog box. Finally, Flash compresses the entire file, including data for the shapes, symbols, and the timeline.

Playing Movies

There are three methods for playing a Flash movie. The first is to open a Flash format file (*.fla*) with Flash, and choose Play from the Control menu. This isn't a viable method of distributing a movie as you can't expect all users to have Flash.

The other two options both make use of the Shockwave Flash format file. You create a Shockwave Flash file file by using the File > Export Movie with the Save File As Type option set to Shockwave Flash.

You can play Shockwave Flash files (*.swf* files) with the standalone Shockwave Flash Player from a local hard drive or local network drive. You also can embed Shockwave Flash movies in HTML pages—stored on a local network drive or on the Web—that anyone can play with a browser and the ActiveX or Netscape plug-in versions of the Shockwave Flash Player.

You also can view Shockwave Flash files inside other programs (e.g., Authorware or Director) that support Windows ActiveX controls. An Xtra that incorporates Shockwave Flash into Authorware packages is already available, and one that does the same for Director movies was demonstrated at the Macromedia User Conference in October, 1997.

Using the standalone Shockwave Flash Player

If you have a self-contained movie that isn't embedded in HTML documents, play it with the standalone Shockwave Flash Player. The standalone Player supports all of the Flash movie functions, except for three Actions: `Get URL`; `Get URL and Goto`; and `Get URL, Goto and Play`.

Controlled situations such as kiosks, presentations, and trade show demonstrations are typical uses of the Player. Movies prepared for the Player also play using a browser with the Netscape plug-in or an ActiveX version of the Player. Save movies intended for the Player first as a Shockwave Flash file, and then copy the file to the computer from where it will play. If you have the Player installed on the computer, you can play the movie by double-clicking its icon.

Play Shockwave Flash movies on any computer that has the standalone Shockwave Flash Player installed, or a browser with the Netscape plug-in or ActiveX version of the Shockwave Flash Player installed. The standalone Shockwave Flash Player only can play movies from the user's local hard drive or from a network volume mounted as a drive on the user's computer.

There are two major considerations when developing movies for use with the standalone Shockwave Flash Player and/or for use in a web environment. The first is file size. Movies played from a hard drive, or even a local network volume, don't have the same file size constraints as movies played from the Web. The vector artwork in Flash movies helps keep all files relatively small. Consequently, the faster file loading of Flash movies played from a hard disk or CD-ROM (as opposed to a 28.8K modem) means that you can increase significantly the amount of other media—specifically, sound. You can do this by boosting the quality of the sound, or by simply using more of it.

Increased movie loading speed does not necessarily mean you can pack more vector graphics or bitmaps into Flash movies. While the Shockwave Flash Player loads outlines significantly faster from a hard disk than across slower network or Internet connections, the computer processor governs the speed with which Flash moves or adds color information to those outlines—a process not affected by loading the file from the hard disk.

The second consideration is that files played with the standalone Shockwave Flash Player must be self-contained. All actions of a standalone presentation need to refer to scenes and frames within a single Flash movie file. Flash movies played inside a browser, on the other hand, can use `Get URL` actions to open and play other movies, and go to other web pages.

Turning a Flash movie into a movie for the standalone Shockwave Flash Player is exactly the same process as that for creating a Shockwave Flash movie for the Web. However, keep in mind the limitations of the Player and the advantages of fast downloads while planning and creating the movie.

To create a Shockwave Flash movie for the standalone Player:

1. Open the movie in Flash.

2. Choose **Export Movie** from the File Menu to open the Export Movie dialog box.

3. Choose **Shockwave Flash** from the **Save As File Type** pop-up menu, and type a name for the movie in the entry field. Do not enter a file name extension (*.swf*), Flash adds it automatically. Click **Save**.

Macintosh users should get into the habit of saving Flash movie files with extension names (.fla). If the original Flash file doesn't have an extension and you enter the same file name into the Export Movie dialog box expecting Flash to add the .swf extension, a warning that reads "Replace existing file" displays; if you click the Replace button, the original file is unusable, even though you saved the Shockwave Flash file properly and with a different name.

4. Choose the options from the Export Shockwave Flash dialog box that are appropriate to your movie and click **OK**.

You now can open the Shockwave Flash movie with the standalone Shockwave Flash Player by choosing **Open** from the File menu, or by double-clicking the file's icon.

Shockwave Flash: Netscape Plug-in and ActiveX Control

The primary delivery vehicle for Flash movies is a World Wide Web browser. The movie plays as part of an HTML page or loaded directly into the browser. The more common method is for an HTML page to encapsulate the movie with `<OBJECT>` and/or `<EMBED>` tags; each method has its advantages.

When a Shockwave-enabled browser opens a Shockwave Flash movie without a surrounding HTML page, the movie automatically scales to fit the window or frame with no border. A typical URL for accomplishing this task is: `http://www.server.com/flashmovie.swf` A link or an HTML frameset contains the URL, and you can design the URL to load a specific frame of an HTML document. You can also open Shockwave Flash movies with the browser locally.

File dialog boxes in Windows typically have a pop-up menu that determines the types of files shown in the dialog box. This is also a feature in the Macintosh version of Internet Explorer. If only HTML files appear in the dialog box, choosing All Files from the pop-up menu exposes the names of Flash movies. On the Macintosh, another solution is to hold down the Option key while choosing Open File from the File menu; doing so displays all types of files, not just the default types.

Movies that are contained in HTML pages through the use of `<OBJECT>` or `<EMBED>` tags have advantages over movies directly loaded into the browser. Among the most important of these is the capability to send and receive instructions from browser scripting languages such as JavaScript and VBScript. You can use such scripting methods to control the scene and frame that display, to start and stop the movie, to zoom in on a frame, or to pan-in a zoomed frame. (For specifics on how to use browser scripting methods with Shockwave Flash, see Appendix D, "Browser Scripting and Shockwave Flash Movies.")

JavaScript control of a Shockwave Flash movie on the Windows95/NT operating system requires Internet Explorer 3.0 or later, or Navigator 3.0 or later. A Macintosh PowerPC requires Navigator 3.0 or later. JavaScript control of Flash movies is not possible with Windows 3.1 or Macintosh 68K-series computers.

Browser scripting provides Flash with capabilities not available with simple actions. You can create games and other complex projects that communicate with and control multiple Shockwave Flash movies using scripting languages.

To create a Shockwave Flash movie for use in an HTML page:

1. Follow steps 1 to 4 above for creating a Shockwave Flash movie for the Player.

2. To incorporate the movie into an HTML page, copy the Shockwave Flash file to the same folder that contains the HTML file. The HTML file should follow this skeleton structure (replace italic items with names relevant to your movie or web page):

```
<HTML>
<HEAD>
 <TITLE>Title of Web Page</TITLE>
</HEAD>
<BODY>
<SCRIPT LANGUAGE="JavaScript">
<!-
// any JavaScript methods appear between this line and
// the SCRIPT tag delimiter
//->
</SCRIPT>
<SCRIPT LANGUAGE="VBScript">
<!-
// any VBScript methods appear between this line and
// the SCRIPT tag delimiter
->
</SCRIPT>
<OBJECT
  ID="movieref"
  CLASSID="clsid:D27CDB6E-AE6D-11cf-96B8-444553540000"
  CODEBASE="http://active.macromedia.com/flash2/cabs/
  swflash.cab#version=2,0,0,0" WIDTH="100%"
HEIGHT="100%">
  <PARAM NAME="Movie" VALUE="flashmovie.swf">
  <PARAM NAME="Play" VALUE="false">
  <PARAM NAME="Quality" VALUE="best">
  <EMBED NAME="movieref" mayscript="mayscript"
  SRC="flashmovie.swf" WIDTH="100%" HEIGHT="100%"
  salign="t" quality="best" play="false"
  pluginspage="http://www.macromedia.com/shockwave/
  download/index.cgi?P1_Prod_Version=ShockwaveFlash2">
</EMBED>
</OBJECT>
<NOEMBED>
//browsers that support plug-ins or ActiveX controls will
//ignore HTML appearing between these tags, only browsers
//that don't support EMBED or OBJECT tags will see
//the text and graphics tags here.
</NOEMBED>
</BODY>
</HTML>
```

The values for the parameters in the `<OBJECT>` and `<EMBED>` tags change from movie to movie. (See Appendix C, "`<OBJECT>` / `<EMBED>` Tag References," for a complete list of parameters and what they do.) Generally, the parameters that need modifying are the Movie parameter of the `<OBJECT>` tag, the SRC parameter of the `<EMBED>` tag, and the width and height parameters of both tags. In all cases, the movie, width, and height parameters of the `<OBJECT>` tag should match the corresponding SRC, WIDTH, and HEIGHT parameters of the `<EMBED>` tag.

One disadvantage to `<OBJECT>` and `<EMBED>` tags is that there isn't an equivalent of the ALT parameter for the `<IMG>` tag. The ALT parameter displays text when an image is missing or when the user turns off the image loading feature of the browser. Browsers that properly interpret the `<OBJECT>` tag (Internet Explorer 3.0 or later for Windows, and forthcoming versions of Navigator) can automatically download and install the latest Shockwave Flash viewer. Older browsers display the broken plug-in icon. (A number of strategies to combat that problem exists, see Appendix E, "Hiding Broken Plug-in Icons," for details.)

Virtually any HTML tag, text, images, and even other Flash movies can appear in the body of the HTML document before or after the `<OBJECT>` and `<EMBED>` tags. Keep the HTML file and any embedded Shockwave Flash files in the same folder when publishing on a web server.

Load order

Flash draws each frame of the movie in the order that the objects and shapes for the frame appear in the file. Use the Load Order option in the Export Shockwave Flash dialog box to build suspense (by loading Bottom up so that background elements display first), or to inform (by loading Top down so that the most important items display first). The Load Order options control the organization of data in the movie's first frame. Each object or shape displays on screen in the order specified by the Load Order selection (Bottom up or Top down.) Load order does not affect movies viewed with the standalone Player.

Beware that there's no way to determine how long the elements of the first frame might take to load and draw on a user's machine.

If the hard drive reads the file quickly, and if there are no complex shapes to draw, the Load Order has little apparent effect. If movie data streams from a web server, or if the shapes are too complex to draw quickly, the items on the screen appear in the manner prescribed by the Load Order during the first frame of the movie.

If you use the Bottom up option, the movie background draws first, next canvas-level shapes from the bottom layer draw, and then the layer's overlay objects (in their stacking order from back to front). Next, the layer whose name is directly above the last layer in the layer list draws, and then each of the other layers loads and draws in the same manner. This process repeats until all layers load and draw.

The Top down option does roughly the opposite. The movie background color chosen in the Movie Properties dialog box always displays first, then each object in the frame appears in the selected load order.

To see an example of how Load Order can affect the same movie, use your browser to open the file *exer10a.html.*

Protection

If you save your Shockwave Flash movie without protecting it, anyone that can view the movie can import all of its shapes, pictures, and some of its animation. Using the File > Import command, and then selecting a Shockwave Flash movie file from a web browser's cache, records an unprotected Shockwave movie frame by frame to a new Flash movie. While importing does not preserve sounds, actions, layers, buttons, symbols, and other information, it does preserve artwork and bitmap images, making it easy for others to steal your work.

You can prevent importation of a Shockwave Flash file by another Flash program by clicking the Protect from Import button in the Export Shockwave Flash dialog box when you export your *.fla* movie as a *.swf* movie. Protection does not affect a movie's playback.

Compression

There are two types of compression available in the Export Shockwave Flash dialog box: JPEG and sound compression. All bitmap images compress with the JPEG algorithm when you save the image data as part of the movie file. The sound compression options control both the overall quality of the sound and the amount of sound compression. (Individual settings for sounds, as set in the Sound Properties dialog box override these settings.)

JPEG compression

JPEG (Joint Photographic Experts Group) is a method of compressing image data that was developed to make photographic-style images smaller.

Because of the way it compresses pictures, JPEG is not particularly useful for compressing line-art images, where colors have well-defined edges. It works best on pixel-based or continuous-tone images, where colors blend into one another rather than abruptly changing.

Line-art bitmaps, logos, and cartoons, are ideal candidates for conversion to vector objects using Modify > Trace Bitmap. Decide whether you should convert bitmap images to vectors or leave them before you import them. Photographic images, images with subtle shading, and 3D-rendered images usually produce smaller files as JPEG bitmap images than as vector graphics that contain the same amount of detail.

The Export Shockwave Flash dialog box controls the default compression applied to JPEG images in the movie. The Library menu's Properties dialog box also allows individual images to have specific settings applied to them. JPEG compression is a tradeoff between quality and size, with larger files allowing for more color and detail.

There's no simple method for determining what an image looks like at a particular JPEG Quality setting, so try different settings. As an example of what to expect, look at Figure 10.1, which compares two imported bitmap images—one photographic and the other line art—as they appear in a Shockwave Flash movie at various levels of JPEG Quality compression.

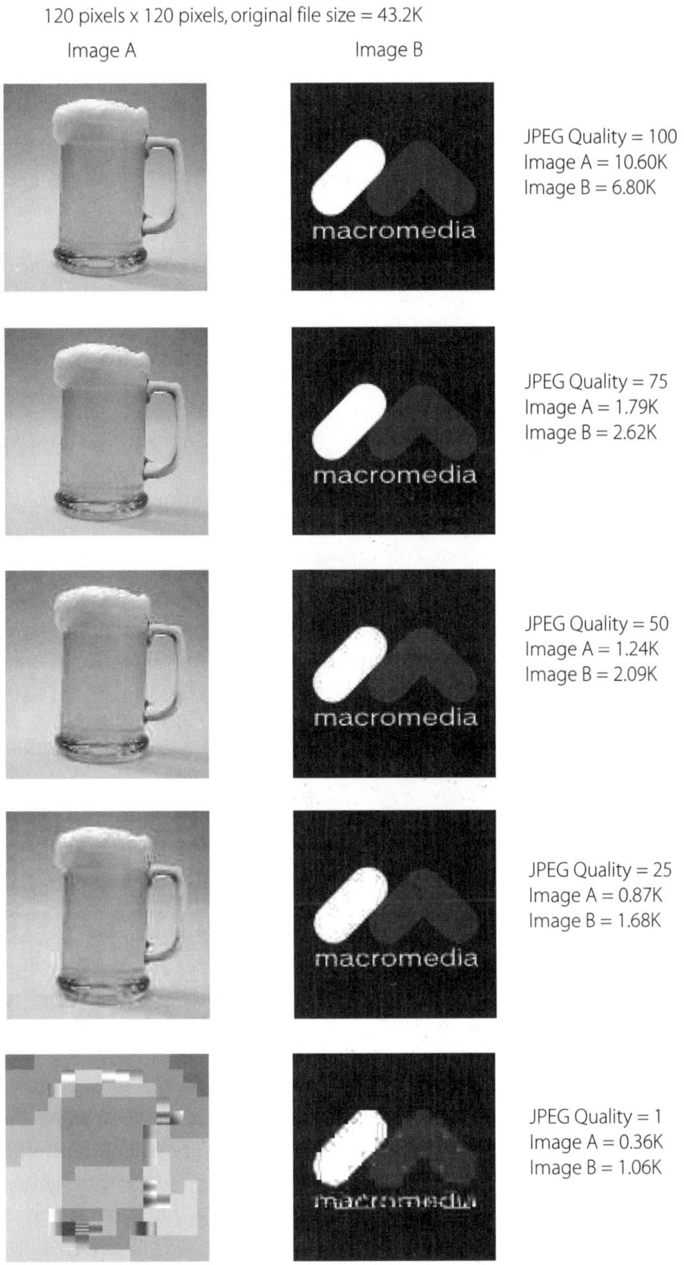
120 pixels x 120 pixels, original file size = 43.2K
Image A
Image B
macromedia
JPEG Quality = 100
Image A = 10.60K
Image B = 6.80K
JPEG Quality = 75
Image A = 1.79K
Image B = 2.62K
JPEG Quality = 50
Image A = 1.24K
Image B = 2.09K
JPEG Quality = 25
Image A = 0.87K
Image B = 1.68K
JPEG Quality = 1
Image A = 0.36K
Image B = 1.06K

Figure 10.1
A comparison of two bitmap images. The numbers indicate the size (in kilobytes) of the image after compression.

The edges of both images begin to degrade, acquiring what are known as *artifacts*, in places where the compression becomes obvious. Artifacts are usually more obvious in a line art image. This is because the sharpness of the edges between colors emphasizes the artifacts to a greater degree than the smoother gradations of the photographic image. By the time the JPEG Quality level is set to 1, neither image looks very good.

You can view the color versions of these images in the Shockwave Flash files, *exr10-2a.swf* (JPEG Quality = 1) through *exr10-2e.swf* (JPEG Quality = 100).

Sound compression

Flash uses ADPCM (Adaptive Differential Pulse Code Modulation) compression to compress sounds. Compressing (and decompressing) sound is trickier than compressing bitmaps or program files.

A sound wave is constantly changing in amplitude—changes that make noise. Figure 10.2 shows a very short portion of a sound, the "h" sound of the word "hello." The top view shows the entire "h" sound, the lower view displays a close-up of the soundwave shown in the black box.

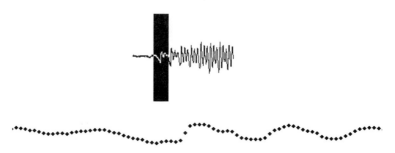

Figure 10.2
A short section of a sound wave, shown at different resolutions.

The sound wave in Figure 10.2 is a 16-bit, 11.025 kHz sample. (See Chapter 9, "Sound" for an explanation of sampling depths and rates.) Each of the diamond shapes in the lower view represents 16 bits of information about the amplitude of the sound. There are 11,025 such 16-bit groups for each second of the sound. Sound needs to decompress at least as fast as the sound plays. Otherwise, the sound sputters and pops, as the demand for the sound occurs faster than the decompression of the sound.

ADPCM compression

The ADPCM compression strategy looks at the amount the sound changes over time and finds patterns in those changes. The compressor examines those changes and approximates them. The decompressor reads the codes generated by the compressor and generates the sound data. Naturally, this process needs to happen very fast.

The ADPCM process for sound is—like JPEG compression for images—a lossy compression technique. The more the sound is compressed, the less it sounds like the original. The Export Shockwave Flash dialog presents four options for ADPCM sound compression that range from 2-bit to 5-bit compression. Two-bit compression produces the lowest-quality, smallest-file compression; five-bit compression produces the highest quality sound. Different settings are available for Audio Streams and Audio Events. You can compress background audio used as streams with a low-quality setting. Shorter event sounds should be compressed at a higher-quality setting.

As with JPEG compression, some types of sounds take better to compression than others. Clear, spoken text typically can withstand compression better than music. Short sound effects (such as those used for button clicks) often sound fine when compressed with 2-bit ADPCM, or they could sound like static bursts. Experimentation is the best solution.

The Export Shockwave Flash dialog box also enables you to set the final sampling rate of sounds. Ideally, you should import sounds into Flash at a high-quality level, with no compression. This allows you to add resolution and compression as a part of the Shockwave Flash export process.

The example movie *exer10c.swf* contains examples of three sound types at different levels of compression: a short musical sequence, spoken word, and a sound effect. Compare how different values in the Export Shockwave Flash dialog box affect quality.

Compression considerations

Compression of an image affects the amount of memory it occupies in the movie file, as does compression of sound. However, there are slightly different considerations to keep in mind when using bitmaps and sounds in Flash movies on the Web and on local drives.

The most obvious consideration is file size. To deliver an image or sound across a 28.8K modem, you should expect delivery of 2–3K of data per second. A double-speed CD ROM can deliver 300K per second. Newer CD-ROMs and hard drives are much faster, as are many local area network connections.

After a network or hard drive reads and decompresses an image (usually while it downloads), it occupies a set amount of memory (based on the image's size in pixels rather than its compressed size) during the time it draws on screen. In other words, once a bitmap reaches the computer where it displays, it doesn't make any difference whether or not it downloaded from a local hard disk or a web server anywhere in the world. Once the bitmap image downloads, its display and animation depend on the capability of the local computer to move, rotate, scale, and perform any other tasks (such as drawing vector shapes) Flash asks the processor to perform.

The effects of compressed sounds on movie performance is a little trickier to judge. Short sounds download quickly and generally don't affect the performance of a movie radically. Longer sounds can affect the performance of a movie because the sound must decompress while the movie draws shapes and bitmaps on the screen.

How much compression should you apply to bitmaps and sounds is often a judgment call as to how much quality you can sacrifice for smaller files. You usually can leave files loaded from hard drives, CD-ROMs, or diskettes intact, with a minimum amount of compression. This is because the movie's size has less bearing on the speed at which the movie plays than it does for movies delivered on the Web.

Size Reports

Another feature useful for creating optimized Shockwave Flash movies is the Movie Size Report. Generate reports by checking Generate Size report in the Export Shockwave Flash dialog box. When you check Generate Size Report, Flash saves a text file with the Shockwave Flash file that details the amount of memory used for each frame, scene, symbol, bitmap, sound, and font outline in the movie file. When you open the report as a text file, Movie Report appears in the title bar.

While you can use the Size Report to track down a problem with a specific movie, it is also useful before you create your movies to understand how Flash stores shapes, symbols, and sounds. You can plan how to make files smaller and more efficient before you draw a single curve. To use the report in this way, it's necessary to know how the files are put together.

The basic unit of a vector graphic is a single curve. (A straight line drawn with the pencil tool has one curve, a circle has eight.) Data for each curve in a frame requires a certain amount of file space, as does the data for any stroke applied to the curve, and any fill applied to a shape.

Each movie frame also requires a small amount of file space. Key frames store data for objects drawn on the canvas layer or grouped as overlays (see Figure 10.3).

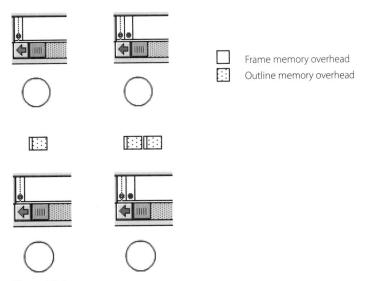

☐ Frame memory overhead
⬚ Outline memory overhead

Figure 10.3
Two key frames that contain the same artwork not saved as a symbol (right), use roughly twice the amount of memory as a single key frame with the same artwork (left), or two key frames using the same artwork saved as a symbol.

Flash stores the data for a symbol in the first key frame in which the symbol appears. Once you have saved the data for a symbol in the file, the key frames in which the symbol appears need to store only information about the position, scaling, rotation, etc. of the symbol. Flash stores animated symbol data in the same way it stores frame-by-frame animation.

Bitmaps are stored in the movie file in a similar manner to symbols, as is text data. Flash stores sound in two ways. Event sounds are stored like symbols, appearing in a single frame, and available thereafter. Flash saves streaming sounds piece by piece in each frame they appear, and then they are reconstituted into a single audio stream as each piece plays back.

The following lines are from a Movie Report generated by saving the file *exer10c.fla* as a Shockwave Flash file (some of the report was deleted to show only the significant portions).

```
Movie Report
- - - - - - - - - - - -

Frame #  Frame Bytes Total Bytes  Page
- - - - - - -  - - - - - - - - - - - -  - - - - - - - - - - - -  - - - -
 * 1        174          174         Scene 1
   2        157          331         2
   3        155          486         3
   4        150          636         4
 * 5        145          781         5
   6        143          924         6
   7        137          1061        7
   8        133          1194        8
   9        116          1310        9
 * 10       2            1312        10
   11       2            1314        11
   12       2            1316        12
   13       513          1829        13
   14       19           1848        14
. . .
 * 20       19           1962        20
   21       24           1986        21
. . .
   26       24           2106        26
   27       19           2125        27
. . .
 * 31       19           2201        31
. . .
 * 35       19           2277        35
   36       2            2279        36
. . .
   46       2            2299        46
   47       8            2307        47
Symbol               Shape Bytes  Text Bytes
- - - - - -              - - - - - - - - - - -  - - - - - - - - - -
Venutian Cup         1119         0
x Part-
Venutian Guy         500          0
```

Frames 1 to 9 of the Size Report show between 116 and 174 bytes used for each frame; this represents the portion of the animation in which the top of the cup rotates counter-clockwise. In the timeline, each of those frames is a key frame in the Cup layer.

Frames 10 to 12 require only 2 bytes of storage; no changes occur in those frames of the timeline, in either layer.

Frame 13 appears to have no changes onscreen, but the Size Report indicates that it requires 513 bytes of storage capacity. This marks the first key frame in which the venutian guy layer has artwork in it. This artwork hides behind the bottom of the cup.

Frames 14 to 27, only need 19 to 24 bytes of memory to handle the tweening anima-tion of the venutian guy layer.

Figure 10.4 shows significant frames of the movie (marked by asterisks in the Size Report). Figure 10.5 displays the timeline of the symbol used in the animation.

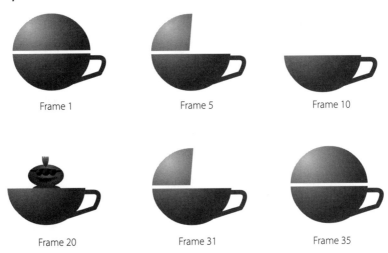

Frame 1   Frame 5   Frame 10

Frame 20   Frame 31   Frame 35

Figure 10.4
Significant frames from the Venutian Cup movie displayed.

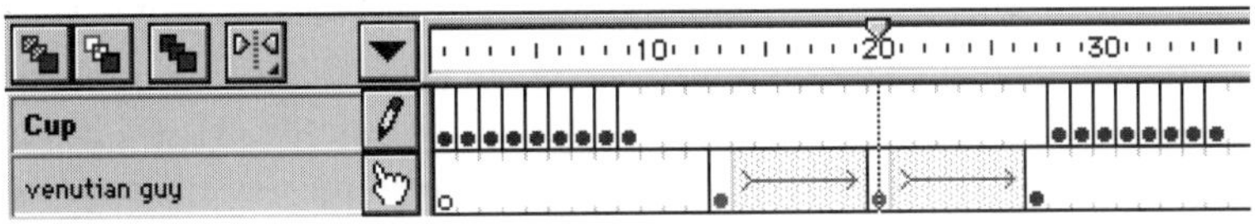

Figure 10.5
The timeline of the Venutian Cup symbol.

The total number of bytes used for this animation is 2307. You can improve on that number. A quick examination of the Size Report can help a Flash developer understand what he can do to make the file smaller.

In the case of this movie, the obvious place to examine for savings is in the first 9 frames. The other frames only require between 2 and 24 bytes each, except for frame 13 where the artwork for the venutian guy first appears.

The change that takes place in frames 1 to 9 is the opening of the top half of the cup. In the original version of the symbol, the shape used for the cup is modified in each of the key frames. The result is a new set of outlines saved for the cup in every key frame.

The bottom half of the cup doesn't change, however; so there's no reason to resave it. By creating a new layer and cutting and pasting the bottom of the cup into the first frame of the new layer (see Figure 10.6), you can gain a small savings in file size. The difference in the exported Shockwave Flash file is only about 100 bytes, not a significant difference.

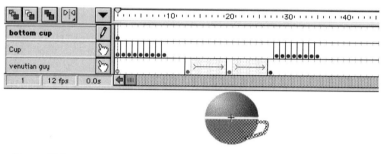

Figure 10.6
The bottom half of the cup copied to its own layer makes a small difference in the amount of data stored in each key frame of the "Cup" layer.

Key frames 28 to 25 of the "Cup" layer are duplicates of those in frames 1 to 8, with the sequence reversed. Flash can keep track of that fact. And if no changes are made to the outlines in those key frames, the movie refers to the data for the original frames when needed. Even small changes made to the outlines in those frames increases the bytes needed to store data for those frames.

You can get more substantial savings by animating the top of the cup differently. This animation consists of eight separate circular wedges, ranging from a complete half-circle in frame 1 (and frame 35) to a thin sliver in frame 8 (and frame 28). Store each of those wedges in the file with the outline and fill data for the shape. The top half of the cup, however, doesn't actually move. You could mask part of the top of the cup to hide it, rather than create a new shape in every key frame.

Figure 10.7 shows how you can create the same animation by putting a layer between the one that contains the bottom of the cup and the one that contains the top. Place a simple white rectangle shape on this layer and rotate the rectangle. (The white rectangle is shaded gray for clarity.) Making the rectangle a symbol produces further savings in file size.

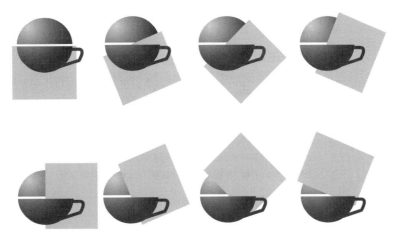

Figure 10.7
Create the animation for the top of the cup by placing a rotating box over it.

This technique can't be used in every case. It works in this case because the cup doesn't appear over other shapes.

To create the same effect:

1. Create another layer in front of the layer with the top of the cup, and name it **white rect**.

2. Draw a rectangle slightly wider than the cup and just a little taller than the top half of the cup and position it as shown in the first image of Figure 10.7. Use the background color for a fill, and then create a symbol from the rectangle.

3. Choose **Modify > Transform > Edit Center** from the menu and move the crosshair icon representing the center of the shape to the middle of the top edge of the rectangle (see Figure 10.8). A rotating shape rotates around its center point.

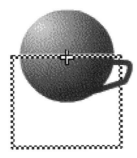

Figure 10.8
Edit the center of the symbol to determine the point the rectangle revolves around.

4. Create a key frame in frame 35, for the final position of the rectangle. Duplicate its position in frame 1,

5. Insert a key frame at frame 9, and then rotate the white rectangle 180° counter-clockwise. This completely hides the top of the cup.

6. Insert another key frame at frame 28, duplicating frame 9 and the rotated rectangle.

7. Tween the sequences of frames beginning in frame 1 and frame 28 in the "white rect" layer (see Figure 10.9).

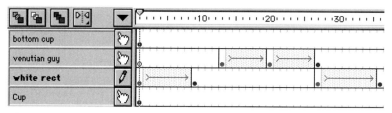

Figure 10.9
The completed timeline of the revised symbol.

8. To complete the effect, move the "venutian guy" layer in front of the "Cup" and "white rect" layers to prevent the rectangle from obscuring it.

This version of the movie uses each set of outlines only once: the bottom of the cup, top of the cup, and rectangle appear in frame 1; the venutian guy's outline appears in frame 13. Flash performs the animation through transformations applied to symbols, not by the direct manipulation of outlines. The Size Report for this movie looks like this:

```
Movie Report
- - - - - - - - - - - -
Frame #  Frame Bytes  Total Bytes  Page
- - - - - - -  - - - - - - - - - - -  - - - - - - - - - - -  - - - -
      1  271          271          Scene 1
      2  28           299          2
      3  29           328          3
      4  28           356          4
      5  27           383          5
      6  28           411          6
      7  29           440          7
      8  28           468          8
      9  27           495          9
     10  2            497          10
     11  2            499          11
     12  2            501          12
     13  513          1014         13
     14  19           1033         14
    ...
     19  19           1128         19
     20  19           1147         20
     21  24           1171         21
    ...
     26  24           1291         26
     27  19           1310         27
     28  28           1338         28
     29  29           1367         29
     30  28           1395         30
     31  28           1423         31
     32  28           1451         32
     33  29           1480         33
     34  29           1509         34
     35  28           1537         35
     36  19           1556         36
     37  2            1558         37
    ...
     46  2            1576         46
```

```
Symbol           Shape Bytes  Text Bytes
- - - - - -      - - - - - - - - - - -  - - - - - - - - - -
Venutian Cup     173          0
white rect       37           0
x Part-
Venutian Guy     500          0
```

This version of the movie is 1576 bytes, only 68 percent of the original size. It requires a bit more storage in frame 1, to accommodate the overhead of the extra layers; but handling the animation with symbols and tweening rather than individual key frames makes for a significant reduction in movie size.

In addition to the frame-by-frame information examined earlier, movie Size Reports include a standard set of information apart from the frame-by-frame information examined above. The following example covers the first 15 frames of a 400-frame movie, the timeline of which appears in Figure 10.10.

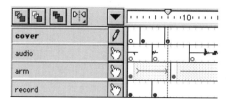

Figure 10.10
The timeline showing the first 14 frames of a 400-frame movie.

The movie contains three sounds (two event sounds and a streaming sound), a bitmap, and four symbols. This movie was set to play at 3 frames per second. A picture of the Shockwave Flash movie structure emerges when you examine the timeline (see Figure 10.10 above) and the movie Size Report together.

```
Movie Report
- - - - - - - - - - - -

Frame#¹        Frame Bytes²   Total Bytes³   Page⁴
- - - - - - -  - - - - - - - - - -  - - - - - - - - - -  - - - -
1              4137           4137           Scene 1
2              28             4165           2
```

Frame 1 contains artwork in the "arm" and "record" layers in the timeline these are represented by the filled circles indicating key frames. There is also a sound in the first frame of the "audio" layer. The sound ("Latch Slide 2") accounts for most of the data stored in the frame. Even through the event sound extends through a couple of frames, its data is stored in the first frame in which it appears. No changes occur in Frame 2, except for the tweening in the "arm" layer. This needs only 28 bytes.

---

[1] Frame number; [2] bytes used for that frame; [3] total bytes used in the movie up to and including this frame; and [4] scene number when new scene appears, frame number during a scene.

Frame #	Frame Bytes	Total Bytes	Page
3	4230	8395	3

The bitmap image in the "cover" layer appears at Frame 3. At 4136 bytes, it takes up most of that frame's byte allotment.

4	28	8423	4

Frame 4 is another frame in which nothing much is added to the movie.

5	957	9380	5

The other sound, Safe Tumbler 1, takes up most of the 957 bytes in frame 5.

6	54	9434	6
7	526	9960	7

The text (504 bytes) appears in frame 7. At this point, all of the items in the movie are loaded except for the streaming sound. Then, a couple of frames go by with just the animation of the "arm" layer and the "record" symbol.

8	54	10014	8
9	54	10068	9
10	2377	12445	10

Frame 10 shows the beginning of the streaming sound (which does not appear with the rest of the sounds in the report). At the chosen compression level, the movie averages about 2.4K per second (generally a sustainable rate on a full-speed 28.8K modem connection).

11	2360	14805	11
12	2360	17165	12
13	2360	19525	13
14	4707	24232	14

Occasionally, the movie packages extra sound data into a single frame, as in frame 14, which is slightly over twice the size of the other frames. If the sound had been placed as an event sound, the data for the entire sound would have been stored in a single frame, potentially stalling the movie.

15	2355	26587	15

...

The Page data section of the Size Report shows the size of data stored directly with the frames of each scene. Flash stores any artwork that isn't part of a symbol as part of the scene data. No lines or shapes have been drawn directly in the scene, but a line of text appears in frame 7 of the "cover" layer, so the value for the Scene is 48 bytes. Embedded Objects track the data needed for the embedded objects. In this movie there are two embedded objects, the two event sounds.

Page	Shape Bytes	Text Bytes
Scene 1	0	48
Embedded Objects	0	2

The Symbol section contains the list of symbols appearing in the movie's Library. During export, Flash does not save any unused symbol in the Library. In this movie, "almost" and "safari" were not used, so their sizes do not display. None of the symbols have any text, so there are no values listed under text bytes.

Symbol	Shape Bytes	Text Bytes
almost	0	0
arm	121	0
record	7008	0
safari	0	0

The Bitmaps section lists the bitmaps used in the movie. Bitmaps are shown by their name in the Library list, displayed with the number of bytes after compression, the number of bytes they originally required, and the JPEG quality level with which they were compressed.

Bitmap	Compressed	Original	Compression
cursefront.jpg	4136	102400	JPEG Quality=20
Stream sound:	11KHz	Mono,	5-bit ADPCM
Event sounds:	11KHz	Mono,	2-bit ADPCM

Data on sounds appears in the next section of the report. The report indicates the compression levels set in the Export Shockwave Flash dialog box, and then lists each event sound individually, with the number of bytes after compression and the compression quality for each.

Sound Name	Bytes	Format
Safe Tumbler 1	2276	11kHz Mono, 5-bit ADPCM
Latch Slide 2	3998	11kHz Mono, 5-bit ADPCM

The data for embedded font characters appears in the last section. Here embedded fonts display by name, the number of bytes used by these characters, and the actual characters stored in the file are listed. In the example, the words "99th Wave" appear in the movie, but "9" only appears once in the list of embedded characters because Flash can use the same outline for the character twice.

Font Name	Bytes	Characters
Kino MT	407	9Waehtv

Moving On...

Designing Flash movies is both an art and a science. Most of this book focuses on the art, but hopefully this chapter has encouraged an analytical look at the craft of designing Flash movies to fit different delivery methods.

Now it's back to the art side. The next chapter discusses strategies for integrating Flash into web sites.

CHAPTER 11

Flash Sites

Producing Flash movies for

a web site can have its challenges.

By its very nature, all multimedia takes more time to create and play than simple HTML documents. In a Flash movie, things change from moment to moment, so it needs more graphic images. Sound needs to be coordinated with the movie. Buttons must be created and actions assigned, etc. Maintaining a site with many Flash movies requires more work than putting an HTML page on a server.

Again, planning is a key ingredient to managing a Flash site (as with any site!). This chapter describes how to integrate Flash into web sites, and examines some issues designers should know when planning Flash sites.

What you'll learn...

Integrating Flash into a web site

What a webmaster needs to know about Flash

Making Flash sites friendly to the unFlashed

Once you become a Flash enthusiast, you're ready to turn everything on your site into Shockwave Flash movies. But Flash isn't always the best vehicle for every message. Moreover, a single, great interactive Flash movie can be more rewarding to visitors than having everything on the site rendered in anti-aliased text, no matter how pretty it looks.

How much Flash to use, of course, depends on your goals. Some sites might use a single Flash movie on its entry page, providing an animated welcome. Others might incorporate Flash into every aspect of the site, using movies for navigational bars, content, advertising banners, etc.

Several factors need to be considered as you determine how much of a site to convert to Flash movies:

- How much time will it take to create the Flash movies?

- How much of the site will be accessible to users who don't have Flash?

- How closely will the movies be integrated with the content?

There are a number of reasons why Flash movies usually take longer to produce than static HTML pages—even well-designed HTML pages. Although Flash movies allow precise, resizable layouts, they typically have more interactivity than the static page. Button rollovers, animated objects, user interaction, and actions require more artwork, planning, and just plain work to put together than static images and text.

So a Flash designer (or project manager, in a larger team) needs to balance how much time to devote to Flash movies and how much time to devote to other elements. Will every page or frame carry a little bit of Flash content? Or will Flash be used in large dollops at significant places within the site?

When starting out, it's probably best to experiment to get determine the ratio between what you can do without multimedia and what you can do with Flash. As you increase your use of Flash, the site's basic art elements are added to Flash libraries, user familiarity increases, and the ratio will weigh more and more in Flash's favor.

Flash for the unflashed

The truth must be told. Not all users have installed the Flash Player in their browser—yet. Users who avoid plug-ins, who have older browsers, or who browse the Web with Unix computers or PDAs (Personal Digital Assistants, like the Newton) don't have the capability to see Flash movies. If you create an entire site with Flash, those people will see either the broken plug-in icon or an empty page.

How far to go in the direction of providing content for the multitude of options is based largely on availability and the competence of the person maintaining the site. If they simply put up a batch of Flash movies and a page saying "Don't pass here unless you have Flash," they only have to worry about the time it takes to make Flash movies. If they need to show something to other users, however, they need not only the Flash movies, but something for other people to see.

Appendix E, "Hiding Broken Plug-in Icons," shows one method for displaying Flash movies to people who have the Player installed, and displaying something else to other viewers. In October, 1997, Macromedia released Aftershock, a utility for public beta-testing, which automates the process of making decisions about which groups of people see the movies, and what the rest of the world sees instead. It automatically builds the `<OBJECT>` and `<EMBED>` tags for Shockwave Flash movies, and presents a graphical interface for setting the options for those tags. Aftershock also incorporates the code for the Flash Java Player, which plays Flash movies on systems without the plug-in or ActiveX control.

NOTE *The beta version of the Aftershock utility can create animated or static GIF files from selected frames of a Shockwave movie, and export a client-side image map file for browsers that don't support Flash.*

Flash integration

Aside from how much Flash to use, how those movies work with each other and the HTML portion of the site is another issue. Do all of the site's links get incorporated into a single Flash navigation bar? Should all the text appear in Flash movies so that it looks really good?

Using Flash as the only navigational tool prevents search engines like Excite, Yahoo, or Altavista from indexing some sections of the site. This is because some pages link only to actions, which the search engines can't read. Similarly, if the text in a Flash movie doesn't exist outside the Flash movie, it can't be indexed. So pages created entirely in Flash don't appear in the databases of the search engines.

NOTE *This dilemma isn't limited to Flash. A search engine also can't read words and URLs embedded in any non-text object (e.g., Java applets, streaming digital video, even GIF and JPEG images).*

If a site is updated frequently, updating the links in a single Flash navigation bar can be more of a task than originally anticipated.

This is an area where planning how much time you will devote to Flashing the site, and how non-Flash viewers see the site makes a difference. By making a site friendly to those with Flash and to those with their image loading turned off, you maintain maximum accessibilty to search engines.

There isn't a fast way to export all the text and URLs in a Flash movie—yet. (The beta version of Aftershock does have an option to export URLs, however.) If a movie has numerous text objects that haven't been broken apart, they can be copied and pasted into a text file. Although this is a daunting task if there are many of them.

To make sure that search engines can find words that appear in Flash movies, index terms can be added to the first portion of the HTML document in which the page appears. The <META> tag has a number of uses; one is to provide indexing information about items which would be unindexed otherwise. The <META> tag goes between the <HEAD> tag and its delimiter. In this example, the words *21st century*, and *living* are added to a the top of an HTML document, just after the <TITLE> tag, which controls the text displayed in the window bar. The viewer doesn't see the index words unless the source HTML for the page is viewed.

```
<HEAD>
  <TITLE>Atomic  City Apartment Home Page</TITLE>
  <META NAME="keywords"
       CONTENT="21st century living">
</HEAD>
```

If alternate text versions of the site are provided for those without Flash, there's no need for this extra step.

Remember that when it comes time to make changes to a movie, if you change the movie's URL, or a whole section of the site moves to a new location, there's no fast and easy method to update all of the movie's URLs. Each frame or button action needs to be individually edited, and it can be surprisingly easy to miss one.

Setting Up the Server

When setting up a web site, make sure that the server can transmit movies correctly. If the server is not configured to serve Flash movies, the movie usually appears in the browser as garbled text. A MIME-type setting identifies a file to a browser as a Shockwave Flash movie. (See Appendix A, "Configuring a Web Server to Serve Flash Movies," for specific information on setting up web servers and the Shockwave Flash MIME type.)

If, for some reason, you can't configure the server to serve Flash movies, try adding the parameter `TYPE="application/x-shockwave-flash"` to the `<EMBED>` tag of an HTML document (see Chapter 8, "Actions," for specifics about the parameters of the `<EMBED>` tag). Some browsers interpret the parameter's information to replace the default MIME type sent from the server.

Uploading Files to the Server

Once the server is configured and HTML and Shockwave Flash files are ready to add to a web site, you must get the files from the computer where you created them to the server (a process typically called *uploading*). For users who have physical server access, uploading files is as simple as copying files to the right folder on the machine where the server runs.

This is usually accomplished via a FTP (File Transfer Protocol) client. There are a number of different tools you can use to send files to an FTP server, including most recent versions of web browsers. By typing in a FTP URL (rather than an HTTP URL) as a destination for the browser, you can send files to the FTP server by dragging them from the desktop into the browser window.

To open a connection to an FTP server from Netscape Navigator:

1. Select **File > Open Location** to display the Open Location dialog box.

2. In the Open Location field, enter an address to an FTP server in the form:
   ftp://name:password@ftp.surftrio.com/movies/
   Replace the name, password, and FTP address with the appropriate settings for your server.

NOTE *FTP users need to ensure that they transfer files in binary— rather than ASCII—format. Most FTP clients have this option in their preferences.*

The Payoff

The payoff for creating sites with Flash is that they present a far more interactive experience—with less work—than any other web authoring tool available. Because Flash is a very visual tool, it appeals to people who can draw and design with the computer more than the typical "programmer-oriented" tools.

Nevertheless, the Flash user (and everyone else) needs to keep real-world constraints in mind when designing a site. Start small with a single movie on a page, and build from that.

The world of the Web is still in its infancy, even compared to other forms of multimedia. But its tools are still developing, so don't be surprised if you find you've bitten off more than can be safely chewed in Flash. Spit some of it out, and concentrate on making the remaining portion truly Flashy.

Moving On...

How is Flash being used on the Web? What types of projects have used Flash and what can you tell about them just from looking? Come along for a visit to some Flash sites that have caught the eyes of the folks at Macromedia!

CHAPTER 12

Flash Examples

One way to figure out what

you might want to do with Flash is to look at what other people have already done, with an eye to examining not just what it looks like but how it was done.

This chapter showcases a variety of approaches to Flash movies. We'll examine their integration with the Web and puzzle out the techniques their creators employed. The movies themselves span a gamut from simple linear presentations to complex interactive games.

Think of these as signposts marking notable Flash sites (and check out others available at this book's companion web site). Then go out and blaze new trails into the world of multimedia, adding to your own creativity and experiences, and abilities.

Happy Flashing!

Macromedia, Inc.

URL: http://www.macromedia.com/

Naturally, one of the first web sites to be extensively Flashed was Macromedia's own. Macromedia's use of Flash falls into two categories: navigational and informational. The image above is from Macromedia's Shockzone (http://www.macromedia.com/shockzone/), an area dedicated to the networked Shockwave technologies (including Flash, Director, Authorware, Freehand, and xRes).

The site's navigational aspect can be seen in the screenshot at the bottom of the image. This navigation bar is enclosed in a separate frame of an HTML frameset and appears throughout the Shockzone area, providing quick access to the main level of the Macromedia site (the "up arrow" or "home" symbol at the left), as well as to the major subsections of the Shockzone itself. Other navigational elements are used in different portions of the site. The movie itself is simple, with button rollovers indicating the current user choice.

The informational content appears in the center portion of the screen, and presents a long, self-running loop featuring current hot topics at the site. These informational movies link directly to other portions of the site and generally contain one or two minutes of content. The movie showing in the window above is less than 40K.

Macromedia uses a combination of scripting and HTML techniques to provide alternate images to browsers that don't have the Flash player installed.

The Microsoft Network

URL: http://www.msn.com/

The Microsoft Network (MSN) was an early adopter of Flash technology, and its producers have used it extensively on their site. The image above is from MSN's On Stage area, where continuous features of the network display.

Two navigational Flash movies are seen in the screenshot. The main navigation bar for the MSN site appears at the top of the screen in a separate frame. It controls two frames below that divide each subsection's navigation bar (at left) from its content (on the right).

As with the Macromedia site, a large informational movie loop plays while the viewer decides which selection to choose from the navigation bars.

MSN requires the Flash Player to view the site, and does not provide any alternate images.

WebTV Networks, Inc.

URL: http://www.webtv.com/

WebTV supports the Flash technology. Its consumer web-browser platform uses Flash because of its limited memory requirements and capability to provide compelling animation without extensive programming.

The WebTV site uses Flash mainly for informational content. In the screenshot, navigational elements at the top and left are animated using JavaScript and GIF images, while the looping movie in the middle of the screen uses Flash. Flash provides longer, smoother animations than those possible using GIF or any other bitmap-image animation.

WebTV uses a server-side detection mechanism to decide whether Flash or bitmap versions of the site display.

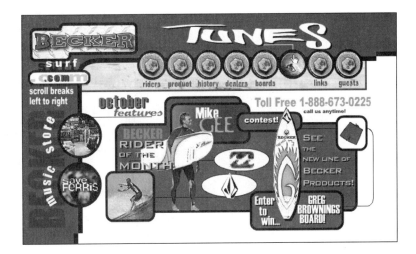

Becker Surf

URL: http://www.beckersurf.com/

The Becker Surf web site uses Flash exclusively to deliver its message about surf boards, shorts, shirts, and hats. Each page is a single Flash movie that incorporates navigation, informational material, and rollovers for highlights. The entire movie in the screenshot is a 70K Shockwave Flash movie.

The Becker Surf movie includes a navigational bar with rollover buttons along the top of the screen. Virtually every item that the cursor moves across causes a highlight to appear on screen.

The Becker Surf site is available only to viewers with Flash, and it uses no detection scripts. The entry page to the site informs visitors that the Flash Player is required.

Hunterkillerdog

URL: http://www.hunterkillerdog.com/

The Hunterkillerdog site is another example of Flash used as an interface to the Web. The interface was created entirely as a Flash movie, with rollover buttons and an animated loop playing in the screen's main portion. The screenshot is from the site's main menu area.

Hunterkillerdog uses Flash throughout the site for navigational bars and graphics. The site also employs standard HTML and animated GIFs.

An informational page displays to let viewers know that the site uses Flash.

Art Gallery of Ontario Edvard Munch Web Project

URL: http://www.ago.net/

The Edvard Munch Web Project in the Archives of the Art Gallery of Ontario contains information about and artwork by the painter of the famous "Scream." Flash is the primary interface to the site, which displays inside the large frame of an HTML frameset.

The Munch site contains little animation once the visitor enters, but it is very deep, with many areas to explore.

The site informs visitors that they need the Flash Player to see the content. It uses no detection mechanism.

Spumco's "The Goddamn George Liquor Program"

URL: http://www.spumco.com/

While the Flash movies on the Spumco site aren't interactive, they are marvelous—and sometimes disgusting—examples of the animation quality possible with Flash graphics. Created by the studio that originated the "Ren & Stimpy" cartoon series, "The Goddamn George Liquor Program" episodes are about 5 minutes long. Each episode is a single Flash movie approximately 600K, and includes a cheery soundtrack.

The bulk of the Spumco site is made up of standard HTML and bitmap images, but the cartoons push the quality of web animation—not to mention good taste—to the limits.

Spumco advises viewers to download the Flash Player before viewing their movies. The site does not use a detection script.

Hide Needs Sake

URL: http://www.visual-shock.com/game.html

Games are not easy to write in Flash. An interactive Flash movie needs to contain at least one frame for every possible action outcome. Even for a simple game like tic-tac-toe, the possible results of each turn run into the thousands. For a game like chess, the variations are in the billions. That's a lot of frames.

With realistic goals and a little innovation, games like "Hide Needs Sake" can be created with Flash. In this game, the player clicks on a target—hopefully the right one, or Hide smacks them in the face. Each correct click takes the player to a new level, while any wrong click stops the game. Five correct target clicks win the game. Each correct click takes the player to a new set of frames (or a new scene), effectively keeping track of the number of correct clicks. Keeping track of the incorrect clicks would make the movie much more complex.

"Hide Needs Sake" plays only with the Flash Player and does not use a detection script.

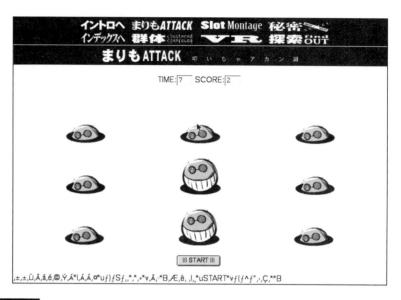

URL: http://www.ultra-q.co.jp/SWF/top.htm

Perhaps the most amazing example of complex interaction between Flash and browser scripting languages comes from Japan's Aegagropila World, which features a heavily-Flashed site that uses the programmability of JavaScript and VBScript to create complex games.

The site features a variety of grid-based games. It uses multiple Flash movies for the graphics and browser scripting to keep track of the scoring and other game information. In the screenshot, a navigation bar occupies the top frame of the browser, the game occupies the middle frame, and some text occupies the bottom frame.

The TIME and SCORE counters above the game are HTML fields, and the START button below is an HTML button. The START button sends a message to a browser script to start the timer, and as the little balls pop out of their holes you try to hit them. Each ball is a separate movie, which sends a message to the browser script if it's hit while out of its hole.

Browser script communication with embedded objects isn't an entirely reliable technology yet, but this type of project points toward the truly amazing capabilities of Macromedia Flash.

Configuring a Web Server to Serve Shockwave Flash Movies

To deliver Shockwave Flash

movies on a web page via a web server (versus opening them directly from a CD-ROM, diskette, or hard drive), you need to configure the server to properly serve the files.

In addition to the actual data for an HTML file, bitmap image, or Shockwave Flash movie, the server must first send to the browser information about the type of file it is sending. This information is known as the MIME (Multipart Internet Mail Exchange) type. The browser uses it to determine how to interpret the data for the file. In the case of a Shockwave Flash movie, a browser with the Shockwave Flash Player installed (as a plug-in or ActiveX object) recognizes the MIME type and engages the Player to display the Shockwave Flash movie.

Web servers typically use the extension appended to a file's name to determine which MIME type designation to use. A Shockwave Flash file intended for use on the Web should always have the .swf extension appended to its file name. The Flash program automatically appends the proper extension when you export a Shockwave Flash file.

TIP *Macintosh users can use any file name for files intended for delivery by local disks or networks. They should, however, avoid the practice of using spaces or slashes (/) in Shockwave Flash file names destined for web sites. This rule holds true for all files destined for the web, not just Shockwave Flash files.*

The actual MIME type information sent from a server is a pair of words that describe the general type of data it is sending, as well as the specific format of the file. The two terms are separated by the slash (/) character (e.g., text/html).

To serve Shockwave Flash files, the server should have the following additions made to its MIME type configuration file:

	Flash 2.0	*Flash 1.0 & FutureSplash Animator*
File Extension	.swf	.spl
MIME Type	application/ x-shockwave-flash	application/futuresplash
Action (Macintosh servers)	BINARY	BINARY
File Type (Macintosh servers)	SWFL	TEXT
File Creator (Macintosh servers)	SWF2	FSPL

Each server has its own method for adding MIME type configurations. These methods range from editing a text file to a web-based administration interface. See the documentation for your server if you're entering MIME type configurations yourself. The essential task is to associate the extension with the proper MIME type.

MIME type information for Flash 1.0 movies is presented here for compatibility with older movies and Flash 2.0 movies exported in the FutureSplash Player format. MIME type information is case-sensitive, and should appear in lower-case characters. The File Type and Creator information for Macintosh servers is also case-sensitive—you should enter it exactly as it appears.

NOTE *The File Type and Creator information shown for Macintosh servers uses an asterisk [*] wild card character instead of the data shown in the Flash manual. Files created by a Macintosh application contain information about what type of data the file contains (File Type), and which application created the files (File Creator), which is not dependent on the file name extension. Macintosh servers can use File Type and Creator information to distinguish between different types of files with the same extensions and supply the proper MIME type. Because files created on other operating systems do not save File Type and Creator data, Macintosh servers set to look for specific File Type and Creator data, in addition to the file name extension, might not supply the proper MIME type when it serves the file.*

Transmission Speed

The speed at which a

Shockwave Flash movie downloads
from a web server depends on a number
of factors: the data-delivery capabilities of the user's
connection to the Internet, the speed of the server
connection, the amount of traffic at the server, and
traffic at any or all points between the user and the
server. The maximum possible speed—assuming a
good connection between user and server—is determined by the slowest connection in its data flow. The
size of a Shockwave Flash movie should take into
account the amount of time you expect a user to wait
for part or all of the movie to download.

The following table displays the speed (in K per
second) at which files open from disks or download
from the Internet.

Download Speeds					
User Connection	*Server Connection*				
	14.4K modem	**28.2K modem**	**ISDN (single-channel)**	**T-1 (Full)**	**N/A**
14.4K modem	1K/sec	1K/sec	1K/sec	1K/sec	—
28.8K modem	1K/sec	3–4K/sec	3–4K/sec	3–4K/sec	—
ISDN (single-channel)	1K/sec	3–4K/sec	10–12K/sec	10–12K/sec	—
T-1 (Full)	1K/sec	3–4K/sec	10–12K/sec	1,500K/sec	—
2x CD-ROM	—	—	—	—	300K/sec
12x CD-ROM	—	—	—	—	3,600K/sec
Ethernet	—	—	—	—	approx. 10,000K/sec
SCSI hard drive	—	—	—	—	20,000–40,000K/sec

\<OBJECT>/
\<EMBED>
Tag References

The following format

accommodates the \<OBJECT> tag
used by ActiveX-enabled versions of the
Microsoft Internet Explorer browser, and the \<EMBED>
tag used by plug-in-enabled Netscape Navigator browsers
and browsers without ActiveX or plug-in capabilities.
Use the formats presented below to insert a Shockwave
Flash movie into a web page. You need to change the
text displayed in bold characters for each movie. See
the following \<OBJECT> and \<EMBED> charts, for the
particulars of each parameter.

```
                    classid="clsid:D27CDB6E-AE6D-11cf-96B8-444553540000"
                    codebase="swflash.cab#version=2,0,0,0"
                    ID="movie" Width=100% Height=120>
            <PARAM NAME="Movie" VALUE="movie.swf">//
            <PARAM NAME="Loop" Value="True">
            <PARAM NAME="Play" Value="True">
            <PARAM NAME="BGColor" Value="ffffff">
            <PARAM NAME="Quality" Value="AutoLow">
            <PARAM NAME="Scale" Value="ShowAll">
            <PARAM NAME="SALign" Value="L">
            <PARAM NAME="Base" Value="http://www.server.com/base/">
            <PARAM NAME="Menu" Value="True">
            <EMBED SRC="movie.swf" WIDTH=100% HEIGHT=130
              NAME="movie" LOOP="True" PLAY="True" BGCOLOR="ffffff"
              QUALITY="AutoLow" SCALE="ShowAll" SALIGN="L"
              BASE="http://www.server.com/base/" MENU="True"
              PLUGINSPAGE="http://www.macromedia.com/shockwave/
            download/index.cgi?P1_Prod_Version=ShockwaveFlash2">
            </OBJECT>
            <NOEMBED>
              <IMG src="alternate.gif" width=100% height=120>
            //HTML between the <NOEMBED> tags is displayed by
            //browsers without the capability to use <OBJECT>
            //or <EMBED> tags.
            </NOEMBED>
```

<OBJECT> and <EMBED> Tag Parameters

<OBJECT>	*<EMBED>*	*Function*	*Value*
Movie	SRC	Provides URL for Shockwave Flash movie.	Can be a complete URL (beginning with "<://"), an absolute URL (beginning with "/"), or a relative URL (beginning with an alphanumeric character).
Width	WIDTH	Determines width of movie window in browser frame.	Can specify numeric value indicating pixels, or a percentage relative to the frame.
Height	HEIGHT	Determines height of movie window in browser frame.	Can specify numeric value indicating pixels, or a percentage relative to the frame.
classid, codebase	pluginspage*	Provides URL and information for download of Shockwave Flash ActiveX control or plug-in.	
ID*	MAYSCRIPT NAME*	Identifies the movie for access with browser scripting.	Use the name assigned as a value for this parameter in JavaScript and VBScript commands and functions; if used with the <EMBED> tag, needs to have an accompanying MAYSCRIPT parameter.
Play*	PLAY*	Controls automatic play of the movie.	Can be **True** or **False. True** = movie begins playing after first frame loads (default). **False** = movie stops at first frame.
Loop*	LOOP*	Controls action of movie after it reaches last frame.	Can be **True** or **False. True** = movie returns to first frame after reaching last frame (default). **False** = movie stops at last frame.

<OBJECT>	<EMBED>	Function	Value
Quality*	QUALITY*	Controls display quality of movie.	Can be **AutoLow, Low, High,** and **AutoHigh. AutoLow** = movie begins play with anti-aliasing off; then turns anti-aliasing on if Player supports it (default for multiframe movies). **Low** = movie plays with antialiasing off; **High** = movie plays with anti-aliasing on (default for single-frame movies); **AutoHigh** (default) = movie begins play with anti-aliasing on; then turns anti-aliasing off if the computer's processing capabilities can't match the desired frame rate (set in Movie Properties dialog box).
BGColor*	BGCOLOR*	Controls the color of the movie background (can override the color assigned to the movie background in the Movie Properties dialog box).	Can be a six-digit hexadecimal value for red, green, and blue components in the form **rrggbb**. Each digit belongs to the sequence **0123456789abcdef**. The value 000000 represents black, ffffff represents white. Values composed entirely of digits from the sequence **0369cf** represent "browser-safe" colors from the 216-color browser palette.

<OBJECT> and <EMBED> Tag Parameters (continued)			
<OBJECT>	*<EMBED>*	*Function*	*Value*
Scale*	SCALE*	Controls how the movie resizes to fit the allocated browser space.	Can be **ShowAll, No Border, Exact Fit. ShowAll** = the entire movie is visible in the specified area. Maintains the width and height proportions of the original movie. No distortion occurs. Borders might appear on two sides of the movie. This is the default value (see Figure C.1). **NoBorder** = scales the movie proportionally so it fills the entire movie window (see Figure C.1). **ExactFit** = scales the movie non-proportionally so it fills the entire movie window (see Figure C.1.).
SAlign*	SALIGN*	Determines placement of the movie within the movie window if it does not completely fill the window (e.g., Scale= SHOWALL). (See Figure C.2.)	Values can be **T, B, L, R, TL, TR, BL,** and **BR. T** = aligns movie centered horizontally on top edge of movie window (default). **B** = aligns movie centered horizontally on bottom edge of movie window. **L** = aligns movie centered vertically on left edge of movie window. **R** = aligns movie centered vertically on right edge of movie window. **TL** = aligns top left corner of movie with top left corner of movie window. **TR** = aligns top right corner of movie with top right corner of movie window. **BL** = aligns bottom left corner of movie with bottom left corner of movie window. **BR** = aligns bottom right corner of movie with bottom right corner of movie window.

<OBJECT> and <EMBED> Tag Parameters (continued)

<OBJECT>	*<EMBED>*	*Function*	*Value*
Base*	BASE*	Establishes a reference address for relative URLs in the movie.	Value is a URL. The default reference URL is the directory of the HTML document in which you have embedded the Shockwave movie, or the directory of the Shockwave movie itself, if it is addressed directly.
Menu*	MENU*	Controls the options available on the pop-up menu available in the browser. (Clicking on a movie with the right mouse button in Windows, or clicking the mouse while holding down the Control button on the Macintosh, makes the pop-up menu appear.)	Values can be **True** or **False.** **True** = displays the Shockwave Flash Player pop-up menu with all items available (default). **False** = displays the Shockwave Flash Player pop-up menu with only the About Shockwave Flash option available.

*optional parameter

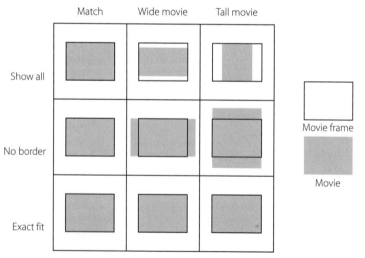

Figure C.1
The SCALE parameter controls how the movie scales to fit the movie frame. This chart compares the proportions of the movie dimensions (set in the Movie Properties dialog box) to those of the WIDTH and HEIGHT parameters in the <OBJECT> or <EMBED> tag.

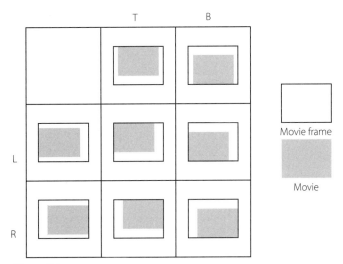

Figure C.2
The SALIGN parameter controls the placement of movies within
the movie frame, if the movie doesn't completely fill the frame.

Browser Scripting & Shockwave Flash Movies

You can create complex

interactions in Shockwave Flash movies by combining frame and button actions. Using JavaScript and VBScript, you can add additional complexity to your movies. With scripting, you can write HTML pages with controls that affect movies, movies can initiate browser scripts, and movies can even control other movies. Use the following table to determine browser and machine compatibilities and the scripting capabilities of each.

Browser	Shockwave Flash Player Platform				Scripting Language	
	Macintosh 68K	*Macintosh PPC*	*Windows 3.1*	*Windows 95*	*JavaScript*	*JScript VBScript*
Internet Explorer 2.0				X		X
Internet Explorer 3.0				X		X
Internet Explorer 4.0		X		X		X
Netscape Navigator 2.0		X			X	
Netscape Navigator 3.0		X		X	X	
Netscape Navigator 4.0		X		X	X	

Because of the variety of scripting capabilities, using browser scripting can restrict the number of people who can see movies that depend on scripting to operate, and you may need to perform extensive testing on multiple platforms to ensure compatibility in mixed environments. Browser scripting can supply Flash movies with an intelligence they do not currently have.

Shockwave Flash movies can communicate with the browser via a `Get URL` action attached to a frame or button. By supplying the action with the FSCommand, instead of a URL, `Get URL` can call JavaScript functions. By supplying a Flash button or action with the FSCommand instead of a Get URL command, the action can find a specific JavaScript function within an HTML document and execute it.

For browser scripting to communicate with Flash movies, embed the movie in an HTML page with a ID parameter (for `<OBJECT>` tags) or a NAME parameter (for `<EMBED>` tags). The actions that browser scripting can perform on Flash movies are *methods*, and they fall into three categories:

- **Informational.** Supplies some information about the movie;

- **Frame Control.** Moves the current frame indicator to a particular frame and controls playback;

- **Display Control.** Determines what portion of the movie frame displays.

Shockwave Flash browser scripting methods initiate only after the Player starts playing. Only after the first frame of the movie loads are browser scripting methods called. To ensure these conditions, attach scripting methods to buttons within the movie itself.

The ID or NAME parameter determines how the movie is referred to by browsers using the `<OBJECT>` or `<EMBED>` tags. For browsers using the `<OBJECT>` tag, the proper object reference for a movie with an ID parameter value of "flashmovie", is: `window.flashmovie`

For a browser using the `<EMBED>` tag, the object reference is: `window.document.flashmovie`

The Tables below use this example and demonstrate the methods available.

Informational Methods			
Method	*Purpose*	*Navigator Example*	*Internet Explorer Example*
IsPlaying()	Determines if the movie is playing (**true**) or paused (**false**).	window.document. flashmovie.IsPlaying()	window.flashmovie. IsPlaying()
TotalFrames()	Returns the total number of frames in all scenes of the movie.	window.document. flashmovie.TotalFrames()	window.flashmovie. TotalFrames()
Percent Loaded()	Returns a value representing the amount of the movie that has been downloaded.	window.document. flashmovie. PercentLoaded()	window.flashmovie. PercentLoaded()

Frame Control Methods			
Method	*Purpose*	*Navigator Example*	*Internet Explorer Example*
Play()	Starts to play the movie from the current frame.	window.document. flashmovie.Play()	window.flashmovie.Play()
StopPlay()	Stops playback of the movie at the current frame.	window.document. flashmovie.StopPlay()	window.flashmovie.StopPlay()
GotoFrame (*integer*)	Specifies a frame as the current frame of the movie. The frame must download by the time this method is used or an error results.	window.document. flashmovie. GotoFrame(24)	window.flashmovie. GotoFrame(24)
Rewind()	Returns the movie to its first frame.	window.document. flashmovie.Rewind()	window.flashmovie.Rewind

Frame Control Methods

Method	Purpose	Navigator Example	Internet Explorer Example
SetZoomRect (*integer, integer, integer, integer*)	Specifies a selected portion of the movie in the current frame to fill movie window.*	window.document. flashmovie.SetZoomRect (200,200,1000,1100)	window.flashmovie. SetZoomRect (200,200,1000,1100)
Zoom(*integer*)	Enlarges or reduces the movie window's view of the movie. Numbers less than 100 enlarge the artwork; numbers greater than 100 reduce the artwork.	window.document. flashmovie.Zoom(37)	window.flashmovie. Zoom(37)
Pan(*integer, integer, integer*)	Moves the movie window across the current frame. The first value provides the horizontal pan amount, the second provides vertical pan amounts, and the third should be **0** (if pan values are in pixels), or **1** (if pan values are in percentages).	window.document. flashmovie.Pan(20,15,1)	window.flashmovie. Pan(20,15,1)

* The four values specified are in TWIPs (20 TWIPs = 1 point). Use the rulers in Flash to determine positions in points and multiply by 20 to derive the correct values.

The example below demonstrates many of the methods defined in the table above, placed within the context of a typical script:

```
<SCRIPT LANGUAGE="JavaScript">
<!—
//  Decides between

// Internet Explorer and Navigator

var doObject = navigator.appCodeName.indexOf("MSIE") !=
-1;

// for Macintosh vs. Windows

if doObject {

  var doObject = navigator.appVersion.indexOf ("Mac")
!= -1
  }
function parsezoomargs(zoomargs,whatarg) {
//converts string value to integers for SetZoomRect
method
  var zoom1 = zoomargs.indexOf(",")
  var zoom2 = zoomargs.indexOf(",",zoom1+1)
  var zoom3 = zoomargs.indexOf(",",zoom2+1)
  var zoom4 =
zoomargs.substring(zoom3+1,zoomargs.length)
  var zoom3 = zoomargs.substring(zoom2+1,zoom3)
  var zoom2 = zoomargs.substring(zoom1+1,zoom2)
  var zoom1 = zoomargs.substring(0,zoom1)
  if (whatarg==1) {
    return (parseInt(zoom1))
  } else if (whatarg==2) {
    return (parseInt (zoom2))
  } else if (whatarg==3) {
    return (parseInt (zoom3))
  } else if (whatarg==4) {
    return (parseInt (zoom4))
  }
}

function parsepanargs(panargs,whatarg) {
//converts string value to integers for Pan method
  var pan1 = panargs.indexOf(",")
  var pan2 = panargs.indexOf(",",zoom1+1)
  var pan3 = panargs.substring(zoom2+1,panargs.length)
  var zoom2 = panargs.substring(zoom1+1,zoom2)
  var zoom1 = panargs.substring(0,zoom1)
  if (whatarg==1) {
    return (parseInt (pan1))
  } else if (whatarg==2) {
    return (parseInt (pan 2))
  } else if (whatarg==3) {
```

```
          return (parseInt (pan 3))
   }
}


//  DoFSCommand handles all the JavaScript FSCommand
messages
// in a movie. It s prefixed with "Do" to differentiate
// from the VBScript function below
// To adapt this code block for your own movie, replace
// flashmovie with the ID/NAME of your embedded movie
function flashmovie_DoFSCommand(command, args) {

// sets fmovie to correct object depending on doObject
   var fmovie = doObject ? window.fmovie :
window.document.fmovie;

//  This statement evaluates the command string and
decides
// what to do
   if ( command=="play" ) {
     fmovie.Play();
   } else if ( command=="stopplay" ) {
     fmovie.StopPlay();
   } else if ( command=="gotoframe" ) {
     fmovie.GotoFrame(parseInt(args));
     //need to convert arg value to an integer
   } else if ( command=="rewind" ) {
     fmovie.Rewind();
   } else if ( command=="isplaying" ) {
     return fmovie.IsPlaying();
   } else if ( command=="totalframes" ) {
     return fmovie.TotalFrames();
   } else if ( command=="percentloaded" ) {
     return fmovie.PercentLoaded();
   } else if ( command=="setzoomrect" ) {
     fmovie.SetZoomRect(parsezoomargs(args,1),
parsezoomargs(args,2), parsezoomargs(args,3),
parsezoomargs(args,4)); }
   } else if ( command=="pan" ) {
     fmovie.Pan(parsepanargs(args,1), parsepanargs
(args,2), parsepanargs (args,3)); }
   } else if ( command=="zoom" ) {
     fmovie.Zoom(parseInt(args)); }
   }
//This script handles only the built-in methods of
//a Shockwave Flash movie. Other commands can be used
//with FSCommand to accomplish more than one task by
//combining methods and adding them to this script.
}
//->
</SCRIPT>
<SCRIPT LANGUAGE="VBScript">
<!-
```

```
//  This command sends the FSCommand parameters from
ActiveX VBScript to JavaScript
Sub flashmovie_FSCommand(ByVal command, ByVal args)
  call flashmovie_DoFSCommand(command, args)
end sub
->
</SCRIPT>
```

See Figure D.1 for an example of how to send a command and
parameters to the above script.

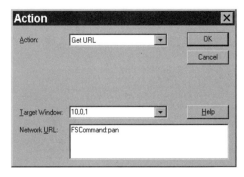

Figure D.1
An Action dialog box configured to send parameters to a JavaScript function that
pans the movie 10 percent of the movie's width to the right. Values controlling the
pan are in the Target Window field: 10 right, 0 vertical, 1 indicates value of pan is in
percentages.

Hiding Broken Plug-in Icons

There are a number of strategies for keeping the casual visitor from seeing the man behind the curtain—otherwise known as the broken plug-in icon. After you have a strategy for using Flash on a web site (see Chapter 11, "Flash Sites"), you can decide how to cope with unFlashed visitors. Choices range from ignoring them to going all-out to make the site's content accessible to everyone.

Ignoring unFlashed Users

This is the simplest and easiest strategy to implement, requiring virtually no work on the part of the web designer. Placing a Shockwave Flash movie on the page with an `<OBJECT>`/`<EMBED>` tag (see Appendix C, "`<OBJECT>`/`<EMBED>` Tag References") does the trick. Depending on the platform and browser, what the user sees varies from nothing (browsers dating before the `<EMBED>`/`<OBJECT>` tag specification) to the broken plug-in icon—browsers that can interpret the `<EMBED>` tag, but do not have the Shockwave Flash Player installed—to a dialog box inviting the user to download the Shockwave Flash ActiveX control. (The ActiveX version of the Shockwave Flash Player is currently available for only Internet Explorer 3.0 and later on Windows95.) Put a "Get Shockwave" badge (see Figure E.1) on the page and link to Macromedia's Shockwave page (http://www.macromedia. com/shockwave/download/index.cgi?P1_Prod_Version=Shockwave) to encourage downloading the Shockwave Flash Player.

Figure E.1
The "Get Shockwave" badge
on a web page.

Create Two Versions

This strategy requires that you create two versions of each page that uses Flash. An additional page played before each pair of pages acts as a gateway, allowing the user to choose whether they want to see the Flash version or not. You can duplicate the pages with one that shows GIFs or JPEGs instead of a Flash movie. An entire site can have a single gateway, or a gateway that leads to sections of the site that contains Flash movies.

This technique relies entirely on the user choosing an option. It is easy to implement for smaller sites, but can become difficult for larger sites, as you must produce each page twice. This also requires that you make any changes twice and that links to pages reflect the different versions (Flash versions of the pages need to link to Flash pages, non-Flash pages link to other non-Flash pages). Additionally, visitors that circumvent the gateways (through links on other web sites or search engines, for instance) might come directly to a version of the page that is wrong for them.

Semi-Intelligent Detection of the Shockwave Flash Player

This method uses browser scripting to determine if the user has Shockwave Flash installed in their browser; or, if the browser is capable of downloading and installing the ActiveX control (as in the case of Windows95 versions of Internet Explorer). It is called *semi-*intelligent because this strategy can cause immense headaches if you try to accomodate the wide variety of browsers in the world.

Scripting has advantages and disadvantages—not the least of which is that not every browser supports scripting in the same way (see Appendix D, "Browser Scripting & Shockwave Flash Player").

Scripting does have the advantage of requiring only one version of each page. Current pitfalls include:

- Inability to use the `<OBJECT>` tag with Macintosh versions of Internet Explorer;

- Inability to detect Shockwave Flash installations with Macintosh versions of Internet Explorer (3.0 and earlier);

- Inability of early versions of Navigator to detect installed plug-ins (version 2.0 and earlier); and

- Inability of some browsers capable of supporting Flash to properly execute browser scripts.

To use scripts to hide `<OBJECT>` and `<EMBED>` tags from viewers without Flash:

1. Determine which browser is displaying the page.

2. Determine if the computer running the browser supports ActiveX controls.

3. Determine if the Shockwave Flash Player is installed, if possible.

4. Write the `<OBJECT>`/`<EMBED>` combination into the document if you detect ActiveX support or Flash Player installation, otherwise write alternate HTML.

5. Provide alternate HTML between NOSCRIPT tags for browsers that don't support scripting.

An added benefit of this type of script is that you can use a single line with the values for the parameters to embed the movie in the page because the script generates the `<OBJECT>` and `<EMBED>` tags. This saves a lot of typing. In the example below, one line of code embeds the movie, near the end of the script. Values you need to change are in bold.

```
<HEAD>
  <SCRIPT LANGUAGE="JavaScript">
    function writeObEm
(movie,nmid,wide,high,play,loop,qual,bgco,scal,alig,base,menu)
{
        if ((navigator.appName.indexOf("Microsoft") != -1
&&  //browser is Internet Explorer
            navigator.userAgent.indexOf("Windows 3.1")
== -1 &&  //not Windows 3.1
            navigator.userAgent.indexOf("mac") == -1) ||
//not Macintosh
            (navigator.mimeTypes && //or the plugin is
installed
            navigator.mimeTypes["application/x-
shockwave-flash"] &&
            navigator.mimeTypes["application/x-
shockwave-flash"].enabledPlugin)) {
        //following lines write <OBJECT> and <EMBED>
tags automatically from arguments
        var ObEmTag = "<OBJECT CLASSID= clsid:D27CDB6E-
AE6D-11cf-96B8-444553540000'"
        var ObEmTag = ObEmTag + " ID=" + nmid
        var ObEmTag = ObEmTag + " WIDTH=" + wide + "
HEIGHT=" + high
        var ObEmTag = ObEmTag + " <PARAM NAME= MOVIE
VALUE= " + movie + "'> "
        var ObEmTag = ObEmTag + " <PARAM NAME= PLAY
VALUE= " + play + "'> "
        var ObEmTag = ObEmTag + " <PARAM NAME= LOOP
VALUE= " + loop + "'> "
        var ObEmTag = ObEmTag + " <PARAM NAME= QUALITY
VALUE= " + qual + "'> "
        var ObEmTag = ObEmTag + " <PARAM NAME= BGCOLOR
VALUE= " + bgco + "'> "
        var ObEmTag = ObEmTag + " <PARAM NAME= SCALE
VALUE= " + scal + "'> "
        var ObEmTag = ObEmTag + " <PARAM NAME= SALIGN
VALUE= " + alig + "'> "
        var ObEmTag = ObEmTag + " <PARAM NAME= BASE
VALUE= " + base + "'> "
        var ObEmTag = ObEmTag + " <PARAM NAME= MENU
VALUE= " + menu + "'> "
        var ObEmTag = ObEmTag + "<EMBED SRC=  " + movie
```

```
+ "' WIDTH=" + wide
        var ObEmTag = ObEmTag + " HEIGHT=" + high
        var ObEmTag = ObEmTag + " MAYSCRIPT NAME=" +
nmid
        var ObEmTag = ObEmTag + " PLAY=" + play
        var ObEmTag = ObEmTag + " LOOP=" + loop
        var ObEmTag = ObEmTag + " QUALITY=" + qual
        var ObEmTag = ObEmTag + " BGCOLOR=" + bgco
        var ObEmTag = ObEmTag + " SCALE=" + scal
        var ObEmTag = ObEmTag + " SALIGN=" + alig
        var ObEmTag = ObEmTag + " BASE=" + base
        var ObEmTag = ObEmTag + " MENU=" + menu
        var ObEmTag = ObEmTag + " pluginspage= http://
www.macromedia.com/shockwave/download/
index.cgi?P1_Prod_Version=ShockwaveFlash2'"
        var ObEmTag = ObEmTag + "> </EMBED> </OBJECT>"
return ObEmTag
        }
      else {
        return "alternate HTML"
      }
    }
  </SCRIPT>
</HEAD>
<BODY>
  <SCRIPT LANGUAGE="JavaScript">
    //URL, name/id, width, height, play, loop, quality,
background color, scale, alignment, base location, menu
    document.write(writeObEm("movie.swf","mname",400,200,"TRUE",
"TRUE","LOW","000000","SHOWALL","T","http://
www.server.com/flashmovs/","TRUE"))
  </SCRIPT>
  <NOSCRIPT>
    alternate HTML
  </NOSCRIPT>
</BODY>
```

Keyboard Shortcuts

Animation

Action	Windows	Macintosh
Play movie/Stop movie	Enter/Return	Enter/Return
Step forward one frame	> or .	> or .
Step back one frame	< or ,	< or ,
Stop movie	Esc or Enter	Esc or Enter
Insert frame	F5	F5
Delete frame	Shift-F5	Shift-F5
Insert key frame	F6	F6
Insert blank key frame	F7	F7

Moving Selections

Movement of selections is relative to the size of the movie on the screen.

Action	Windows	Macintosh
Move selection one pixel left	Left Arrow	Left Arrow
Move selection eight pixels left	Shift-Left Arrow.	Shift-Left Arrow
Move selection one pixel right	Right Arrow	Right Arrow
Move selection eight pixels right	Shift-Right Arrow.	Shift-Right Arrow
Move selection up one pixel	Up Arrow	Up Arrow
Move selection up eight pixels	Shift-Up Arrow.	Shift-Up Arrow
Move selection down one pixel	Down Arrow	Down Arrow
Move selection down eight pixels	Shift-Down Arrow.	Shift-Down Arrow

Choosing Tools

Action	Windows	Macintosh
Select arrow tool	A	A
Select text tool	T	T
Select ink bottle tool	I	I
Select pencil tool	P	P
Select paint bucket tool	U	U
Select brush tool	B	B
Select dropper tool	D	D
Select eraser tool	E	E
Select Lasso tool	L	L
Select magnifier tool	M	M

Activating Grid

Action	Windows	Macintosh
Snap to grid when dragging	Shift	Shift

Changing Scenes

Action	Windows	Macintosh
View previous scene	Page Up	Page Up
View next scene	Page Down	Page Down
View first scene	Home	Home
View last scene	End	End

Editing Text - Insertion Point

Pressing the Shift key will select the text between the insertion point's original position and the new position.

Action	Windows	Macintosh
Move insertion point one character to left	Left Arrow	Left Arrow
Move insertion point one character to right	Right Arrow	Right Arrow
Move insertion point one line up	Up Arrow	Up Arrow
Move insertion point one line down	Down Arrow	Down Arrow
Move insertion point to beginning of line	Shift+Home	Shift+Home
Move insertion point to end of line	Shift+End	Shift+End
Move insertion point to beginning of text block	Ctrl-Home	Ctrl-Home or Option-Home
Move insertion point to end of text block	Ctrl-End	Ctrl-End or Option-End

Editing Text - Kerning

Kerning commands are relative to size of the movie on the screen.

Action	Windows	Macintosh
Decrease space between selected characters by 1/2 pixel	Control-Left Arrow	Ctrl-Left Arrow or Option-Left Arrow
Increase space between selected characters by 1/2 pixel	Control-Right Arrow	Ctrl-Right Arrow or Option-Right Arrow
Decrease space between selected characters by 2 pixels	Shift-Control-Left ArrowArrow	Shift-Ctrl-Left or Shift-Option-Left Arrow
Increase space between selected characters by 2 pixels	Shift-Control-Right Arrow	Shift-Ctrl-Right Arrow or Shift-Option-Right Arrow

Action	*Windows*	*Macintosh*
File menu	Alt-F	
File>New	Ctrl-N, Alt-F (N)	Command-N
File>Open	Ctrl-O, Alt-F (O)	Command-O
File>Open as Library	Ctrl-Shift-O, Alt-F (L)	Command-Shift-O
File>Close	Ctrl-W, Alt-F (C)	Command-W
File>Save	Ctrl-S (S)	Command-S
File>Save As	Ctrl-W, Alt-F (A)	Command-W
File>Import	Ctrl-R, Alt-F (I)	Command-R
File>Export Movie	Ctrl-Shift-R, Alt-F (M)	Command-Shift-R
File>Export Image	Alt-F (E)	
File>Page Setup	Alt-F (U)	
File>Print Preview	Alt-F (V)	
File>Print	Ctrl-P, Alt-F (P)	Command-P
File>Preferences	Alt-F (F)	
File>Assistant	Alt-F (T)	
File>Exit/Quit	Alt-F (x)	Command-Q
Edit Menu	Alt-E	
Edit>Undo	Ctrl-Z, Alt-E (U)	Command-Z
Edit>Redo	Ctrl-Y, Alt-E (R)	Command-Y
Edit>Cut	Ctrl-X, Alt-E (T)	Command-X
Edit>Copy	Ctrl-C, Alt-E (C)	Command-C
Edit>Paste	Ctrl-V, Alt-E (P)	Command-V
Edit>Paste in Place	Ctrl-Shift-V, Alt-E (N)	Command-Shift-V
Edit>Paste Special	Alt-E (S)	
Edit>Clear	Delete, Alt-E (L)	Delete
Edit>Duplicate	Ctrl-D, Alt-E (D)	Command-D
Edit>Select All	Ctrl-A, Alt-E (A)	Command-A
Edit>Deselect All	Ctrl-Shift-A, Alt-E (E)	Command-Shift-A
Edit>Edit Symbols	Ctrl-E, Alt-E (Shift-E)	Command-E
Edit>Edit Selected	Alt-E (D)	

Menu Shortcuts (continued)

Action	*Windows*	*Macintosh*
Edit>Edit All	Alt-E (T)	
Edit>Insert Object	Alt-E (I)	
Edit>Links	Alt-E (K)	
Edit>Object	Alt-E (O)	
View Menu	Alt-V	
View>Goto	Alt-V (G)	
View>Goto>First	Home	Home
View>Goto>Previous	Page Up	Page Up
View>Goto>Next	Page Down	Page Down
View>Goto>Last	End	End
View>100%	Alt-V (1)	
View>ShowFrame	Ctrl-2, Alt-V (F)	Command-2
View>Show All	Ctrl-3, Alt-V (A)	Command-3
View>Outlines	Alt-V (O)	
View>Fast	Alt-V (F)	
View>Smooth	Alt-V (S)	
View>Smooth Text	Alt-V (M)	
View>Timeline	Ctrl-Shift-L, Alt-V (L)	Command-Shift-L
View>Work Area	Ctrl-Shift-W, Alt-V (W)	Command-Shift-W
View>Rulers	Alt-V (R)	
View>Tabs	Alt-V (B)	
View>Grid	Alt-V (R)	
View>Snap	Alt-V (P)	
Insert Menu	Alt-I	
Insert>Create Symbol	F8, Alt-I (C)	F8
Insert>Layer	Alt-I (L)	
Insert>Motion Guide	Alt-I (M)	
Insert>Frame	F5, Alt-I (F)	F5
Insert>Delete Frame	Shift-F5, Alt-I (D)	Shift-F5
Insert>Key Frame	F6, Alt-I (K)	F6
Insert>Blank Key Frame	F7, Alt-I (B)	F7

Action	Windows	Macintosh
Insert>Scene	Alt-I (S)	
Insert>Remove Scene	Alt-I (R)	
Modify Menu	Alt-O	
Modify>Element	Alt-O (E)	
Modify>Scene	Alt-O (S)	
Modify>Movie	Ctrl-M, Alt-O (M)	Command-M
Modify>Font	Ctrl-T, Alt-O (F)	Command-T
Modify>Paragraph	Ctrl-Shift-T, Alt-O (F)	Command-Shift-T
Modify>Kerning	Alt-O (K)	
Modify>Kerning>Narrower	Ctrl-Left Arrow, Alt-O (K) (N)	Command-Left Arrow
Modify>Kerning>Wider	Ctrl-Right Arrow, Alt-O (K) (W)	Command-Right Arrow
Modify>Kerning>Reset	Ctrl-Shift-K, Alt-I (K) (R)	Command-Shift-K
Modify>Transform	Alt-O (T)	
Modify>Transform>Scale	Alt-O (T) (S)	
Modify>Transform>Rotate	Alt-O (T) (R)	
Modify>Transform>Scale and Rotate	Ctrl-Shift-S, Alt-O (T) (C)	Command-Shift-S
Modify>Transform>Rotate Left	Alt-O (T) (L)	
Modify>Transform>Rotate Right	Alt-O (T) (T)	
Modify>Transform>Flip Vertical	Alt-O (T) (V)	
Modify>Transform>Flip Horizontal	Alt-O (T) (H)	
Modify>Transform>Remove Transform	Ctrl-Shift-Z, Alt-O (T) (T)	Command-Shift-Z
Modify>Transform>Edit Center	Alt-O (T) (E)	
Modify>Arrange	Alt-O (A)	
Modify>Arrange>Bring to Front	Ctrl-Shift-Up Arrow, Alt-O (A) (F)	Command-Shift-Up Arrow
Modify>Arrange>Move Ahead	Ctrl-Up Arrow, Alt-O (A) (A)	Command-Up Arrow
Modify>Arrange>Move Behind	Ctrl-Down Arrow, Alt-O (A) (E)	Command-Down Arrow

Menu Shortcuts (continued)

Action	Windows	Macintosh
Modify>Arrange>Send to Back	Ctrl-Shift-Down Arrow, Alt-O (A) (B)	Command-Shift-Down Arrow
Modify>Curves	Alt-O (C)	
Modify>Curves>Smooth	Alt-O (C) (S)	
Modify>Curves>Straighten	Alt-O (C) (T)	
Modify>Curves>Optimize	Ctrl-Shift-C, Alt-O (C) (O)	Command-Shift-C
Modify>Trace Bitmap	Alt-O (B)	
Modify>Align	Ctrl-K, Alt-O (L)	Command-K
Modify>Lock	Alt-O (L) (L)	
Modify>Unlock All	Alt-O (U)	
Modify>Group	Ctrl-G, Alt-O (G)	Command-G
Modify>Ungroup	Ctrl-U, Alt-O (U)	Command-U
Modify>Break Apart	Ctrl-B, Alt-O (K) (K)	Command-B
Modify>Remove Colors	Alt-O (E)	
Control Menu	Alt-C	
Control>Play	Enter	Enter, Return
Control>Rewind	Ctrl-0, Alt-C (R)	Command-0
Control>Step Forward	>, Alt-C (F)	>
Control>Step Backward	<, Alt-C (B)	<
Control>Loop Playback	Alt-C (L)	
Control>Play All Scenes	Alt-C (A)	
Control>Enable Frame Actions	Alt-C (F) (F)	
Control>Enable Buttons	Alt-C (B)	
Control>Play Sounds	Alt-C (S)	
Xtras menu	Alt-X	
Xtras>Libraries	Alt-X (L)	
Xtras>Lessons	Alt-X (E)	
Xtras>Samples	Alt-X (S)	
Window menu	Alt-W	
Window>New Window	Alt-W (N)	
Window>Arrange All	Alt-W (A)	

Action	Windows	Macintosh
Window>Cascade	Alt-W (C)	
Window>Toolbar	Alt-W (T)	
Window>Controller	Alt-W (O)	
Window>Colors	Alt-W (L)	
Window>Library	Ctrl-L, Alt-W (L) (L)	Command-L
Help menu	Alt-H	
Help>Flash Help	F1, Alt-H (F)	F1
Help>Help Pointer	Shift-F1, Alt-H (H)	Shift-F1
Help>Overview	Alt-H (O)	
Help>Reference	Alt-H (R)	
Help>Troubleshooting	Alt-H (T)	
Help>How To	Alt-H (O) (O)	
Help>Web Links	Alt-H (W)	
Help>Sample HTML	Alt-H (S)	
Help>Register	Alt-H (G)	
Help>About Flash	Alt-H (A)	

I N D E X

3D shapes, importing, 35

A

absolute URLs, 182
action commands, 3
Action dialog box, 163–165, 282
action frames, 17
actions, 159, 162, 175
   adding to buttons, 171–172
   associated with frames, 17
   buttons, 159
   complex, 201–205
   executing, 3, 163
   loading upper frames, 202–204
   play, 163
   removing, 165
   standalone Shockwave Flash Player, 221
   web browsers and, 3
adding movie elements, 9
ADPCM (Adaptive Differential Pulse Code
   Modulation) compression, 230, 231
advanced animation, 138–144
   animating symbols, 140–141
   color animation, 138–139
   tweening on paths, 141–144
Aegagropila World web site, 260
Aftershock, 247
AI files, exporting frames as, 2
AIFF files, 208
aliasing, 5
Align (Ctrl/Command-K) keyboard shortcut,
   93
Align dialog box, 92
amen.html file, 194
amen.swf movie, 194
amplitude, 209
animated GIF (Graphics Interchange
   Format), 3, 40
animation
   accelerating and decelerating, 134–136
   advanced, 138–144
   color, 138–139
   frame-by-frame, 121, 126–131
   key frames, 6
   keyboard shortcuts, 289
   layers, 155–158
   making movie smaller, 235–238
   pre-rendered bitmap images, 3
   rendering images on-the-fly,
   synchronizing sounds, 216–217

   timeline, 6
   tweening, 6–7, 121, 131–137
   viewing as filmstrips, 130–131
   animation sequencer, 2
   anti-aliasing, 5
Arrange submenu, 10, 11
arrow tool, 24–25, 167
   adding to selection, 80–81
   deselecting shapes, 79
   duplicating line, 80
   Magnet modifier, 24
   modifiers, 24–25
   modifying curves, 88, 89
   move selection cursor, 79
   moving corners, 88
   moving fills, 79
   Reshape Curve mode, 89
   Rotate modifier, 25, 91, 105, 128, 129,
      130, 133, 143
   Scale modifier, 25, 93, 105, 133
   selecting all connected outlines, 82
   selecting corner of shape, 65
   selecting lines with, 84, 85
   selecting objects, 78–85, 109, 113
   selecting Play button, 169
   Smooth modifier, 24, 88, 89, 90
   Snap modifier, 91
   Straighten modifier, 24, 88, 89, 90, 107
Art Gallery of Ontario Edvard Munch Web
   Project, 257
artifacts, 230
audio compact discs, 209
authoring program, 2
Authorware, 45, 49
automatic snap feature, 24

B

Becker Surf web site, 255
bitmap files, exporting movies as series of,
   3
bitmap objects, 103–112
bitmaps
   artifacts, 230
   breaking apart, 106–109
   compression comparison, 229
   conversion to vector graphics, 228
   converting to fill, 107
   converting to vector graphics, 109–112
   copying to FreeHand file, 37
   different shape fills, 109

exporting, 42-46
fills, 106
file size, 2
frames, 2
FreeHand, 41
how closely trace follows, 111
imported artwork, 34
importing, 40-42, 104-106
large file size, 103
linking to master bitmap, 105
modifying, 105
modifying fills, 27, 107-109
in movies, 104
moving to scene, 105
pixellated, 2, 4
pre-rendered, 3
previewing, 23
saved as JPEG graphics, 228
selecting portion to use as fill, 29
size, 4
size created by trace, 111
storing, 22-23, 233
storing master copy of imported, 104
storing on disk, 4
tiling, 106
tracing, 109-112
uses for, 103
viewing, 22
blank frames, 122, 156
blends, 21-22
BMP graphics, 2
<BODY> tag, BGCOLOR parameter, 189
bold fonts, 25
bottom menu layer, 149
Break Apart (Ctrl/Command-B) keyboard shortcut, 107
browser scripting
display control methods, 276, 279
example, 280-282
frame control methods, 276, 278
hiding <EMBED> and <OBJECT> tags, 285-287
informational methods, 276, 277
methods, 276
problems, 285
Shockwave Flash movies, 275-282
unFlashed users, 285-287
variety of capabilities, 276
browser-safe colors, 72, 75
brush strokes, 60-63

brush tool
Brush Color modifier, 27
Brush Mode modifier, 26, 60, 63, 64, 65
Brush Shape modifier, 27, 61
Brush Size modifier, 27, 60
Fill Color modifier, 63, 64, 65, 73
Fill Color palette, 60
Line Color modifier, 73
Lock Fill modifier, 27
modifiers, 26-27
modifying color palettes, 73
Normal option, 63
Paint Behind option, 64
Paint Fills option, 64
Paint Inside option, 65
Paint Mode modifier, 64, 65
Paint Normal option, 60
Paint Selection option, 65
painting shapes, 59-66
Pressure modifier, 27
Round Brush option, 61
sensitivity, 27
brushes
modifying outlines of, 62-63
button effects, 194-200
simulating virtual reality, 195-198
virtual objects, 195-200
buttons, 159, 166-173
active or hit area, 168
adding actions, 171-172
adding looping action to scene, 170-171
adding sounds, 217-218
adding to new scene, 173
artwork, 166
assigning action to, 168-169
button states, 168
common actions, 170-173
controlling virtual reality effect with, 198-200
displaying all frames of, 23
multiple scenes, 169
previewing, 23
special frames, 166
Stop All Sounds action, 214
stopping and starting movies, 167-169
viewing, 22

C

Canvas, 14
canvas level, 3
converting bitmap to fill on, 107
layers, 147

returning overlay objects to, 97
characters, spacing between, 10
clients, 178
clipping path, 109
closed shapes, 52
color animation, 138-139
color palettes
browser-safe colors, 72
default, 74
deleting colors, 75
modifying, 19, 73
number of colors in, 74
Color window, 19-22
assigning color to color pointer, 76, 77
Change button, 20, 22, 75, 78
color list, 20, 22
color pointers, 76
Color pop-up menu, 75, 76, 77
color preview, 20
defining radial fill, 76
Delete button, 20, 22
deleting colors, 75
editing radial fill gradient, 76-77
editing width of bands in gradient, 78
gradient creation, 75
Gradient mode, 21-22
gradient preview, 21
Gradient tab, 19, 75
Gradient Type, 21, 76
Gradient-Definition bar, 21, 76
master pointer, 77
New button, 20, 22, 74, 75
Numeric Color Picker, 20, 22
R, G, and B fields, 76
Radial option, 76
red pointer, 77, 78
solid colors, 20, 73-75
Solid mode, 20
Solid tab, 19, 20, 73
Visual Color Picker, 20, 21
white pointer, 76, 77
white-to-black gradient, 75
color-coding layers, 154
colors
browser-safe, 72
brushes, 27
changing, 72-78
deleting, 75
deleting position on list of, 20
displaying available, 20
dithering, 72
enforcing 216-color web palette on, 20

fonts, 25
index, 4
large patch of selected, 20
lines, 26
new position on list of, 20
numbers for values, 20
Pencil tool, 26
pixels, 3–4
positioning in gradients, 21
selecting hue and saturation, 20
solid, 73–75
solid for lines and fills, 20
verifying change in, 20
web-safe, 20
complete URLs, 181, 182
complex actions, 201–205
compressing movies, 228–232
ADPCM (Adaptive Differential Pulse Code Modulation) compression, 230, 231
bitmap image comparison, 229
compressed sound effects, 232
compressing sound, 230–231
considerations
file size, 232
JPEG (Joint Photographic Experts Group), 228
constraining lines, 55
Control menu, 11
control points, 6
Control > Enable Buttons command, 168, 169, 187, 199, 217
Control > Enable Frame Actions command, 165
Control > Loop Playback > Play command, 126
Control > Play All Scenes command, 162
Control > Play commands, 220
control.fla movie, 202
Copy (Ctrl/Command-C) keyboard shortcut, 93
copying
artwork between Flash and FreeHand, 32–33
artwork to FreeHand file, 37
fills, 28
line styles, 28
objects, 93
Create Symbol (F8) keyboard shortcut, 118
Ctrl key, 80
curved lines, 233
anti-aliasing, 5
changing line properties, 63
defining, 2, 55–56

drawing, 56–57
modifying, 88, 89
Curves submenu, 11
custom line styles, 54

D

default fonts, 25
default.htm file, 187
Delete key, 93
Deselect All (Shift-Ctrl/Command-A) keyboard shortcut, 79
digital sound, 208
digital type design, 39–40
digital video, exporting, 47–49
to Authorware, 48
to Director, 45, 48
disabling pressure-sensitive capabilities, 61
display control, 9
methods, 276, 279
display layer, 147, 149
dithering, 72
domains, 177
Down frame, 168
drawing
behind text, groups, and symbols, 52
curved lines, 56–57
line on top of line, 52
lines with pencil tool, 52–57
on layers, 52
outlines for shapes, 52–57
ovals, 59
rectangles, 59
shape recognition and, 58
shapes, 57–59
straight lines, 54–55
triangles, 58
drawing tools, 23
dropper tool, 28, 70–72
determining fill and line attributes of shape, 70
Fill Color preview area, 108, 109
icons appearing with, 70
line attributes, 71, 83
over fill or line, 70
pencil icon, 71
Transform Fill modifier, 108
DXF files
exporting frames as, 2
importing, 35

E

Edit menu, 8
Edit Multiple Frames button, 15
Edit > Copy command, 37, 93, 169, 173
Edit > Cut command, 149, 198
Edit > Deselect All command, 79
Edit > Edit Movie command, 141, 144, 168, 199, 217
Edit > Edit Selected command, 97, 119
Edit > Edit Symbols command, 97, 119, 140, 168, 197, 217
Edit > Paste command, 22, 93
Edit > Paste In Place command, 149, 169, 173
Edit > Select All command, 93, 151, 173, 197, 198
Edit Symbol/Movie (Ctrl/Command-E) keyboard shortcut, 119, 120, 140
editor, 13, 14
elements
adding and removing, 9
applying line styles and colors, 82
<EMBED> tag, 190, 223, 224
BASE parameter, 272
BGCOLOR parameter, 270
disadvantage of, 226
HEIGHT parameter, 226, 269
hiding, 285–287
LOOP parameter, 269
MAYSCRIPT NAME parameter, 269
MENU parameter, 272
movie values, 226
NAME parameter, 276, 277
PLAY parameter, 269
pluginspage parameter, 269
QUALITY parameter, 270
SALIGN parameter, 271
SCALE parameter, 271
SRC parameter, 269
template, 189
TYPE parameter, 249
WIDTH parameter, 226, 269
EMF files, exporting frames as, 2
empty frame, 17
empty key frame, 17
Enter key, 126
EPS (Encapsulated PostScript), 2–3
eraser tool, 28
deleting portions of lines and shapes, 87–88
Erase Normal option, 87
Eraser Mode modifier, 28, 87
Eraser Shape modifier, 28

Eraser Size menu, 87
Faucet modifier, 28, 87, 88, 91
modifiers, 28
reshaping, 28
Escape key, 79
event sounds, 213, 214
storing data, 233
event-driven sounds, 210
Export Adobe Illustrator dialog
box, 38, 39
Export dialog box, 36
Export Image dialog box, 37, 43
Export Movie dialog box
Adobe Illustrator Sequence
option, 38, 39
File Save As Type pop-up
menu, 39
Save As File Type pop-up
menu, 222
Save As Type pop-up menu,
44, 47
Save button, 38, 39, 222
Save File As Type pop-up
menu, 38
Shockwave Flash type, 164,
222
Export QuickTime dialog box, 48
Export Shockwave Flash dialog
box, 223
Generate Size Report
checkbox, 232
JPEG Quality value, 228
Load Order option, 226–227
Protect from Import button,
227
setting final sampling rate of
sounds, 231
sound compression, 231
exporting
animated GIF files, 40
artwork to Extreme 3D, 36
artwork to Fontographer,
39–40
artwork to FreeHand, 36–39
bitmaps, 42–46
bitmaps to Authorware, 45
bitmaps to Director, 45
bitmaps to Extreme 3D, 45
bitmaps to FreeHand, 46
bitmaps to xRes, 44
digital video, 47–49
digital video to Authorware,
49
digital video to Director, 48
entire movie as sequence of
files, 38–39
frames, 2, 43

frames to FreeHand, 37–38
GIF files, 103
JPEG files, 103
movie as sequence of bitmap
files, 44
movies, 3, 220
movies with characters for
Fontographer, 39–40
vector graphics, 36–40
external files, 8
Extreme 3D
bitmap as Material element, 45
Edit Texture dialog box, 45
Export File dialog box, 35
File Format menu, 42
File > Export > DXF
command, 35
File > Import > DXF
command, 36
File Selection dialog box, 45
importing bitmaps from, 41–
42
importing files from, 35
importing Flash artwork, 36
importing Flash bitmaps, 45
<< button, 45
Render > Render to Disk
command, 41
Render > Set Background
command, 45
Render to Disk dialog box,
41–42
Save File dialog box, 42
Windows > Materials palette
command, 45

F

File menu, 8
File > Export Image command,
37, 43
File > Export Movie command,
38, 39, 44, 47, 164, 188, 192,
220, 222
File > Export > Image command,
36
File > Import command, 33, 35,
41, 42, 47, 104, 211, 227
File > Open Location command,
249
files
creating, 8
external, 8
importing, 117
sizes and symbols, 116
transmission speeds, 265–266
filled shapes, 26

filling outlines, 27
fills
copying, 28
determining attributes, 70
erasing, 28
modifying gradients and
bitmaps, 27
modifying gradients or blends,
21–22
moving, 79
reshaping, 78–87
selecting, 78–87
solid colors, 20
zoom tool before, 72
filmstrips, viewing animation as,
130–131
fla files, 220
Flash ActiveX control, 176
Flash example web sites
Aegagropila World, 260
Becker Surf, 255
Hide Needs Sake, 259
Hunterkillerdog, 256
Macromedia, 252
MSN (Microsoft Network), 253
Spumco's "The Goddamn
George Liquor Program",
258
WebTV Networks, Inc., 254
Flash for Windows floating
windows, 19
Flash movies integration into
web sites, 247–249
Flash Player, 2
playing movies back, 2
web site users without, 247
Flash plug-in, 176
floating windows, 19
Fontographer, importing Flash
artwork, 39–40
fonts, 25
fps (frames per second), 122
frame actions, 159, 162–166
loading HTML page in lower
frame, 204–205
frame control methods, 276, 278
frame rate, 122
<FRAME> tag
MARGINHEIGHT parameter,
186
MARGINWIDTH parameter,
186
NAME parameter, 186
SCROLLING parameter, 186
SRC parameter, 186
frame-by-frame animation, 121,
126–131

color, 138
creation of, 126-127
key frames, 126
onion-skinning, 127-130
sequence of key frames
    containing artwork, 126-127
tweening and, 135
frames, 2, 122, 182
action, 3, 17
adding, 122-124, 132
adding to movie, 122-124
AI files, 2
appearing as outlines only,
    129
assigning actions to, 3
bitmap images, 2
blank, 122
BMP graphics, 2
borders, 182
changes to visual elements on
    this layer, 17
controlling display, 124
controlling rate, 18
converting to key frame,
    124-125
copying artwork to FreeHand
    file, 37
copying between scenes,
    161-162
current, 19
displaying all simultaneously,
    128-129
displaying graphics as outlines,
    15
displaying graphics for range
    of, 14
DXF files, 2
editing graphics in onion skin,
    15
EMF files, 2
empty, 17
enlarging or reducing, 24
EPS (Encapsulated PostScript)
    graphics, 2
exporting, 2
exporting as bitmap, 43
file space, 233
FreeHand Xtra, 2
GIF graphics, 2
graphics from current, 13
gray area surrounding, 14
illustration files, 2
information on range of, 14
inserting into multiple layers,
    153-154
intermediate, 17
JPEG graphics, 2

modifying, 17
movie controlling, 187-189
no change from previous, 17
no visual elements on this
    layer, 17
number of current, 18, 125
PICT files, 2
playing specific, 164
removing actions, 165
replacing in web browser, 176
scrollbars, 182
selecting irregular areas of, 29
sending movie's current frame
    indicator to, 176
Stop All Sounds action, 214
Stop synchronizations, 214
timeline, 6, 16
transparent, 182
tweened, 17, 122
types, 17
updating multiple, 201-205
viewing objects within, 14
visible in timeline, 16
WMF files, 2
<FRAMESET> tag, 186
framesets, 182-194, 201-202
actions to load upper frames,
    202-204
movies, 185
nesting, 183
for Shockwave Flash menubar,
    185-187
Shockwave Flash movie that
    controls frames, 187-189
FreeHand
Adobe Illustrator 5.5 format,
    33
bitmaps, 41
Copy command, 32
Edit > Paste command, 37
entire movie as sequence of
    files, 38-39
Export command, 33
Export File dialog box, 34-35
File > Import, 46
importing artwork from,
    32-35
importing documents from,
    33-34
importing Flash artwork,
    36-39
importing Flash bitmaps, 46
importing movie frame, 37-38
Xtras > Create > Flash Image
    command, 34
FreeHand Xtra, exporting frames
    as, 2

FTP (File Transfer Protocol)
    client, 249
FTP Web server, uploading
    movies to, 249-250
FutureSplash Player files, 220

G

Get URL, Goto, and Play action,
    176, 221
Get URL action, 176, 221, 276
Get URL and Goto action, 176,
    204, 221
GIF files
    exporting, 103
    exporting frames as, 2
Goto action, 164, 205
Goto and Play action, 164-166,
    171
GotoFrame method, 278
gradient fill locked to canvas, 71
gradient shapes, 27
gradients
    assigning color to, 76
    creating, 75
    defining radial fill, 76
    deleting selection on list, 22
    displaying, 21
    editing radial fill, 76-77
    editing width of bands, 78
    handles on fills, 27
    hue, 21
    imported artwork, 34
    lightness, 21
    Linear, 21
    modifying, 21-22, 22
    modifying fills made of, 27
    new selection on list, 22
    numeric color values, 22
    positioning, 21
    radial, 21
    saturation, 21
    selecting color from Solid
        Color List, 22
    transforming, 90
    white-to-black, 75
graphics
    altering, 68-69
    anti-aliasing, 5
    buttons, 166
    copying between Flash and
        FreeHand, 32-33
    current frame display of, 13
    displaying as outlines for
        frame range, 15
    displaying for range of frames,
        14

editing in all onion skin frames, 15
execution of actions, 3
manipulating layers, 150-154
mathematical equations as, 2
moving between layers, 149-150
registering between frames, 14
rendering on-the-fly, 3
time spent downloading, viii
turning into symbol, 132
tweening, 133
grid keyboard shortcuts, 289
Group (Ctrl/Command-G) keyboard shortcut, 113
grouping groups, 115
groups, 112
  converting to individual items, 113
  creating, 113
  duplicating, 116
  grouping, 115
  removing from display layer, 149
  rotating, 128

H

Help menu, 12
Hide Needs Sake, 259
hiding layers, 151-153
Hit frame, 168
home.htm file, 193
home.swf movie, 192
  HTML document for, 193-194
hood.htm file, 194
hood.swf movie, 194
HTML documents
  framesets, 182-194, 201-202
  for home.swf movie, 193-194
  movie for, 190-192
  outlining frameset, 183-185
  simple web page, 179-180
HTML files holding Shockwave Flash file, 189-190
HTML (HyperText Markup Language), 178-182
  tags, 178-180
HTML pages
  embedded movies, 224-226
  embedding Shockwave Flash files, 221
  frame action loading in lower frame, 204-205
  playing movies, 2, 7

http (HyperText Transfer Protocol), 177
hue, 20
  gradients, 21
Hunterkillerdog web site, 256

I

illustration files, 2, 3
<IMG> tag ALT parameter, 226
Import (Ctrl/Command-R) keyboard shortcut, 34, 104
Import dialog box, 42, 47
  Adobe Illustrator option, 33
  File Type pop-up menu, 104
  List Files of Type pop-up menu, 33
  Open button, 33, 211
Import File dialog box, 35
imported artwork bitmaps and gradient fills, 34
importing
  3D shapes, 35
  Adobe Illustrator 5.5 format, 33
  animated GIF files, 40
  artwork from vector-based clip art libraries, 32
  bitmaps, 40-42, 104-106
  copying artwork between Flash and FreeHand, 32-33
  DXF files, 35
  Extreme 3D bitmaps, 41-42
  Extreme 3D files, 35
  files, 117
  Flash movies with FreeHand Xtra, 34
  FreeHand artwork, 32-35
  FreeHand documents, 33-34
  outlines, 32
  overlay objects, 33
  sequence of files, 34
  SoundEdit 16 sounds, 46-47
  sounds, 46-47
  sounds into movies, 211-212
  vector graphics, 32-35
  xRes bitmaps, 40-41
index.htm file, 187
index.html file, 187
informational methods, 276, 277
ink bottle tool, 71
  affecting lines attached to shapes, 68
  applying line styles and colors to elements, 82

black option, 69
changing curve properties, 63
changing line properties, 63
changing parts of lines, 83
Color modifier, 82
Fill Color modifier, 73
Line Color modifier, 26, 63, 69, 73
Line Style modifier, 26, 63, 69
Line Thickness modifier, 63, 82
Line Width modifier, 26, 69, 84
modifiers, 26
modifying color palettes, 73
modifying letter outlines, 72
modifying outlines of brush strokes, 62-63
outlining shapes, 82
Solid option, 69
Insert Frame (F5) keyboard shortcut, 123, 140
Insert Key Frame (F6) keyboard shortcut, 127, 140
Insert menu, 9
Insert > Create Symbol command, 118, 132, 167, 196, 203
Insert > Frame command, 132
Insert > Key Frame command, 126, 132
Insert > Scene command, 160
interactive movie files, 2
interactive multimedia files, 2
interactivity, 2
intermediate frames, 17
Internet and URLs, 176-178
Internet Explorer 176, 221, 223, 224, 226, 267-273
IsPlaying() method, 277
italic fonts, 25

J

Java Player Flash Edition, 7
JavaScript control of movies, 224
JPEG files
  compressing before importing, 40
  exporting, 103
  exporting frames as, 2
JPEG (Joint Photographic Experts Group) format, 228

K

Kerning submenu, 10
kerning text keyboard shortcuts, 289
key frames, 6, 16, 17, 122, 132, 155
  changes to, 133
  converting frames to, 124–125
  current frame indicator pointing to, 124
  derived from tweened frame, 17
  empty, 17
  file space, 233
  frame-by-frame animation, 126
  moving, 137
  removing sounds, 214
  sequence containing artwork, 126–127
  storing data for symbols, 233
  tweening, 17, 131, 134
keyboard shortcuts
  animation, 289
  grid, 289
  menus, 292–296
  moving insertion point, 289
  moving selections, 289
  scenes, 289
  tool selection, 289

L

labels, 97–101
  converting text blocks back to, 100–101
  creation of, 98–99
  line breaks, 98
  modifying style, 101–102
  styling, 101–103
  width, 98
  lasso tool, 29, 79
  selecting objects, 85–86, 113
layer names, 16
Layer Properties dialog box, 148–149, 195, 211
layers, 3
  adding, 147–149
  altering, 16
  animation, 155–158
  Blue Outlines option, 154
  canvas level, 3, 52, 147
  color-coding, 154
  Current Mode, 153
  Current option, 149
  Delete Layer option, 153

deleting, 151–153
differences from levels, 97
drawing on, 52
editable, 149
file size and, 157
Green Outlines option, 154
Hidden option, 151
Hide Others option, 150
hiding, 151–153
identifying contents, 150
identifying in timeline, 16
immobile movie parts, 155
Insert Layer option, 148
inserting frames into multiple, 153–154
key frames, 16, 155
last frame, 16
levels, 3
Lock Others option, 151
Locked option, 151
locking, 151
manipulating, 150–154
Modify Layer button, 16, 148, 149
Modify Layers pop-up menu, 148, 150, 151, 152, 153, 154
Modify Level pop-up menu, 153
moving artwork between, 149–150
moving forward or backward, 147
naming, 152
Normal mode, 149
objects appearing in, 16
organization of, 14
overlay level, 3
overlay levels, 147
performance, 157
Properties option, 152
Red Outlines option, 154
scenes, 147
selecting elements on, 151
shapes intersecting on, 147
Show All option, 150, 153
showing, 151–153
sounds, 17
state of, 16
symbols, 147
thumbnails of objects in, 16
timelines, 147
transparent portions, 146
tweened animation, 147
tweened frames, 155
unused, 148
uses for, 146

legend layer, 149
levels differences from layers, 97
Library: Buttons-Geometric window, 217
Library (Ctrl/Command-L) keyboard shortcut, 104, 107
Library window, 22–23, 104, 107, 116–120
  adding items to, 117
  Duplicate option, 198
  duplicating VR01 button, 198
  Edit command, 119
  editing symbols, 119
  identifying items in, 117
  Library list, 212
  Library pop-up menu, 23, 198, 212
  List, 23
  listening to sound, 117
  moving bitmap to scene, 105
  name of item, 117
  opening, 116
  Play button, 23, 117
  Preview area, 23, 117
  Properties option, 212
  sound symbol, 212
  Status line, 23, 117
  Symbol Edit mode, 142
  symbols, 117
  View Bitmaps button, 22, 105
  View buttons, 117
  View Sounds button, 22
  View Symbols button, 22
  viewing button symbols, 167
lightness, 21
line breaks in labels, 98
Line Style dialog box, 55
Linear gradients, 21
lines, 26
  applying styles and colors in elements, 82
  changing, 84
  changing line properties, 63
  colors, 26, 53
  constraining, 55
  controlling portion erased, 28
  copying style, 28
  custom styles, 54
  defining curved, 55–56
  defining straight, 52–54
  deleting portions, 28
  determining attributes, 70
  drawing on top of lines, 52
  duplicating, 80
  erasing, 28
  joining, 52
  modifying, 26, 87–94

pencil tool drawing, 52–57
reshaping, 78–87
selecting, 78–87, 79, 84
simplifying, 24, 59
solid colors, 20
styles, 26, 54
thickness, 54
width, 26
Link Properties: Button dialog
box, 169
Action pop-up menu, 169,
171, 172, 187, 203
Get URL option, 187
Goto and Play option, 171,
172
Goto option, 203
Network URL field, 188
Next Frame option, 172
Next Page option, 172
Play option, 169
Previous Frame option, 172
Scene pop-up menu, 171
Target Window field, 188
Link Properties: Symbol dialog
box, 138, 139, 191, 192
locking layers, 151–153
looping sounds, 213
lossy compression, 231

M

Macintosh
File Creator, 263
File dialog boxes, 223
file names, 262
File Type, 263
GIF bitmaps, 40
JPEG bitmaps, 40
PICT files, 40
saving flash movie files with
fla extension name, 223
servers, 263
Macromedia Authorware.
See Authorware
Macromedia Director.
See Director
Macromedia Extreme 3D.
See Extreme 3D
Macromedia Flash. See Flash
Macromedia Flash ActiveX
control, 48, 49
Macromedia Fontographer.
See Fontographer
Macromedia FreeHand.
See FreeHand
Macromedia SoundEdit 16.
See SoundEdit 16

Macromedia web site, x
Flash examples, 252
Shockwave page, 284
ShockZone, 252
Macromedia xRes. See xRes
magnifier tool, 28
manipulating layers, 150–154
marquee-selecting objects, 81
menu.htm file, 190
menus, 7
Arrange submenu, 10, 11
Control, 11
Curves submenu, 10, 11
Edit, 8
File, 8
Goto submenu, 9
Help, 12
Insert, 9
Kerning submenu, 10
keyboard shortcuts, 292–296
Modify, 10, 11
Modify Frames pop-up menu,
9
Modify Layers pop-up menu, 9
Transform submenu, 10
View, 9
Window, 12
Xtras, 11
<META> tag, 248
MIDI sound, 208
MIME (Multipart Internet Mail
Exchange) type, 261–262
modification commands, 8
Modify Frame View pop-up
menu, 15
Modify Frames pop-up menu, 9,
17
Modify Layers pop-up menu, 9,
16
Modify menu, 10, 11
Modify Movie dialog box, 90
palette, 191
Modify Onion Markers pop-up
menu, 15
Modify > Align command, 92
Modify > Arrange menu, 114
Modify > Arrange > Move Ahead
command, 115
Modify > Arrange > Send to Back
command, 115
Modify > Break Apart command,
97, 106, 107, 120
Modify > Curves command, 59
Modify > Curves > Optimize
command, 88, 89
Modify > Curves > Smooth
command, 24

Modify > Curves > Straighten
command, 24, 107
Modify > Element command,
138, 141, 169, 171, 172, 187,
191, 192, 203
Modify > Group command, 113,
115
Modify > Movie command, 90,
196
Modify > Movie menu, 14
Modify > Paragraph command,
102
Modify > Scene command, 160
Modify > Trace Bitmap
command, 109, 228
Modify > Transform > Edit Center
command, 128
Modify > Transform > Flip
Horizontal command, 92
Modify > Transform > Rotate
command, 25, 91
Modify > Transform > Scale
command, 25, 136
Modify > Ungroup command,
113
motion guide layer, 142–144
Movie Properties dialog box, 18
Frame Rate setting, 122, 127
Grid Spacing, 196
Ruler Units option, 103
View Grid checkbox, 196
Movie Size Report, 232–240
Bitmaps section, 242
Embedded font section, 242
Embedded Objects, 242
exer20c.fla movie, 234, 239
making movie smaller,
235–238
movie structure, 240–243
Page data section, 242
Sound data section, 242
Symbol section, 242
symbol timeline, 235
tracking movie problems, 232
movie window, 13, 14
movies, 2
adding elements, 9
adding frames, 122–124, 132
adding key frames, 124–125
adding layers, 147–149
adding sounds, 209, 215
animated GIF (Graphics
Interchange Format) files, 3
automatically playing,
163–164, 164
bitmaps in, 104

compressed, optimized format, 220
compression, 228–232
controlling frames in frameset, 187–189
controlling operation of, 13
controlling speed of, 122
depth, 146
desired playback speed, 18
displaying all frames of, 128–129
elapsed time to reach current frame, 18
embedded in HTML pages, 224–226
enlarging view of, 28
EPS (Encapsulated PostScript) files, 3
exporting, 220
exporting as sequence of bitmap files, 44
exporting frame to FreeHand, 37–38
exporting frames, 2
exporting to FreeHand as sequence of files, 38–39
exporting with characters for Fontographer, 39–40
formats for exportation, 3
frame file space, 233
frame rate, 122
frames, 2, 122
framesets, 185
halting playback, 19
how much to use, 246
for HTML documents, 190–192
ignoring unFlashed users, 284
illustration files, 3
importing sounds, 211–212
integration into web sites, 245, 247–249
interaction, 11
interactive files, 2
JavaScript control, 224
key frames, 132
modifying color palette, 19
modifying playback order, 165
Movie Size Report, 232–240
multiple sound usage, 212
numeric data about, 18
organization of layers, 14
Play button, 167
playback, 2, 11, 18–19
playing, 220–228
playing from current frame indicator, 176

playing inside HTML (HyperText Markup Language) pages, 7
playing specific frame, 164
predicting playback speed, 216
protection, 227
QuickTime digital video files, 3
range of frames information, 14
reducing view of, 28
removing bitmap data from, 112
removing elements, 9
reordering scenes, 162
scenes, 2
separate version for unFlashed users, 284
series of bitmap files, 3
single, empty key frame, 123
sounds, 207
speed, 220
standalone Shockwave Flash Player, 221–223
starting, 126, 167–169
starting and stopping, 126
Stop button, 167
stopping, 126, 167–169
streaming, 7
structure, 240–243
testing with sound, 216–217
time required to create, 246
timeline, 141
uploading to server, 249–250
user interaction, 166
web site users without Flash Player, 247
where to make smaller, 235–238
moving
    insertion point keyboard shortcuts, 289
    key frames, 137
    selections keyboard shortcuts, 289
MSN (Microsoft Network) web site, 253
multimedia, viii, 2
multimedia files, 2

N

Netscape Navigator 176, 221, 224, 226, 267-73
New button, 20, 22, 74, 75
Normal mode, 149
Numeric Color Picker, 20, 22

O

<OBJECT> tag, 223, 224
    Base parameter, 272
    BGColor parameter, 270
    classid parameter, 269
    codebase parameter, 269
    disadvantage of, 226
    Height parameter, 189, 226, 269
    hiding, 285–287
    ID parameter, 269, 276, 277
    Loop parameter, 269
    Menu parameter, 272
    Movie parameter, 226, 269
    PARAM NAME parameter, 189, 190
    Play parameter, 269
    Quality parameter, 270
    SAlign parameter, 271
    Scale parameter, 271
    template, 189
    Width parameter, 189, 226, 269
objects
    accelerating and decelerating, 134–136
    adding to selection, 80–81
    altering appearance of, 10
    appearing in layers, 16
    arrow tool selection, 78–85
    copying, 93
    defining motion with motion guide, 143–144
    deselecting everything, 81
    duplicating, 80, 116
    lasso tool selection, 85–86
    marquee-selecting, 81
    pasting, 93
    reshaping, 10, 88–90
    selecting, 24, 83
    selecting all, 93
    stacking order, 114
Onion Skin button, 14
Onion Skin Outlines button, 15
onion skinning, 14, 15, 127–130
onion-skin markers, 15
Open Location dialog box, 250
Option key, 80
outlines
    filling, 27
    gap sizes, 27
    importing, 32
    viewing, 62

outlining shapes, 82
ovals drawing, 57, 59
Over frame, 168
overlay level, 3, 95, 96–97, 112
   adding copy of items to, 118
   editing symbols, 119
   layers, 147
   overlay objects, 96
   rearranging items, 115
   stacking order, 3
   symbol, 3
   text objects, 97
overlay objects, 33, 95–96
   breaking apart, 97
   modifying outlines of, 97
   order of, 96
   returning to canvas level, 97
   stacking, 114–115
   text as, 98
   tweened animation, 132

P

paint bucket tool, 27, 66–68, 87, 90, 197
   altering graphics, 68–69
   changing color of filled area, 66
   Close Small Gaps option, 67
   Color modifier, 81
   Don't Close Gaps option, 67, 68
   Fill Color modifier, 27, 67, 68, 69, 70, 73, 127
   Fill Color palette, 86
   filling enclosed areas with color, 66
   filling letters with gradient, 71
   filling selected shapes, 81–82
   Gap Size modifier, 27, 67, 68
   interpretation of gap size, 67
   Line Color modifier, 73
   Lock Fill modifier, 27
   modifiers, 27
   modifying color palettes, 73
   modifying vector shapes, 66
   rainbow fill option, 70
   Rotate modifier, 91
   selected filled shapes and, 81
   selecting color for, 27
   testing effect of zooming on, 68
   Transform Fill modifier, 27, 91
paintbrush, 60–63
painting
   behind shapes, 64

defining brush stroke, 62
   only part of shape, 65
   over shape without altering outline, 64
   shapes, 59–66
   shapes only inside enclosed area, 65
   tools, 6
palettes, onscreen placement, 12
Pan( ) method, 279
paragraph properties, 25
Paragraph Properties (Ctrl/Command-T) keyboard shortcut, 102
Paragraph Properties dialog box, 102–103
paragraphs, modifying properties, 102–103
Paste (Ctrl/Command-V) keyboard shortcut, 93
pasting objects, 93
paths, 2
   tweening on, 141–144
pencil tool, 26
   color, 26
   Custom option, 55
   defining curved lines, 55–56
   defining straight lines, 52–54
   drawing curved lines, 56–57
   drawing lines, 52–57
   drawing shapes, 57–59
   drawing straight lines, 54–55
   Fill Color modifier, 73
   Hairline option, 54
   Ink option, 59
   Line Color modifier, 26, 53, 55, 73
   Line option, 52
   Line Style modifier, 26, 54, 55
   Line Thickness modifier, 54, 55
   Line Width modifier, 26, 87, 90
   modes, 26
   modifiers, 26
   modifying color palettes, 73
   Oval option, 57, 90
   Pencil Mode modifier, 26, 52, 55, 57, 58, 59, 90
   Rectangle modifier, 196
   Rectangle option, 58, 87
   selecting line color, 53
   Smooth modifier, 55, 142
   Straighten option, 58, 87
PercentLoaded( ) method, 277
PICT files, exporting frames as, 2
pictures, 3–4

pixellated, 2, 4
pixels, 3–4
   varying in color from neighbors, 111
Play action, 164, 170
   adding, 163–164
   assigning, 169
Play button, 167
Play( ) method, 278
playing movies, 220–228
   load order, 226–227
   Shockwave Flash ActiveX control, 223–226
   Shockwave Flash Netscape plug-in, 223–226
   standalone Shockwave Flash Player, 221–223
playing sounds, 213–214
pressure-sensitive tablet, 61
previewing gradients, 21
protection for movies, 227

Q

QuickTime digital video files, exporting movies as, 3

R

radial fill, 76–77
Radial gradients, 21
rearranging scenes, 13
rectangles drawing, 58–59
   relative URLs, 181, 182, 188
reordering scenes, 162
reshaping
   fills, 78–87
   lines, 78–87
   objects, 10, 88–90
   shapes, 10
Return key, 126
Rewind( ) method, 278
rotation handles, 25

S

sample rate, 209
sample size, 209
sampled sound, 208
sampled sound file, 209
saturation, 20, 21
Scale and Rotate dialog box, 136
Scale and Rotate (Shift-Ctrl/Command-S) key combination, 136
scaling handles, 25

Scene Properties dialog box, 160
scenes, 2, 159
  adding buttons to new, 173
  adding looping action, 170-171
  controlling display of, 9
  copying frames between, 161-162
  creatiing, 160-162
  current frame, 19
  displaying name, 160
  Edit Movie button, 119, 120
  imported artwork, 34
  keyboard shortcuts, 289
  last frame of current, 19
  layers, 3, 147
  moving bitmap to, 105
  new, 160
  operation of, 160
  rearranging, 13
  renaming, 160
  switching between, 13
  symbols, 119
screen, speeding redraw of, 154
scripting and Shockwave Flash movies, 275-282
search engines, 248
Select All (Ctrl/Command-A) keyboard shortcut, 93, 115
selecting
  fills, 78-87
  items, 24
  lines, 78-87, 79
  objects, 83
  shapes, 79
selection tools, 23
selections
  adding to, 86
  changing lines in, 84
  rotation handles, 25
  scaling handles, 25
servers, 178
SetZoomRect() method, 279
shape outlines, 26
shape recognition, 58
shapes
  adding lines to, 26
  altering outline, 11
  automatic outlines, 59
  changing color of, 27
  changing fill color of part of, 81
  closed, 52
  combining into group, 113
  controlling portion erased, 28
  deleting portions, 28
  deselecting, 79

determining fill and line attributes, 70
  drawing, 57-59
  drawing outlines, 52-57
  modifying, 87-94
  modifying outlines, 72
  moving filled, 79
  with or without anti-aliasing, 62
  outlining, 82
  ovals, 57
  painting, 59-66
  rectangles, 58
  reshaping, 10
  selecting, 79
  selecting corner of, 65
  shape recognition, 58
  simplifying, 24
  transforming, 90
  viewing outlines, 62
Shift key, 86
Shockwave Flash
  HTML file for holding file, 189-190
  relative URLs, 188
Shockwave Flash ActiveX control, 223-226
  downloading, 284
Shockwave Flash files, 220
  embedding in HTML pages, 221
  saving with standalone Shockwave Flash Player, 221
  standalone Shockwave Flash Player, 221-223
  viewing in other programs, 221
Shockwave Flash menubar frameset, 185-187
Shockwave Flash movies
  configuring web server for, 261-263
  Movie Size Report, 232-240
  scripting browser scripting, 275-282
Shockwave Flash Player, 176
Shockwave Flash plug-in, 7, 223-226
showing layers, 151-153
  solid colors, 20, 73-74
Sound dialog box
  Effect pop-up menu, 214, 216
  Event option, 214, 215, 216, 217
  Frames button, 213
  In/Out points, 213
  Loop values, 213

None option, 214, 216
Play button, 213
sound channel waveforms, 213
sound instances, 212
Sound menu, 217
Sound pop-up menu, 213, 215, 216
Streaming option, 214, 217
Synchronization pop-up menu, 213, 214, 215, 216, 217
waveform preview window, 213
Zoom Out button, 213
Sound Properties dialog box, 211-212
SoundEdit 16, 46-47
sounds, 2, 207
  adding to buttons, 217-218
  adding to movies, 209
  AIFF files, 208
  amplitude, 209
  audio CD-quality, 46
  buttons and, 210
  compression, 230-231
  current frame indicator and, 210
  digital, 208
  displaying frames, 213
  event-driven, 210
  importing, 46-47, 211-212
  instances, 212
  layers, 17
  length, 23
  length in relation to timeline, 17
  listening to, 117
  looping, 213
  MIDI, 208
  multiple, 214
  playing, 213-214
  previewing changes to, 213
  quality of, 210
  removing from key frame, 214
  renaming, 212
  reviewing attributes, 212-213
  sample rate, 209
  sample size, 209
  sampled, 208
  samples constructing sound wave, 210
  sampling, 208
  starting, 210
  Stop synchronizations, 215
  stopping, 214
  storing, 22-23, 116
  streaming, 210

synchronizing, 216-217
synthesized, 208
testing movie with, 216-217
timeline, 17, 213
viewing, 22
volume, 213
WAVE files, 208
spl files, 220
Spumco's "The Goddamn George Liquor Program" web site, 258
stacking order, 3, 11
stacking overlay objects, 114-115
standalone Shockwave Flash Player, 221-223
starting movies, 167-169
Stop action, 169
Stop All Sounds action, 214
Stop button, 167
Stop synchronizations, 214, 215
stopping movies, 167-169
StopPlay( ) method, 278
straight lines
    defining, 52-54
    drawing, 54-55
streaming, 7
    streaming sounds, 210, 213, 214, 233
swf files, 220
switching between scenes or symbols, 13
symbol links, 120
Symbol Properties dialog box, 196
    Button Behavior checkbox, 118, 167, 196, 203
    naming symbols, 167
    symbol names, 118
symbols, 3, 116-120
    animating, 140-141
    assigning actions to, 3
    creating, 118-119
    displaying all frames of, 23
    editing, 119-120
    file sizes and, 116, 157
    layers, 147
    modifying color, 138-139
    number of frames for, 23
    previewing, 23
    rotating, 128
    scenes, 119
    storing, 22-23, 116, 233
    switching between, 13
    symbol links, 120
    timeline, 140, 141, 235
    turning artwork into, 132
    viewing, 22
synchronizing sounds, 216-217

synthesized sound, 208

T

tabs, 13
tags, 178-180
text as overlay object, 98
text blocks
    automatically wrapping, 98
    converting back to labels, 100-101
    converting labels to, 99-100
    modifying style, 101-102
    styling, 101-103
text labels. See labels
text objects, 25
    alignment, 25
    breaking apart, 97
    changing alignment, 102
    digital type design, 39-40
    edit mode, 97, 101
    fonts, 25
    labels, 97-101
    modifying paragraph properties, 102-103
    modifying width, 99
    move-selection cursor and, 99
    overlay level, 97
    paragraph properties, 25
    text blocks, 97-101
    text-edit mode, 99
    units of measurement, 103
text tool, 25, 101
    Alignment modifier, 25, 102
    Bold modifier, 25
    editing text objects, 97
    Font Color modifier, 25, 98
    Font modifier, 25
    Font modifier menu, 98
    Font Size modifier, 25, 98
    Italic modifier, 25, 102
    modifiers, 25
    Paragraph modifier, 25
    Paragraph Properties modifier, 102
    Right option, 102
    text objects and, 97
timeline, 6, 13, 14, 122
    action frames, 17
    Action option, 163, 165, 171
    Add Motion Guide option, 142
    clicking on frame numbers, 140
    controlling spacing between frames, 15
    Copy Frames option, 161

current frame indicator, 125, 128, 133, 143, 163, 197
current frame number, 18
Current Layer option, 169
Edit Multiple Frames button, 15, 130
elapsed time, 18
empty frame, 17
empty key frame, 17
End Onion Skin marker, 129
enlarging, 153
frame insertion marker, 139
frame selection indicator, 216
frame types, 17
frames, 6, 16
header, 16
identifying layers in, 16
Insert Frame option, 123, 153, 168, 191, 197, 203
Insert Key Frame option, 124, 125, 126, 134, 168, 192, 197, 203, 215
Insert Layer option, 195, 211
key frame, 17
layer names, 16
layers, 147
Modify Frame View menu, 131
Modify Frames indicator, 123, 124, 132, 134, 135, 137, 140, 143, 163, 165, 168, 171, 192, 197, 213, 215, 217
Modify Frames pop-up menu, 123, 124, 126, 132, 134, 135, 143, 153, 161, 163, 165, 168, 171, 191, 192, 197, 203, 213, 215, 216, 217
Modify Layers button, 16
Modify Layers pop-up menu, 142, 169, 195, 211
Modify Onion Markers menu, 128
modifying frames, 17
motion guide layer, 142
movie structure, 240-243
movies, 141
moving current frame indicator, 124, 127
moving key frames, 137
new movie, 123
Onion All option, 128
Onion Skin button, 14, 128
Onion Skin Outlines button, 15, 129
Paste Frames option, 161
Preview in Context option, 131

Preview option, 131
Reverse Frames option, 161
Sound option, 213, 215, 216, 217
sound waveform, 214
sounds, 17, 213
Start Onion Skin marker, 129
status bar, 18
Stop option, 215
symbols, 140, 141, 235
thumbnail view of key frames, 130-131
tweened frame, 17
tweened key frame, 17
Tweening option, 132, 134, 135, 139, 143, 192
visible frames in, 16
tool selection keyboard shortcuts, 289
toolbar, 23-24
arrow tool, 24-25
brush tool, 26-27
drawing and selection tools, 23
dropper tool, 28
eraser tool, 28
ink bottle tool, 26
lasso tool, 29
Lock Fill modifier, 61
Macintosh and Windows, 23, 24
magnifier tool, 28
paint bucket tool, 27
pencil tool, 26
Pressure modifier, 61
text tool, 25
tool modifiers, 23
Zoom Control, 24
Zoom factor box, 68
top menu layer, 147
top-level domains, 177
TotalFrames( ) method, 277
Trace Bitmap dialog box, 109-112
Tracing Bitmap progress bar window, 112
tracing bitmaps, 109-112
Transform submenu, 10
transforming shapes and gradients, 90
triangles, drawing, 58
tweened animation, 131-137
accelerating and decelerating, 134-136
altering, 136-137
color, 138

creating, 132-134
layers, 147
modifying, 131
overlay objects, 132
tweened frames, 17, 122, 133, 155
tweened key frames, 17
tweening, 6-7, 121, 131
frame-by-frame animation and, 135
key frames, 131
on paths, 141-144
Tweening dialog box, 132
Easing slider, 132, 134, 135
Motion option, 132, 134, 139, 192
Orient to path direction checkbox, 143
Tween rotation checkbox, 134
Tween scaling checkbox, 132, 134
Tweening pop-up menu, 134, 139, 192

U

Undo (Ctrl/Command-Z) keyboard shortcut, 81
unFlashed users
browser scripting, 285-287
ignoring, 284
separate movie version for, 284
Ungroup (Ctrl/Command-U) keyboard shortcut, 113
unused layers, 148
Up frame, 169
uploading movies to server, 249-250
URLs, 176-178
absolute, 182
complete, 181, 182
embedding in web pages, 180
relative, 181, 182

V

VCR Controller, 19
vector graphics
advantage of, 2
bitmap conversion to, 228
control points, 6
converting bitmaps to, 109-112

converting to anti-aliased bitmaps, 43
copying to FreeHand file, 37
exporting, 36-40
importing, 32-35
painting tools, 6
resizing, 4
resolution, 4
single curve, 233
size, 4
storage space, 4
storing data, 233
vector-based clip art libraries, 32
vector-based drawing program, 2
vectors, 2-5
View 100% (Ctrl/Command-1) keyboard shortcut, 67
View menu, 9
View > 100% command, 67, 68
View > Fast command, 62
View > Grid command, 90
View > Outline Setting command, 88
View > Outlines command, 62, 81, 112, 154
View > Show Frame command, 217
View > Smooth command, 62, 216, 217
View > Snap command, 24, 90, 143, 196, 198
View > Tabs command, 160
View > Work Area command, 13, 14
virtual objects, 195-200
virtual reality
buttons that simulate, 195-198
different buttons that control, 198-200
VR01 symbol, 197

W

web browsers
actions and, 3
dividing windows into frames, 182-183
Flash movies, 223
MIME (Multipart Internet Mail Exchange) type, 261-262
movie scaling to fit window, 223
new window, 176
opening files on hard drive, 178

playing movies back, 2
replacing frame in, 176
Shockwave Flash movies and, 176
Shockwave plug-in, 7
web pages
    browser-safe colors, 72
    embedding URLs in, 180
    referring to movies, graphics or other pages, 180
    tags, 178-180
web servers
    configuring for Shockwave Flash movies, 261-263
    default document name, 187
    MIME (Multipart Internet Mail Exchange) type, 262
    transmission speeds, 265-266
    uploading movies, 249-250

web sites
    Flash movie integration, 247-249
    how much Flash to use, 246
    ignoring unFlashed users, 284
    integrating movies, 245
    server transmitting movies, 249
    time required to create movies, 246
    users without Flash Player, 247
web-safe colors, 20
WebTV Networks, Inc. web site, 254
Window menu, 12
Window > Colors command, 73, 75
Window > Library command, 104, 117, 212
windows, 19
    onscreen placement, 12

Windows systems, 40
WMF files, exporting frames as, 2
Work Area, 14
World Wide Web
    frames, 182
    framesets, 182-194
    HTML (HyperText Markup Language), 178-182
    URLs, 176-178

X-Z

xRes, 40-41, 44
Xtras folder, 11
Xtras menu, 11
Xtras > Libraries > Buttons-Geometric command, 217
Zoom() method, 279
zoom tool, 72

Licensing Agreement